SALVATION BY
ALLEGIANCE
ALONE

SALVATION BY ALLEGIANCE ALONE

Rethinking Faith, Works,
and the Gospel of Jesus the King

MATTHEW W. BATES

Baker Academic

a division of Baker Publishing Group
Grand Rapids, Michigan

Published by Baker Academic
a division of Baker Publishing Group
P.O. Box 6287, Grand Rapids, MI 49516-6287
www.bakeracademic.com

Printed in the United States of America

Library of Congress Cataloging-in-Publication Data
Names: Bates, Matthew W., author.
Title: Salvation by allegiance alone : rethinking faith, works, and the gospel of Jesus the King / Matthew W. Bates.
Description: Grand Rapids, MI : Baker Academic, a division of Baker Publishing Group, [2017] | Includes bibliographical references and index.
Identifiers: LCCN 2016039060 | ISBN 9780801097973 (pbk.)
Subjects: LCSH: Salvation—Christianity.
Classification: LCC BT751.3 .B38 2017 | DDC 234—dc23
LC record available at https://lccn.loc.gov/2016039060

In keeping with biblical principles of creation stewardship, Baker Publishing Group advocates the responsible use of our natural resources. As a member of the Green Press Initiative, our company uses recycled paper when possible. The text paper of this book is composed in part of post-consumer waste.

23   7

With gratitude and love to my marvelous parents,
Michael G. Bates and Linda K. Bates

CONTENTS

FOREWORD

"The Church's one foundation is Jesus Christ her Lord," proclaims the hymnist Samuel Stone. Upon the absolutely secure foundation of Jesus, the true gospel sits as a secondary substructure, undergirding the universal church. So when the gospel is compromised, despite its unshakable foundation, the building leans, sways, and slides. Unfortunately the gospel preached in much of the Western world has corroded and destabilized the church—and the deconstruction continues at an alarming pace. But the problem is not just the pseudogospel that is being preached. It runs deeper. How so? The gospel message also includes a proper response, and misunderstandings about what constitutes an adequate response are further compromising the church and her mission to the world.

Without dismissing the real gains and genuine growth, few would deny that the church in the West is not what it could have been and ought to be. Attendance is down; holiness is wanting; love is superficial; discipleship is thin; seminaries are struggling to find a young generation even interested in church ministry. The attempt to bolster attendance, to press for more holiness, to summon more to be shaped by love, and the constant plea for more focus on discipleship and deeper theological preparation proves that criticisms of the church are on target. But the solutions aren't working. Why? Jesus the foundation is rock-solid, but the secondary and tertiary substructures are weak. When the gospel and its proper response have been eroded, recarpeting the foyer, rearranging the pews, and reshingling the roof will not help. The changeless foundation of the church can never be moved; it is the shoddily built "gospel" and "faith" substructure that is in need of renovation.

Salvation by Allegiance Alone is an exciting book because it takes us to that place of renovation: a rediscovery of the genuine gospel and its truly fitting response. As Matthew Bates shows, the gospel is the power-releasing story of *how Jesus became king* and the only adequate response is *allegiance alone*. But unfortunately the clarion call to allegiance in the New Testament has all too often been muted by misguided teachings about grace, or worse, grace-ism.

Regarding this grace-ism, who has not heard that grace means "God's riches at Christ's expense" or that it means "pure gift" or "God's unconditional love" or, from a different angle, "God's mercy to those who don't deserve it." One also hears what follows: you don't have to do a thing, you don't have to worry, it's all been done for you, just sit back and relax in this unconditional grace of God. One wonders if proponents of such theological understandings have spent much time examining what grace means in the New Testament (and the Old Testament, where it is also taught).

Among other stimulating insights in *Salvation by Allegiance Alone*, Matthew Bates helpfully brings to our attention the important work of John Barclay on grace, *Paul and the Gift*. We discover that grace is more complex than we might have otherwise imagined. In fact, Bates, following Barclay, contends there are six dimensions of grace that different authors and theologians may or may not "perfect" or take to their extreme limit. (For these six dimensions and some implications, see chap. 5, sec. "Grace and Allegiance Alone?") Yet for many today, grace has been reduced to only two or three of these six themes. Grace *only* means God's superabundance, God's priority, and most especially the incongruity of God's gift to sinners. Anything else is not grace. But listen to what we discover: *gift-giving, or grace, in the ancient world always required reciprocation.*

Grace, then, was according to the apostle Paul's contemporary, the philosopher Seneca, much like playing a game of catch:

> There is no doubt that when the ball is dropped it could be the fault of either the thrower or the catcher. The game goes along nicely when the ball is thrown and caught by both in a suitable manner, back and forth between the hands of thrower and catcher. But a good player needs to throw the ball differently to a tall partner and to a short one. It is the same with granting benefits: unless it is adjusted to the social roles of both parties, the giver and the recipient, the benefit will not actually be given by the one nor be received by the other in the right manner. (*On Benefits* 2.17; Griffin and Inwood)

Continuing, Seneca then explains the image, helping us to better understand the true nature of grace or gift-giving during the New Testament era: just as we "give" the short player a low throw so that he can make the catch and return the throw, but we "give" the tall player something different, so it should be with all cases of grace or gift-giving. Seneca suggests that all givers and receivers should monitor and adjust the gift-giving so that the cycle of grace can be perpetuated.

Notice that in antiquity a gift *implicated* the person who received the gift to respond with some kind of gift given back to the original giver. Of course, the receiver of a gift responds by beginning with gratitude, but ideally gratitude turns into a reciprocal gift. Matthew Bates demonstrates in this book that grace in the New Testament fits this pattern: God's superabundant, prior gift is granted without regard to our relative worth, but the reception of God's gift demands a return gift from us, a response of grateful discipleship marked by allegiance to King Jesus.

Allegiance, then, is at the heart of grace as it was perceived in the ancient world. Grace was not simply—or ever—pure gift in spite of what some say today. One must define terms by their usage not by our contemporary beliefs or usages. Grace can both be one hundred percent gift *and at the same time* summon the gifted person with an obligation, a heartfelt and intentional duty, to respond in gratitude and behavior in accordance with the new social bond created by the gift-giver's gift. This grace runs right through the Old Testament, through Judaism, and into the New Testament. What distinguished the kind of Judaism that did not believe in Jesus and the one that did was not the appearance or absence of *grace itself* but *how grace was understood*. It is, then, a popular misunderstanding of Paul to conclude that grace did not obligate the Christian—the one who received God's gift of Christ and redemption—to respond to God through real behavioral change. Grace in fact required a life of gratitude, praise, and—here's the language from Matthew Bates's outstanding book—"*allegiance* to Jesus as king."

Some theologians (past and present) think that any kind of obligation attached to grace must somehow entail a dangerous works righteousness. Such people are wrong. But you'll have to read *Salvation by Allegiance Alone* to see how deftly and biblically Matthew Bates dismantles this worry about works while simultaneously offering fresh proposals regarding how a gospel-infused allegiance connects with righteousness.

I want to approach the obligation of grace from another angle, that of Dietrich Bonhoeffer. As a college student I became a voracious reader and, so, as a sophomore I began reading Bonhoeffer, beginning with (what was then called) *The Cost of Discipleship*. Perhaps his most enduring contribution to Christian theology, at least Christian ethics, is his section on "costly grace," a concept that put into words my deepest convictions and concerns about the church I was then witnessing. The church was marked by sanctimonious attendance, judgmentalism on all outsiders, expressed certitude of the security of the believer because of a single act of accepting Christ into one's heart, and rigor in theological propositions. It was also a church pockmarked body-wide with a lack of love, a lack of genuine holiness, and an inability to foster discipleship in the heart of the true believer. Sadly, what it lacked was created by its deficient gospel: "if you just believe" was its watchword and safety net. But "believe" meant mental acceptance and a single act of reception, and never meant what the term also means in the whole Bible: the kind of faith that is also faithfulness.

The superficiality of American evangelicalism's gospel-obsession with security and assurance has led me at times to wonder if we should not teach justification by *discipleship*. Or justification by *faithfulness*. But Matthew Bates has landed on a beautiful and biblically sound term: *allegiance*. When Jesus first called the four disciples along the Sea of Galilee he didn't say "receive me into your heart" but "follow me." When a crisis arose among his followers he didn't say "you're safe" or "get your orthodoxy on" but "deny yourself and take up your cross." Moreover, when he finished the greatest sermon on earth, the Sermon on the Mount, Jesus didn't say "Repent and believe these things" but "the one who hears these words of mine and *does* them." So, too, the apostles Paul, Peter, and John called their listeners to a life swamped by the Spirit, a life of holiness amidst suffering, and a life of living in the light of love. These apostolic expressions are all condensed in this book into the term "allegiance."

King Jesus summons people into a kingdom where he alone is king, and kings expect one thing from their subjects: *allegiance*.

Scot McKnight
Julius R. Mantey Professor in New Testament
Northern Seminary
Lombard, Illinois

ACKNOWLEDGMENTS

This book has been on my heart for nearly ten years—often with a burning-in-the-bones urgency as I mulled preliminary ideas. Write. Write. Write. Yet even though this book restlessly loomed as a fire waiting to be kindled, circumstances required that the flint, steel, and tinder be stowed away for several years. I am grateful to have had the opportunity to complete the task.

As I began working on this manuscript, conversation proved to be steel striking flint. Without the shower of sparks generated by contact with others, progress would not have been possible. I am unable to thank everyone who has helped nurture the flames, but I would like to give special recognition to some individuals and groups.

I have a number of friends to thank. First, I would like to single out Jonathan Miles, associate professor of philosophy at Quincy University. This book has been forged, hammer and tongs, by a constant engagement with his sharp mind and Christian spirit. Second, I extend a special thank you to Scot McKnight. Not only was Scot's research an important stimulus for my own, he contributed significantly to this project. He expressed enthusiastic support for the initial outline and was generous to supply a thought-provoking foreword. Many other professionals also provided invaluable comments on the whole or a portion: David Downs, Joshua Jipp, Kent Lasnoski, Matthew Lynch, Eric Rowe, Daniel Smith, and Daniel Strudwick. Several church leaders read initial chapters and discussed them with me, including Andrew Cashman and Zeke Nelson. Quincy University was kind to reduce my teaching load by three credit hours for the spring of 2014, which accelerated the drafting of several chapters. Special thanks to president Bob Gervasi, vice president of academic affairs Ann Behrens, and my department chair, Daniel Strudwick.

If this book finds an audience among pastors, scholars, and general theological readers, then much of its purpose will have been met. But it has also been crafted with the college or seminary classroom in mind. If it succeeds in this capacity, then this will be in no small measure due to my students at Quincy University. I'd like to give a grateful shout-out to my Exploring the New Testament classes (spring 2015, 2016) for reading the bulk of the manuscript and testing the "for further thought" questions. Meanwhile, my Romans class (spring 2016) gave useful feedback on chapter 8. Several students went beyond the call of duty in interacting with the manuscript: Sarah Alexander, Bridget Bicek, Andrea Brown, Nick Clark, Michael Crotteau, Sammi Goble, Teresa Gorrell, Brianna Johnson, Katherine Rathgeber, Lacey Rokita, and Genesis Torrens.

The personnel at Baker Academic have stoked coals or applied the damper when appropriate. James Ernest (who has since left Baker Academic) was the initial acquiring editor. I cannot say enough good things about how James handled the acquisition of this project. Not only did he show enormous confidence in me and my ideas from the outset, but he generously invested time by providing sentence- and paragraph-level suggestions that helped me enhance the manuscript—and this, astonishingly, even before the manuscript was under contract with Baker! James passed my project to the extraordinarily capable Bryan Dyer, who helped guide the manuscript into production. Bryan provided sound judgment with regard to the macro-organization, helped tame some overly wild portions, and also provided necessary nuance. I am also grateful to anonymous reviewers who supplied comments to Bryan. Other folks at Baker have been splendid too—Jim Kinney, Eric Salo, David Nelson, Mason Slater, Paula Gibson, and Louis McBride.

My family deserves high praise. Sarah, my wife, has been constant in her love and support. She is also patient. As a woman who needs little practical encouragement toward allegiance alone (she lives her loyalty to the King Jesus daily like none other!), she has nevertheless heard more about it than any mortal should. My children have been a boundless source of joy and entertainment: Tad, Zeke, Addie, Lydia, Evie, and (just arrived!) Anna.

This book is dedicated with much love and heartfelt gratitude to my parents, Mike and Linda Bates. Thanks, Mom and Dad, for all that childhood care—diapers changed, food and lodging provided, meals cooked, baseball games coached—and for all that you continue to do for me. But thanks, Mom and Dad, above all for raising me in a home filled with love—a love so tangible yet transcendent that it could only have one source. God is glorified through you.

Abbreviations

Old Testament

Gen.	Genesis
Exod.	Exodus
Lev.	Leviticus
Num.	Numbers
Deut.	Deuteronomy
Josh.	Joshua
Judg.	Judges
Ruth	Ruth
1–2 Sam.	1–2 Samuel
1–2 Kings	1–2 Kings
1–2 Chron.	1–2 Chronicles
Ezra	Ezra
Neh.	Nehemiah
Esther	Esther
Job	Job
Ps. (Pss.)	Psalm (Psalms)
Prov.	Proverbs
Eccles.	Ecclesiastes
Song of Sol.	Song of Solomon
Isa.	Isaiah
Jer.	Jeremiah
Lam.	Lamentations
Ezek.	Ezekiel
Dan.	Daniel
Hosea	Hosea
Joel	Joel
Amos	Amos
Obad.	Obadiah
Jon.	Jonah
Mic.	Micah
Nah.	Nahum
Hab.	Habakkuk
Zeph.	Zephaniah
Hag.	Haggai
Zech.	Zechariah
Mal.	Malachi

Old Testament Apocrypha

1–4 Macc.	1–4 Maccabees
Add. Esth.	Additions to Esther
Sir.	Sirach/Ecclesiasticus
Tob.	Tobit

New Testament

Matt.	Matthew
Mark	Mark
Luke	Luke
John	John
Acts	Acts
Rom.	Romans
1–2 Cor.	1–2 Corinthians
Gal.	Galatians
Eph.	Ephesians
Phil.	Philippians
Col.	Colossians
1–2 Thess.	1–2 Thessalonians
1–2 Tim.	1–2 Timothy
Titus	Titus

Philem.	Philemon
Heb.	Hebrews
James	James
1–2 Pet.	1–2 Peter
1–3 John	1–3 John
Jude	Jude
Rev.	Revelation

Ancient Writings

Apostolic Fathers

2 Clem.   2 Clement

Augustine

Trin.   Augustine, *De Trinitate*

Ignatius

Ign. *Eph.*   Ignatius, *To the Ephesians*
Ign. *Trall.*   Ignatius, *To the Trallians*

Irenaeus

Epid.   Irenaeus, *Epideixis tou aposto-likou kērygmatos*
Haer.   Irenaeus, *Adversus haereses*

Josephus

Ant.   Josephus, *Jewish Antiquities*
J.W.   Josephus, *Jewish War*

Justin Martyr

1 Apol.   Justin Martyr, *Apologia i*
Dial.   Justin Martyr, *Dialogus cum Tryphone*

Minucius Felix

Oct.   Minucius Felix, *Octavius*

Origen

Cels.   Origen, *Contra Celsum*

Philo

Fug.   Philo, *De fuga et inventione*
Opif.   Philo, *De opificio mundi*
Spec.   Philo, *De specialibus legibus*

Pliny the Younger

Ep.   Pliny the Younger, *Epistulae*

Tacitus

Ann.   Tacitus, *Annales*

Other Abbreviations

BDAG	Danker, Frederick W., Walter Bauer, William F. Arndt, and F. Wilbur Gingrich. *Greek-English Lexicon of the New Testament and Other Early Christian Literature*. 3rd ed. Chicago: University of Chicago Press, 2000
chap(s).	chapter(s)
def.	definition
esp.	especially
LXX	Septuagint
NS	new series
NT	New Testament
OT	Old Testament
par(r).	parallel(s)
s.v.	*sub verbo* (under the word)

INTRODUCTION

Back in 1987 George Michael crystalized an aspect of contemporary spirituality with his hit song "Faith." At the same time that Michael donned his skinny
jeans, waggled around on the stage, and belted out the chorus, "Because I've
got to have faith, faith, faith—I've got to have faith, faith, faith—baby!,"
emerging cultural convictions about faith were being solidified and reinforced.
For Michael in this song, we should have faith, but in what? Seemingly in faith
itself. In fact, when I did an internet search to find the lyrics for the song, I
took a casual glance at the recent comments. The very first comment that I
found distills how this George Michael–infused understanding of faith is still
operative today: "I'm no religious freak. In fact I hate organized religion! But
without faith I'd be lost and I'd be a wreck most of the time. So I'm going to
listen to my mate George Michael and say *!&# the rest, I'll just do my best!
And leave the rest up to faith!"

From a charitable Christian standpoint, although the person who penned
this internet comment may be crass, he surely gets something right. *Faith*,
however we define it, is indeed connected to *good news* for humanity. Moreover,
even if we deeply love the church or other forms of organized religion, we have
all encountered empty religiosity in one form or another—and undoubtedly
we have found it distasteful. Yet much of this commenter's sentiment seems
to be off the mark. But in what way? How has modern-day culture, both
non-Christian and Christian, affected how we think about central Christian
concepts such as faith, works, the gospel, and salvation? What is at risk if the
working ideas that we and others hold with regard to these terms are skewed
with respect to the biblical witness? And pushing deeper, what if we were to
discover that the meaning of *faith* itself needs to be reconsidered not just by
thoughtful Christian leaders but also by professional scholars and theologians?

1

In academic circles a major storm has been churning around what it means to be right with God—that is, what it means to be "justified." Because of its overwhelming importance, the debate has spilled over from learned journals into popular books and mainstream Christian discussions. On the one hand, for instance, N. T. Wright has suggested that the Christian's final declaration of innocence by God will be rendered "on the basis of the whole life"—that is, eternal judgment will be based to some degree on performing good works, albeit clearly not through rule-based effort.[1] John Piper has responded, arguing that the Bible describes eternal life as a present possession for the believer. So our right standing before God in the present moment cannot be treated as if it is merely a fictive anticipation of the future verdict. We do not have to wait for the last day to obtain right standing before God.[2] Subsequently Wright has offered further clarifications in his book *Justification: God's Plan and Paul's Vision*, indicating that his intention is not to deny the reality of our present right standing before God. For Wright the final verdict has been determined in advance already, because those who have faith in the Christ will invariably be found innocent on the day of judgment. In addition to Wright and Piper, many other scholars are involved in ongoing conversations about justification and related matters.[3]

I hope to move the discussion forward by approaching salvation from a different, wider angle. Our understanding of salvation can most profitably be advanced not by endlessly reassessing the details of exactly how justification works but by reconsidering precisely what we mean by some pervasive Christian concepts that were originally sharply focused but have become increasingly blurry—especially faith and the gospel.

A Proposed Surgery

In this book I want to demonstrate that our contemporary Christian culture often comes prepackaged with functional ideas and operative definitions of belief, faith, works, salvation, heaven, and the gospel that in various ways truncate and distort the full message of the good news about Jesus the Messiah

---

1. Wright, *Paul: In Fresh Perspective*, 57. For his first major foray into justification, see Wright, *What Saint Paul Really Said*, 33–35, 95–133. For a further statement, see Wright, *Paul: In Fresh Perspective*, 113–22, 148.

2. Piper, *Future of Justification*, esp. 93–116.

3. It is not possible to list even a fraction of the literature. For a student-friendly primer, see Beilby and Eddy, *Justification*. For recent scholarly syntheses, consider Westerholm, *Justification Reconsidered*; Allen, *Justification and the Gospel*; Wright, *Paul and the Faithfulness of God*, 2:774–1042.

that is proclaimed in the Bible. For example, the gospel cannot be accurately summarized by saying, "I trust that Jesus paid the price for me, so I am saved," or "Faith in Jesus's death for my sins saves me as a free gift apart from my works," or even "I am saved because I am trusting in Jesus's righteousness alone." Although these statements do contain important partial truths, they confuse the content of the gospel, the true nature of "faith" (which is not even the best term to use), the direction in which "faith" must be exercised, the proper interfacing between grace and deeds, and probably also what we are "saved" into and for. Surgery is necessary. The proposed operation could create conditions conducive to healing within the fractured church.

What is this necessary surgical procedure? Although the words "faith" and "belief" are mentioned in virtually every sermon preached in the English language, although they are prominent in nearly all translations of the Bible, although faith is currently so much at the heart of Christianity that the whole tradition is often called "the Christian faith," the persistence of this terminology as it pertains to eternal salvation has had, and continues to have, a misleading effect. The best corrective is that "faith" and "belief," insofar as they serve as overarching terms to describe what brings about eternal salvation, should be excised from Christian discourse. That is, English-speaking Christian leaders should entirely cease to speak of "salvation by faith" or of "faith in Jesus" or "believing in Christ" when summarizing Christian salvation. For the sake of the gospel we need to revise our vocabulary.

Although the Greek word *pistis*, the word that most often stands behind our English translations of "faith" or "belief" in the New Testament, can and does frequently involve *regarding something as true or real*, akin to how we might say "I have faith that God exists" or "my beliefs are different from yours," the word *pistis* (and related terms) has a much broader range of meaning. This range includes ideas that aren't usually associated in our contemporary culture with belief or faith, such as reliability, confidence, assurance, fidelity, faithfulness, commitment, and pledged loyalty. The question is, then, when a person today says, "I am saved by my faith in Jesus," what portion of the range of meaning of "faith" is understood to effect salvation? Are certain portions of the legitimate meaning of "faith" being unwittingly shaded out? In what capacity is Jesus being regarded as the object of "faith"? And what mental images surround the process of salvation?

Let's get to the heart of the matter by exploring a couple examples. When the apostle Paul says, "For it is by grace you have been saved through faith" (Eph. 2:8), what if Paul's idea of "faith" (*pistis*) differs from typical contemporary understandings? More specifically, how might our understanding of salvation and the gospel change if we were to determine that Paul's understanding of "faith" here is nearly the same as in the following selection from 1 Maccabees?

First Maccabees, written about 150 years before Jesus's death, contains a letter from King Demetrius. He is concerned that his rival, Alexander, may have beat him to the punch in forging an alliance with the Jewish people. King Demetrius, in seeking to persuade the Jews to his cause, writes:

> King Demetrius to the nation of the Jews, greetings. Since you have kept your agreement with us and have continued your friendship with us, and have not sided with our enemies, we have heard of it and rejoiced. Now continue still to keep faith [*pistis*] with us, and we will repay you with good for what you do for us. (1 Macc. 10:25–27 NRSV)

Here Demetrius is asking the Jews to continue showing *pistis*—that is, loyalty or allegiance—to him rather than to his rival, promising a reward for the allegiance. Just a few lines later King Demetrius further promises that some Jews will be put in positions demanding loyalty (*pistis*) as administrative leaders in the royal government. Could it be that when Paul and others talk about salvation by "faith," not by works, they intend something close to what Demetrius means by *pistis*—so that we should translate, "It is by grace you have been saved through *allegiance*" (Eph. 2:8)?

N. T. Wright offers a different example that helps us reconsider the first-century meaning of "believe" gospel language. Wright notes that the Jewish general Josephus, in his autobiographical recounting of the events of the Jewish-Roman war in AD 66, reports an incident where he urged a rebel leader to "*repent and believe* in me," using language nearly identical to what we find in the Gospel of Mark with respect to Jesus's proclamation, "The kingdom of God is near! *Repent and believe* the good news" (1:15).[4] Our own cultural experiences might lead us to think that "repent" means to turn away from private sins such as adultery, greed, and exploitation. Meanwhile, in Christian circles "believe" is so often linked to Jesus and the forgiveness of sins that it may be hard to weigh what it means in this example featuring Josephus. But Wright's point is that Josephus was not trying to convince this rebel to turn away from private sins or to "believe" that God can forgive, rather Josephus

---

4. All Scripture translations in this book are my own unless otherwise noted. The other text is from Josephus, *The Life* 110, cited in Wright, *Challenge of Jesus*, 44. The exact phrase in Josephus is *metanoēsein kai pistos emoi genēsesthai*, which Wright renders as "repent and believe in me" but which can be more precisely rendered "to repent and become loyal to me." This example from Josephus features the adjective *pistos*, which derives from the same root as the noun *pistis*. Meanwhile in Mark we find the related verb *pisteuō*: "Repent and believe the good news!" (*metanoeite kai pisteuete en tō euangeliō*).

wanted this man to join him in supporting the Jewish cause—that is, as I would put it, to show *allegiance*. So, what "repent and believe in me" means for Josephus in this context is "turn away from your present course of action and become *loyal* to me."

The needed surgery involves not just an excision of "faith" language but also a transplant. With regard to eternal salvation, rather than speaking of belief, trust, or faith in Jesus, we should speak instead of fidelity to Jesus as cosmic Lord or allegiance to Jesus the king. This, of course, is not to say that the best way to translate every occurrence of *pistis* (and related terms) is always or even usually "allegiance." Rather it is to say that allegiance is the best macro-term available to us that can describe what God requires from us for eternal salvation. It is the best term because it avoids unhelpful English-language associations that have become attached to "faith" and "belief," as well as limitations in the "trust" idea, and at the same time it captures what is most vital for salvation—mental assent, sworn fidelity, and embodied loyalty.[5] But we do not need to avoid the words "faith" and "belief" entirely. For example, they do carry the proper meaning in English for *pistis* with regard to confidence in Jesus's healing power and control over nature; moreover, these terms are suitable when *pistis* is directed primarily toward facts that we are called mentally to affirm. Our Christian discourse need not shift in these contexts but only with regard to eternal salvation.

The opportunity to rethink the gospel, faith, and other matters pertaining to salvation stands before us. Indeed, we have already made a beginning. Yet before we travel further, it might be helpful for the reader to receive additional orientation—to learn more about the aims, assumptions, background, and intended audience that have informed this study. This, I hope, will help clarify why this book has been written in this particular way and what various types of readers can expect.

Gaining Perspective

The reader deserves to know something about my background, for my academic training and ecclesial convictions have undoubtedly shaped this book in

---

5. Although my overarching "allegiance alone" proposal has novel features, it is important to recognize that it nonetheless enjoys appreciable continuity with classic studies that focus on "trust" (or *fiducia*) as part of "faith." For example, Murray, *Redemption—Accomplished and Applied*, 134, speaks of faith as "a whole-souled movement of self-commitment to Christ for salvation from sin and its consequences." He further describes faith as having three components: knowledge, conviction, and trust (133–40). My focus on *pistis* as "allegiance" attempts to show that the "trust" idea captures much of the truth but is too limited in light of the evidence.

ways even I do not fully comprehend. I am a committed Christian who seeks to serve the church and the academy, and this reflects my goals and assumptions in penning this book. Although this book undertakes a substantial rethinking of the gospel, faith, and other matters pertaining to salvation, the intention is to clarify the Christian narrative, not to question its fundamental value. Accordingly, basic truths that are widely accepted by Christians are simply presupposed: God's gracious revelation to humanity; the incarnation; Jesus's death for sins; the resurrection as a genuine historical event; Father, Son, and Spirit as one God; Jesus as the only path to final salvation; and the inspired and authoritative nature of the Bible. So, even while rethinking the meaning and significance of tenets central to Christian theology, the framework and goal of the exploration is for the church.

I consider myself fortunate to have received training as an undergraduate in the Reformed tradition (Whitworth University), at seminary in a trans-denominational Protestant environment (Regent College in Vancouver, BC), and at the PhD level at a Catholic institution (University of Notre Dame). This ecumenism is mirrored in my practices. I am a Protestant. Yet I participate with reasonable comfort in a Catholic context—in fact, I pray the morning office on weekdays with my colleagues in theology at Quincy University, the Franciscan school where I teach. In various seasons of life, I have regularly and gladly worshiped with nondenominational, Baptist, Presbyterian, Mennonite, and Evangelical Free churches. In writing this book I do hope my ecumenical experiences have helped me to engage the Scriptures more sympathetically and from more diverse angles than might have been possible had I been steeped in only one Christian tradition.

However, in the final analysis this book does not claim to speak from or for a specific Christian subgroup or denomination. That is, nothing here intends to be distinctively Catholic, Orthodox, Lutheran, Presbyterian, Methodist, or Baptist, although it may both affirm and critique dimensions of all these traditions. The truth purifies. And to the degree that I have managed to capture it, it is hoped that the reassessment offered in this book will ultimately contribute to the healing of that long-festering wound between Catholics and Protestants. (Not to exclude the need for reconciliation with the Orthodox, but the issues addressed here are generally more pertinent to the Catholic-Protestant divide.) The message of salvation as expressed in the Bible's ancient context will be the primary focus, not because further systematic and philosophical inquiry is irrelevant—on the contrary, it is essential—but because the biblical story should supply contours that direct further inquiry. Moreover, by focusing on the ground common to all Christians—the Bible, especially the New Testament—the exposition should be relevant to all Christians and any other readers of goodwill. This is appropriate because salvation cannot be restricted to any Christian subgroup. The gospel has been entrusted to the whole church for the sake of the entire world.

Yet, since this book has novel dimensions, some may judge that it would have been more appropriate to aim it exclusively at specialists. I have taken a riskier tack, writing for as broad an audience as possible—for students, pastors and clergy, church groups, and general readers, as well as for professional theologians and biblical scholars. I have done this for several reasons. First, while readers will have to make their own judgments about the value of this study, the import of the subject matter is undeniable, so it is fitting to write for a wide audience. Second, any freshness found herein is not primarily in new readings of the biblical details (although there are a number of such moments) but in how the details point to a series of realignments. For example, other biblical specialists are well aware that the Greek word *pistis* has a broader range of meaning than "faith," "belief," and "trust," but biblical scholars and systematic theologians haven't generally connected these insights to the gospel and final salvation in the way done here. Third, in my own teaching I find that students are bored by textbooks that offer the "assured" results of the collective guild—indeed, not just bored but frequently misled as the "assured" results are neither uncontested nor incapable of additional nuance. I find that students, and all other readers for that matter, learn most deeply and eagerly when they are compelled to wrestle with arguments involving new ideas. In short, my hope is that all readers, whether novice or expert, will find that this book has something to offer. Scholars will encounter more personal stories than is customary; church leaders and groups more footnotes. I trust students will find a nice balance of each.

Although this is not a textbook—it is more an exploratory "rethinking" of vital topics designed for a diverse audience—this book has also been tested in the college classroom. I think it is particularly well suited for courses on systematic theology, biblical theology, or the New Testament. It should also prove helpful for specialized offerings in which a component of the course focuses on the gospel and salvation, such as courses on evangelism, mission, apologetics, and homiletics. There are study questions at the end of each chapter that can be used for personal contemplation, to prompt group discussion, or as the basis for written reflection.

Finally, a key pastoral point for all readers to keep in mind throughout: with regard to salvation, we dare not think of God as the one who stands against us. The sin problem is real. But God's love is so great that he sent his Son on our behalf even when our sins had made us his enemies (Rom. 5:6–10), showing that God's ultimate desire is to see *all* saved and *all* come to a knowledge of the truth (1 Tim. 2:4). Although the point that "God loves us" is obvious, it needs to be said at the outset, because at times the false notion that "God is enemy, but Jesus is friend" can be held at a nonrational, deeply emotional level—even though we know that it is not true when we actually stop to think. So as we begin, we should all keep the love of God at the forefront of our minds.

So the aim is to rethink the gospel, faith, and salvation in the church and the academy, but to do so within a broad Christian framework for the sake of the *entire* church. My contention is that salvation is by allegiance alone.

Realigning "Faith" and the Gospel

Nevertheless allegiance is frequently missing in discussions of faith, the gospel, and salvation. Some still need to be convinced that enacted obedience is essential to salvation. Those who are already persuaded need a more robust theological grammar to help articulate this truth. For even among the persuaded, why does the proclamation of the gospel in our churches and in our communities so often leave allegiance out? Or if we are pressed to say what it means to "put our faith in Jesus," why do we frequently revert to confusing slogans such as "faith, not works" and "just believe Jesus died for your sins" that would seem to render enacted loyalty unnecessary? We might intuitively sense that allegiance to Jesus is determinative for salvation, but in trying to articulate the gospel, once saving faith is made to demand specific deeds such as giving to charities, taking care of relatives, or volunteering time, many of us fumble for words or get queasy.

Perhaps in those moments we fall back on a "genuine saving faith will inevitably *produce* good works" statement. But is this cause-and-effect assertion fully satisfactory in light of the biblical testimony? Is preestablished faith really the engine driving the good-works machine? Or, perhaps, could it be that buying into this "genuine faith produces good works" slogan presupposes questionable definitions of "faith" and "works" in the first place? In discussing final salvation we are on the firmest ground when we drop "faith" language altogether, speaking instead of allegiance alone. The adoption of "allegiance" language is pressing for the church, for "faith" and "belief" blot out vitally important dimensions of meaning in the *pistis* word family that need to be recovered.

Allegiance relates closely to the gospel and salvation. But because of the lengthy history of these ideas in the West, misperceptions have crept in, so precisely what is meant by "the gospel" and "salvation" requires sharpening as well. This book attempts to explain in a forthright fashion the central biblical teachings about salvation, faith, works, and the gospel—although the reader will discover that this straightforward rehearsal does not always align tidily with popular presentations and understandings of these topics. My argument, reduced to its simplest terms, is as follows:

1. The true climax of the gospel—Jesus's enthronement—has generally been deemphasized or omitted from the gospel.

2. Consequently, *pistis* has been misaimed and inappropriately nuanced with respect to the gospel. It is regarded as "trust" in Jesus's righteousness alone or "faith" that Jesus's death covers my sins rather than "allegiance" to Jesus as king.

3. Final salvation is not about attainment of heaven but about embodied participation in the new creation. When the true goal of salvation is recognized, terms such as "faith," "works," "righteousness," and "the gospel" can be more accurately reframed.

4. Once it is agreed that salvation is by allegiance alone, matters that have traditionally divided Catholics and Protestants—the essence of the gospel, faith alone versus works, declared righteousness versus infused righteousness—are reconfigured in ways that may prove helpful for reconciliation.

This inadequate identification of the climax of the gospel and faulty aiming of "faith" is not a new problem. Nor is it a problem specific to certain Christian denominations or subgroups. It has been a norm across the full spectrum of the church for many hundreds of years. In fact, both Protestants and Catholics alike generally were invested in this slightly skewed scheme in the sixteenth century—indeed these problems extend at least in part all the way back to Saint Augustine in the fifth. Our task here is not to trace that history but rather to look at the earliest Christian sources with an eye to casting fresh vision for the church today. I hope that the correct identification of the high point of the gospel as Jesus's kingship and a retargeting of "faith" as allegiance will reinvigorate the life and mission of the church today.

My conviction is that the story of what God has done for us through the Christ and the Holy Spirit should above all be welcomed as *good news*. And any news that is as wonderfully marvelous as the story of what God has accomplished for us is worthy of our utmost attention. Yet not everyone thinks that the gospel is truly good news. Some, like the man featured in the next section, have walked away depressed and sad.

One Person's Quest for Eternal Life

The story of the rich young ruler is something of an embarrassment for the contemporary church. In Mark's Gospel, when Jesus is just beginning his fateful journey to Jerusalem, he is suddenly accosted by a wealthy man. The man, who is further described in Matthew's Gospel as young (Matt. 19:20) and in Luke's as a ruler (Luke 18:18), dashes up to Jesus and collapses in a subservient and beseeching posture, saying, "Good Teacher, what must I *do* to inherit eternal life?" (Mark 10:17).

The question asked by the ruler is unambiguous—what *action* is required of me so that I can come to participate in life everlasting? Jesus's reply, however, although it seems clear enough on the surface, has proven disconcerting in at least two ways. First, Jesus says in response, "Why do you call me good? No one is good but God alone" (Mark 10:18). Is Jesus hereby denying his divinity, asserting that God (the Father) alone is good and that the appellation "good Teacher" is therefore inappropriate, because it makes Jesus divine?[6] Or, as is much more likely, is this a test designed to make the man reflect more deeply upon the true meaning of the homage that he has offered to Jesus—as if Jesus were querying, "You have bowed and called me 'good,' a title fully suitable to God alone, but to what degree do you really recognize who I am?"[7]

A second disquieting feature of Jesus's response to the rich young man introduces other central concerns of this book—salvation, faith, and works. For in replying to the man's question, "What must I do to inherit eternal life?" Jesus, to the chagrin of many contemporary pastors, priests, evangelists, and teachers, does not give a response that neatly fits our tidy theological systems. "You know the commandments," Jesus states, "'Do not murder, do not commit adultery, do not steal, do not bear false witness, do not defraud, honor your father and mother'" (Mark 10:19). In other words, Jesus cites from the covenantal center of the Old Testament, the Ten Commandments, and intimates that proper *performance* of these commandments will result in eternal life. Jesus says nothing here about faith, trust, or belief. Rather, Jesus in a relatively straightforward fashion asserts that it is necessary to do certain "works" to attain eternal life.

6. Regarding how and when Jesus's earliest followers came to regard him as divine, see Hurtado, *Lord Jesus Christ*; Bauckham, *Jesus and the God of Israel*; Bates, *Birth of the Trinity*.

7. In seeking to weigh Jesus's intentions, we can compare Mark 10:18 (// Luke 18:19) with Mark 2:7, for only here in the NT do we find the Greek phrase *ei mē heis ho theos* ("but God alone"). In Mark 2:7, "who can forgive sins *but God alone*" serves as evidence that Jesus wields the forgiving power that God alone holds after Jesus is able to supply miraculous healing. The reader is thereby invited to conclude that Jesus is somehow both God and distinct from God. It seems likely that the reader of 10:18 is expected to make the same leap.

As the dialogue continues in Mark's Gospel, the man then promptly replies to Jesus, "Teacher, all these I have kept from my youth" (Mark 10:20). Notice that Jesus does not dispute this young man's claim to adequate performance of the Ten Commandments, nor does he question his ability to meet the demands of the law. Instead Jesus says, "You lack one thing: go, sell whatever you have and give it to the poor, and you will have treasure in heaven—and come, follow me" (10:21). Thus, even when Jesus clarifies that the man still lacks one thing, it is not faith or belief, but rather he is required to perform specific additional "works" beyond the Ten Commandments in response to Jesus's instructions—to *sell* all that he has, *give* the money to the poor, and *follow*. It is reported that the man was greatly discouraged by this and sorrowfully departed.

If this were the lone instance in which Jesus taught the primacy and absolute necessity of good works (including proper performance of the law) for eternal life, then it might be plausible to import the "faith alone" idea into this passage without resorting to special pleading. One could, for instance, argue that Jesus was making these legal demands simply to help the man realize that although he *thinks* he has kept the law blamelessly, the man cannot possibly have met its fullest demands. That is, one could claim, as did John Calvin, that by bringing up the rigorous demands of the law, Jesus was attempting to smash the man's pretentions toward law-based righteousness in order to help him see that faith alone can save him.[8] Alternatively, an interpreter might conveniently skip over Jesus's tacit affirmation that the man must keep certain Old Testament commandments and that the man must *sell* everything and *give*, focusing on Jesus's additional demand to "follow me." Here it might be suggested that the man can only be saved by faith in Jesus alone (as evidenced through his willingness to undertake discipleship) and that his performance of the commandments and the charitable deeds would not contribute in any fashion to his attainment of eternal life, except as a token of his willingness to surrender the self.[9] Yet this ignores Jesus's emphasis on keeping the commandments as the first and primary actions in the sequence of necessary events for the man, not to mention the additional specific "good works" of selling and giving.

An even larger problem for a purely faith-alone interpretation of the story involving the rich young man is that every other passage in the Synoptic Gospels (Matthew, Mark, and Luke)—that is, the Gospels that scholars agree most closely adhere to Jesus's own style of speech—that explicitly describes how to

8. See *Calvin's Commentaries*, 16:394–95.
9. See Lane, *Gospel according to Mark*, 366–68.

attain eternal life emphasizes not "faith alone" but rather the absolute necessity of right action.[10] Even if some of the actions are presented in metaphorical or hyperbolic terms, to find eternal life the *correct action* is without fail required. One must enter through the narrow gate (Matt. 7:13–14 and parr.); take up the cross and follow Jesus (Matt. 10:38–39; 16:25; and parr.); give up homes, families, and possessions in following Jesus (Mark 10:30); remove one's own offending hand or eye (Matt. 18:8); stand firm in testifying to Jesus in the face of persecution (Luke 21:19); provide food, water, hospitality, and clothes for the least of Jesus's brothers; tend the sick; and visit the imprisoned (Matt. 25:31–46). In Luke's Gospel, Jesus says to Zacchaeus, "Today salvation has come to this house, since he is also a son of Abraham," not because Zacchaeus is described as putting his "faith" solely in Jesus, but rather because Zacchaeus declares, "Look, half of my belongings I give to the poor, Lord, and if I have extorted anything from anyone, I am paying it back fourfold" (Luke 19:8–9). It is Zacchaeus's concrete gift to the poor and action to make reparation that prompts Jesus's "salvation" declaration.

Meanwhile, in an earlier passage from Luke's Gospel, a certain lawyer asks Jesus how to gain eternal life. When queried further by Jesus, the lawyer is able to state that the two greatest commands are required: to love God and to love one's neighbor as one's self. In reply Jesus does not say, "Forget the commandments! Have faith in me alone and you will live!" but rather, "You have answered correctly; *do* this, and you will live" (Luke 10:28). Then Jesus proceeds to define what it means to be a loving neighbor by telling the parable of the good Samaritan, all of which reinforces the basic point—that it is necessary to perform concrete acts of service to those who are in need in order to gain eternal life.

Of course, those anxious to harmonize Jesus's teachings with their understanding of Paul's gospel of salvation by grace through faith tend to see any suggestion of the necessity of works as a threat to God's free gift of salvation and an insult to the sufficiency of Jesus's sacrifice. So the specific teachings in the Synoptic Gospels pertaining to eternal life are filtered, often ingeniously, through the lens of Paul in order to explain how they do in fact teach salvation by faith alone—that is, if one reads with enough care. The discerning reader should judiciously evaluate such maneuvering. How many beams of good works must we toss aside as we strain to find the sawdust speck of "faith

10. A. Stanley, *Salvation by Works?*, affirms that Jesus did teach that good works are ultimately necessary for final salvation. For a contrary view stressing the importance of faith alone for salvation in the Synoptics, see Schreiner, *Faith Alone*, 112–16. However, Schreiner's evidence feels strained, as his examples pertain to healing and temporary vindication but not clearly to final salvation. The perspective of the Gospel of John will be discussed subsequently.

alone" before we start to wonder precisely how this salvation house has been constructed? If we have to read the "good works" requirement out of so many of Jesus's teachings about eternal life, might it be the case that the assumed Pauline interpretative lens of "by grace alone through faith alone" and "not by works" is causing the distortion? Or could it be that we have foisted our own questionable contemporary understandings of faith, works, the gospel, and salvation onto both Paul and the Gospels?

For reasons that will become clear in due course, I submit that the gospel is not primarily about the necessity of the human response of "faith" in Jesus's saving work, but rather about how Jesus came to be enthroned as Lord of heaven and earth. *Allegiance alone* is required for salvation.

—— FOR FURTHER THOUGHT ——

1. Where outside of a religious setting have you heard people use the term "faith"? What did it mean in that context?
2. If the word "faith" were instantly forbidden, what words do you think would tend to replace it in the various communities in which you participate (e.g., family, school, church, work)? Why?
3. To what degree are our spiritual and religious journeys bounded by our own horizons of experience? Which of your experiences most control how you presently understand "faith"?
4. What did Josephus mean when he urged the rebel, saying, "Repent and believe in me"? Why might this be important for understanding the overall framework of Jesus's ministry?
5. Can you identify several factors that pressure readers to read all passages in the Bible in a "faith, not works" direction?
6. Do you think it is significant that Jesus does not say to the rich young man, "Just believe in me and you will have eternal life"? Why or why not?
7. Have you ever tried to explain to a friend or acquaintance how faith and works fit together? How did (or would) you explain it?

1

FAITH IS *NOT*

Christianity is all about the human response of faith, or so popular teaching and perception would have us believe. Undeniably, faith is essential to Christianity—right? Or is it? I would argue that like rot in an apple, much of the malaise in contemporary Christianity stems from a rotten core. The gospel, salvation, and the Christian life have little to do with "faith" or "belief" as generally defined or understood, and this is the decay in the interior—so much so that it would be best if these words were abandoned with regard to discussions of salvation among Christians. The Greek word *pistis*, generally rendered "faith" or "belief," as it pertains to Christian salvation, quite simply has little correlation with "faith" and "belief" as these words are generally understood and used in contemporary Christian culture, and much to do with *allegiance*. At the center of Christianity, properly understood, is not the human response of faith or belief but rather the old-fashioned term *fidelity*. Chapters 2–4 will reframe the gospel while developing the concepts of allegiance and fidelity more robustly. Those who are anxious to get to the heart of my argument and evidence are welcome to leapfrog the present chapter. But as I have taught this material in the university classroom, I have found that the best first step is to clear away popular misconceptions. So each subsection in what follows seeks to explain what faith is *not*.

Not the Opposite of Evidence Assessment

Several years ago some zealous young missionaries happened to knock on the door of my sister's apartment where I was visiting. These two young women,

15

the radiance of their faces only surpassed by the gleam of their tracts, were eager to do God's work. As they began to tell us the reason for their mission and the source of their joy, I asked a few probing questions about a sacred text known as *The Book of Abraham*.

The Book of Abraham is a text that Joseph Smith Jr., the leading figure of the Latter-Day Saints (Mormon) tradition, claimed to have discovered when a traveling mummy exhibit came through Kirtland, Ohio, where Smith was living at the time. Smith asserted that the manuscript was an ancient document called *The Book of Abraham*, and, after purchasing it, Smith eventually offered his own interpretative translation. Smith claimed it told the story of Abraham's departure from Chaldea, and that it included nonbiblical traditions, such as Abraham's being bound to an altar to be sacrificed by a pagan priest. According to Smith, it also contained speculation about Kolob, a creation alleged to be near to God's celestial residence. Both the pictographs and Smith's translations are easily available online.

But there are large discrepancies between Smith's claims and subsequent scholarly findings. For example, Smith takes the first image as a representation of a pagan priest seeking to sacrifice Abraham on an altar, translating: "And it came to pass that the priests laid violence upon me [Abraham], that they might slay me also, as they did those virgins upon this altar; and that you may have a knowledge of this altar, I will refer you to the representation at the commencement of this record."[1] So Smith asserts that an image in the manuscript and the words associated with the image describe a pagan attempt to sacrifice Abraham. But scholars of the ancient world have determined *The Book of Abraham* to be from a class of Egyptian funerary documents known from elsewhere as "Books of Breathings," and that this particular document was "copied for a Theban priest named Hor."[2] As to the alleged near-sacrifice of Abraham, it is actually a representation of "the resurrection of the Osiris Hor on the customary lion-headed funerary couch." Meanwhile, an authoritative translation of the words associated with the image reads: "[Osiris, the god's father], prophet of Amon-Re, King of the Gods, prophet of Min who slaughters his enemies, prophet of Khonsu" (and so forth).[3] So there is significant publicly available evidence that Smith's *The Book of Abraham* has nothing to do with Abraham at all if ordinary methods of scholarship and translation are applied.

These young women were unflappable when presented with these evidence-based questions, simply stating, "We believe that we can only know the truth

1. *The Book of Abraham* 1:12 in Smith, *Pearl of Great Price*, 27. *The Book of Abraham* is available on the official Latter-Day Saints website: www.lds.org/scriptures/pgp/abr/1?lang=eng.
2. Ritner, "'Breathing Permit of Hor,'" 162.
3. Ibid., 169.

by faith," and inviting us all to consider through prayer whether or not we might have a warm sensation in our hearts as we considered the truth of their presentation.

I tell this story not to nitpick the Mormon tradition (which is complex and intellectually diverse) but rather because I think this story captures well a fundamental misperception about the nature of faith for many in our contemporary culture. Faith is for many of us, much as it was for these exuberant and well-intentioned missionaries, the opposite of evidence-based assessment of truth. A truth claim had been made—"Mormonism is the one fully true story" (including the role of *The Book of Abraham* in the Mormon worldview since this is an authoritative text as part of *The Pearl of Great Price*)—but the assessment of the truth value of that claim was deemed by these young women to be a matter of faith or belief *totally apart from publicly available evidence that might be pertinent to the value of the truth claim*. Faith or belief was being put forward as the opposite of reasoned judgment in consideration of the evidence. Indeed such evidence was deemed immaterial in advance! Faith was reckoned not just an alternative but a *superior* way of knowing what is true and what is false. Judgment could be rendered on the basis of inward feelings alone. For these women, and they are not alone in our culture, faith is defined as something one simply *must* privately and personally affirm regardless of whatever contrary public evidence exists. In short, for many today faith is defined as *the opposite of evidence-based truth*. This is neither a biblical nor a Christian understanding of faith.

In its more egregious forms, such as in the story of the missionaries just recounted, it is perhaps easy to see that this definition of faith is both naive and dangerous because the error is so overt. However, this private, experiential, anti-evidential notion of faith (often called *fideism* in scholarly circles) is not unique to groups such as the Mormons. It also sneaks into the mainstream church in more subtle modes.[4] For instance, we find belief or faith being defined in this basic manner when an inquirer asks a tough question about evolution and creation (on the basis of data available in the public arena) and receives a curt anti-evolutionary response simplistically affirming, "The Bible says it, and I personally have found the Bible to be true, so I believe it," a response that does not attempt to deal seriously with *all* the available data (including complexities in the Bible itself). Regardless of precisely how one comes down on the complex creation or evolution (or both!) debate, we should all agree that the "faith" God requires of us has nothing to do with ignoring relevant evidence that is easily available when adjudicating truth claims. And

4. See Noll, *Scandal of the Evangelical Mind*.

is it not largely due to this abusive use of "faith" and "belief" that so many, past and present, are quick to dismiss Christianity and religion in general, seeing it as purely "faith" based, while taking "faith" to mean the opposite of evidence-based truth?[5] True Christian faith is not fideism.

Not a Leap in the Dark

As Christians, we are frequently encouraged to *step out in faith*, to do something bold for God or for Jesus that intentionally pushes us outside our comfort zone: to travel halfway around the world, to build an orphanage in a third-world country, to contribute money to a kingdom-growing project beyond what we think our finances can bear, or to befriend the socially disadvantaged. All of these things are undoubtedly worthwhile endeavors—but is this at the heart of *faith*? And is the reason for doing them really that we should "step out"? Is it true that we should—like the hero in *Indiana Jones and the Last Crusade* (in a movie clip that is sometimes shown at churches to encourage such action)—take a step off of a ledge into a dark chasm, obediently following arcane instructions, even when no obvious path to safety can be achieved by making the leap? To be a true Christian, so it is asserted, or at least to foster maturity *in the faith*, we must plunge into the darkness, launching into what appears to be utter nothingness, knowing that the unfailing God will catch us. This, so it is claimed, is not an irrational leap, because we know that God will indeed safely cradle us.

It is not just popular Christianity that would encourage this type of faith. The Danish existential philosopher and theologian Søren Kierkegaard, reacting with strong aversion to the predominant but all-too-easy Christian culture in which he found himself (what he calls *Christendom*), waxes eloquent when he considers Abraham.[6] For Kierkegaard, Abraham is the greatest example of faith in the Bible—a paragon of faith—because of his unquestioning obedience to God's command with regard to Isaac. In Genesis 22, Abraham is commanded to do the unthinkable, to offer his son as a sacrifice to God. And not just his son, but his beloved son Isaac, who, after years of infertility and frustration, was given in fulfillment of God's promise. Contrary to natural paternal instinct and all basic laws of moral decency, Abraham must kill his

---

5. Fideism is not just a contemporary issue but was a problem in early Christianity too. For example, the pagan Celsus speaks derisively about Christians, saying, "Some do not even want to give or to receive a reason for what they believe, and use such expressions as 'Do not ask questions; just believe,' and 'Thy faith will save thee'" (Origen, *Cels*. 1.9 [Chadwick]).

6. Kierkegaard, *Fear and Trembling*.

own son on the altar. For Kierkegaard, Abraham in his unquestioning obedience is a knight of faith, willing to do what is irrational, what is in fact by
mere human standards immoral, in obedience to the divine commandment.
In Genesis 22 it is clear that Abraham never wavers; he is single-mindedly
committed to executing the divine will until the angel calls out, restraining
Abraham's hand even as he is about to plunge the knife. Kierkegaard summons
us to act with the same faith as Abraham, to abandon ourselves recklessly
to the necessary leap in the dark, because it is only in midflight that we truly
encounter God.[7]

This stepping-out-from-security definition captures an essential component
of biblical faith but simultaneously introduces a dangerous half-truth when
it is coupled with an irrational leap-in-the-dark notion. The truth portion
of this half-truth is best illustrated by examining the most straightforward
definition of faith given in the Bible. The author of the Letter to the Hebrews
defines *pistis*, saying, "Now faith [*pistis*] is the underlying substance [*hypostasis*] toward which hope is directed, the conviction of things not seen" (Heb.
11:1). The point of this definition—as is made clear by examples in the rest
of Hebrews 11—is that by means of *pistis*, the true people of God are willing to act decisively in the visible world not for reasons that are immediately
apparent but because an unseen yet even more genuine underlying substance
(*hypostasis*), God's reality, compels the action. This willingness to act on the
deeper, truer, but nonetheless hidden reality is "faith" for the author of Hebrews. And we should eagerly agree that true knowledge of God and saving
"faith" are often bound up with such a notion.[8] For example, Noah was saved
when he acted on things not yet seen, responding to the command of God to
build an ark, even in the absence of tangible, this-present-world evidence (Heb.
11:7)—all of which is instructive for our salvation (1 Pet. 3:20–21; 2 Pet. 2:5).

Yet—and now for the way in which this leap-in-the-dark idea is a dangerous half-truth—it must be remembered that neither Noah nor Abraham
launched out into the void, but rather each responded to God's command.
They acted in response to the call of a promise-fulfilling God with whom
they had experience. Abraham was asked to sacrifice Isaac by the God who
had miraculously provided Isaac—a God who had proven to be trustworthy

7. Kierkegaard's ideas about faith are much more sophisticated than this brief recounting
might suggest. For further analysis, see Westphal, *Kierkegaard's Concept of Faith*.

8. Although I have cautioned against imposing Kierkegaard's existential definition of faith
onto our ancient texts, at the same time I welcome Kierkegaard's insistence on the necessity
of a subjective knowing with respect to God. Kierkegaard does offer a helpful antidote to any
vestige of naive objectivism that remains in the academy and the church—and a way to hold
head and heart together. See Crump, *Encountering Jesus, Encountering Scripture*.

to Abraham through a lengthy life journey together. One might even dare to say that in so acting Noah and Abraham above all *showed allegiance* to God as the sovereign and powerful Lord who speaks all human affairs into existence, but more on this later.

The key point is that true *pistis* is not an irrational launching into the void but a reasonable, action-oriented response grounded in the conviction that God's invisible underlying realities are more certain than any apparent realities. Stepping out in faith is not intrinsically good in and of itself, as if God is inherently more pleased with daring motorcycle riders than with automobile passengers who cautiously triple-check their seatbelt buckles; it is only good when it is an obedient response to God's exercised sovereignty. We are not to leap out in the dark at a whim, or simply to prove to ourselves, God, or others that we "have faith." But the promise-keeping God might indeed *call us* to act on invisible realities of his heavenly kingdom.

If the call is genuine, we may indeed be bruised by the leap. Yet if it is genuine, in gathering the bruises from the hard landing, we can be certain that we will come to look more like the wounded Son, which is the final goal of redeemed humanity. If the call to leap is not genuine but an idolatrous response to a false god of our own making, we may jump into the emptiness only to find ourselves unable to gain secure footing or to reverse course. True *pistis* is not an irrational leap in the dark but a carefully discerned response to God's reign through Jesus over his kingdom and that kingdom's frequently hidden growth.

Not the Opposite of Works

I grew up in a fundamentalist, King-James-Version-only Bible church in Northern California. In this brand of Christianity the Bible sometimes has a way of taking on a certain luminous quality. The Bible was certainly not worshiped, but some of the hymnody perhaps unwittingly encouraged a covert bibliolatry. For instance, each and every Sunday, prior to the Sunday school service, the leader would hold up a worn leather Bible, and the congregation would enthusiastically belt out, "The B-I-B-L-E, yes that's the book for me! I'll stand alone on the Word of God, the B-I-B-L-E!" If no one bowed face-down on the dusty carpet in homage to the book, a few knees might have ever so slightly buckled.

My pastor at that time was (and still is) a kindhearted man, deeply devoted to God, Jesus, the church, the unsaved, his family, and the Bible—perhaps not in that precise order. When I reflect on his role in my life, I can only speak with gratitude. Although my mother had introduced me to Jesus and the Christian life when I was a young child, during my teenage years my pastor's formal teaching awakened something new—a brighter light, a moral rigor, a passion for God's ways, and above all else a reverence for Scripture. I am profoundly grateful for his role in my life.

Yet in retrospect the preached message I heard weekly growing up was subtly confused. No matter what passage of Scripture was being exposited, regardless of the liturgical season (my church was not exactly into following the ecclesial calendar), despite whatever contemporary political or societal affairs might be pressing, virtually every sermon had the same conclusion— a presentation of "the gospel" and an invitation "to accept Jesus into your heart." Now, do not misunderstand: I think the gospel should be preached and invitations to follow Jesus need to be extended—urgently so. However, invariably the good news was presented in its classic "Romans Road" form and accompanied by a stern warning. That is, the gospel was given as follows: (1) we are all perniciously bent on trying to earn our salvation by doing good deeds; (2) yet all have sinned and fallen short of the glory of God—and that includes *you*; (3) but the good news is that Jesus died for your sins; (4) so if you will just believe this and pray along with me, then the free gift of eternal life is yours today. And now the warning: the only thing that you must not under any circumstances do is believe that you can earn your salvation through good works, for this was the mistake of many Jews in Paul's day and is still the error of Catholics today.

Within this version of the gospel, which involves several dangerous distortions, good works end up playing the confusing dual role of friend and foe. Good works are "friend" because they are believed to *flow from* the more primal response of belief and are evidence of genuine faith. In this way, it is still possible for those who adhere to this system to affirm James 2:26, "faith without deeds is dead," because good works are felt to emerge spontaneously from the wellspring of faith. Yet good works are "foe" because they can all too easily lure us, seduce us, become our false security blanket, causing us to rely on ourselves for our own salvation—and then, so it is presumed, we stumble (cf. Rom. 9:30–33). We must instead ever and always just trust, avoiding the seduction of seeking to earn God's favor through moral or religious performance.

In this way faith and works are pitted against one another as opposite paths to salvation, one that is successful (faith) and one that fails (works). Chapter 5 will explain more fully how treating faith and good deeds as opposite and mutually exclusive paths to salvation distorts the gospel. Here I merely want to point out that the faith/works divide taught in churches like the one in which I was raised relies on assumed meanings of "faith" (*pistis*) and "works" (*erga*) that may not be linguistically or contextually sound. If, for instance, we were to discover that Paul is concerned not primarily with "good works" in general but rather with "works of law"—that is, works demanded by the law of Moses—then what difference might that make? Furthermore, if we were to determine that in appropriate salvation-oriented contexts in the New Testament *pistis* most likely means faithfulness, or fidelity, or allegiance, then might not *pistis* by its very definition *include* concrete acts that are inseparable from allegiance? In other words, we might come to discover that faith and works are not mutually exclusive after all.

Not an "It's All Good" Attitude

You just lost your job. Rent is overdue. Utility bills are piling up. Your roommate just told you that she is moving out next month. Then you receive the notice that your tuition payment for next semester is due in three weeks. Enter your well-intentioned Christian friend, who offers the following words of consolation: "Everything is going to be all right—you just need to have faith," or "God brings about these sort of events to test our faith—just believe in God and he will deliver you from this trial."

Now in the most general theological terms, this might in fact be sound advice. Although not everything that happens in life reflects God's *desired will* (most obviously our own sin or the sin of others is not what God would wish to occur), all that happens is allowed within God's *permissive will*. And we also know that whatever God permits, even if evil is allowed to temporarily flourish, it can be turned to good by God for us and for others. This is beautifully illustrated by the story of Joseph, who even after being sold into slavery by his brothers, suffering false accusation, imprisonment, and exile, is still able in the end to say to his brothers, "Although you meant evil against me, God meant it for good, in order that, as it is today, many people should be kept alive" (Gen. 50:20). So in the final analysis we truly can affirm with the apostle Paul that "all things work together for good for those who love God, for those who are called in accordance with his purpose" (Rom. 8:28).

The risk here is that if you, while staring disconsolately at your bank statement, were to accept your friend's advice ("Everything is going to be all right—you just need to have faith") in an unqualified fashion, then you might accept an inadequate definition of faith. You might begin to think of faith as equivalent to "maintaining a positive mindset." As if the hippy tie-dye generation kind of faith—just chill out and relax, because everything is going to be fine—is somehow what is needed in this stressful situation. You might be tempted to think that real Christian faith demands unfettered optimism. No matter what, you must relax and stay positive, so you should deny your real feelings, slap a plastic doll grin on your face, and try to keep up appearances of all-rightness. But this optimism is a bit self-delusional (if not neurotic). If everything does *not* turn out all right and the self-delusion collapses, you might think that you have somehow lost your Christian faith. "After all," you might say, "if I had genuine faith, I would not feel so discouraged."

A few minutes of reflection will probably reveal the inadequacy of a "positive mindset" definition of faith. Faith-as-optimism is an almost entirely vacuous idea (remember the George Michael example in the introduction), because in the final analysis *no concrete object of faith is in view at all*. It is faith merely for faith's sake. The truth is that genuine biblical faith is not a conjured optimism, a pull-a-rabbit-out-of-the-hat, magical feel-goodism, nor is it aimlessly directed at some vague cosmic hope that affirms good karma will somehow prevail in the end. Let me give an example to help illustrate.

As a salute and celebration of the great American auto industry, let's say I currently drive a 1972 Chevy Nova. Not only does its very name suggest that it won't reliably run (*No va* means "it doesn't go" in Spanish), but my own practical experience is that due to its age and lack of maintenance, my car will only start once out of every ten times I jump into it and turn the key. Now, I have a hugely important interview early tomorrow morning. Do I say to myself, "I simply have faith that my Nova will start tomorrow!" and do nothing but blindly hope, or do I make a backup plan? If this interview is truly central to my life goals, I am not going to chance it. Why? Because even if I wanted to channel a deep inner reservoir of "faith," I would not really be able to do it. I would know in my heart of hearts that my car is an untrustworthy junker.

In other words, true faith cannot be spontaneously generated on the basis of wishful thinking, for it is rooted in *a concrete object toward which it is directed*.[9] If the object upon which I am asked to rely (in this example, my Nova) has repeatedly proven to be untrustworthy, then unless I am adept at extreme and willful self-delusion, it will literally be impossible to *really* trust it, even should I desperately wish to trust it. The point is that real biblical faith is not a general positive mindset or a blind optimism but is directed toward

---

9. Morgan, *Roman Faith and Christian Faith*, 4, describes it this way: "*Pistis* is a relational concept whose meaning is always defined in part by the relationship in which it operates: the faithfulness of a slave towards her master is not the same as that of a client towards his patron or that of a believer towards Christ." So, more precisely, *pistis* is a relational term, the quality of which is determined by the subject's ability to invest trust in the object and the object's ability to generate trust in the subject.

a defined object—and it is the trustworthiness of the object that sources and fixes faith's genuineness. So if we want to grow in faith, we should study and contemplate God's extraordinary reliability.

Not Reducible to Intellectual Assent

One of the greatest strengths of the Christian tradition is the depth and rigor of its intellectual heritage. Anyone who thinks that Christianity is nothing more than a naive tale suitable only for simpletons should spend a few hours reading ancient worthies such as Saint Augustine, Thomas Aquinas, and John Calvin, or more recent thinkers such as Karl Barth, Alvin Plantinga, and N. T. Wright. Perhaps partly because this rich intellectual heritage is so compelling, some Christians, both ancient and modern, have felt that salvation depends solely upon knowing the right things, believing certain doctrines to be true.

In the period of the early church, some deviant groups came to believe that they were saved primarily through the acquisition of knowledge. These diverse groups are usually collectively called the Gnostics. Despite considerable variety in what they believed, they shared the conviction that salvation was contingent on the acquisition of esoteric knowledge. In short, without obtaining the requisite secret information, upon death they might not be able to escape from the enslaving material order (usually understood to be crafted by the god of the Old Testament, whom they regarded as an inferior deity) and to return to the spiritual fullness from which they originated—that is, to the most high God, the God of the New Testament as revealed by Jesus. So these Gnostics tended to believe falsely that the god of the Old Testament is different from the God of the New. The Gnostics thought that the latent spark of divinity inside you needed to be fanned into a white-hot flame through the acquisition of secret knowledge, all of which would allow you to pass through the various heavenly spheres as you returned to the fullness. You might even need to have memorized certain passwords so that angels guarding the gateways to the various heavenly spheres would allow you to pass through to the next level in your movement away from the material order and toward the fullness. For the Gnostics, secret knowledge was what was ultimately most necessary for salvation.

In more recent times the so-called free-grace movement approaches this notion of salvation by knowledge. This system asserts that all God requires of a person for eternal salvation is to hold a specific minimalistic belief as factual—that Jesus died for my sins. And the weight of emphasis here is on personal, intellectual assent ("I agree") to the truthfulness ("reality") of a proposition ("that Jesus died for my sins"). In short, if you mentally agree that Jesus died for your sins, then nothing else is required for your salvation—you are on your way to heaven.[10] The problem here is a deficient definition of faith (and for that matter of salvation). Advocates of free-grace salvation have correctly recognized the primacy of God's grace and the necessity of holding certain doctrines as "true" or "real," but by effectively reducing faith to intellectual assent, they have introduced a dangerous error.

Nobody, even in the free-grace movement, wants to claim that the demons in Mark's Gospel—who know Jesus's divine origins and who utter, "I know who you are, the Holy One of God!" (Mark 1:24) and "You are the Son of God" (3:11)—are in actuality saved because of their true knowledge of Jesus. Free-gracers are quick to disavow such a conclusion. All would agree with the Letter of James, which affirms that such "facts" are not enough: "You believe that God is one. You do well. Even the demons believe and shudder" (James 2:19). Nonetheless, problematically, at least some in the free-grace movement want to make salvation depend on nothing but a slight variation of the Son-of-God fact, an affirmation that Jesus died for my sins.

It is correct that we must hold certain intellectual truths as real or factual, including Jesus's saving work, but this is not all God requires. As we seek to recover the Bible's teachings about faith, works, and the gospel, in the next chapter we will explore further what essential "facts" do need to be intellectually affirmed as a necessary condition for salvation along with allegiance to Jesus as king.

—— FOR FURTHER THOUGHT ——

1. Why is it important for Christians to recognize that faith and evidence aren't opposites?
2. Describe a time when you personally encountered a situation in which faith was being defined (overtly or covertly) as the opposite of evidence. Did you or others recognize it as problematic at the time?
3. Have you ever felt that God was asking you to make a leap in the dark? What happened?
4. Why does the leap-in-the-dark idea both approach and depart from the biblical notion of *pistis* ("faith") as described in Hebrews?

10. As representative voices in the free-grace movement, consider Hodges, *Absolutely Free*; C. Stanley, *Eternal Security*.

5. At what point (or points) is the line crossed between a healthy respect for the Bible and an inappropriate bibliolatry (worship of the Bible)?

6. Do your past experiences, especially religious experiences, lead you to see works more as friend or foe? Why?

7. Do you think it is psychologically helpful for a person to have faith just for faith's sake? What are the potential risks and rewards?

8. If you were to catch a Christian friend placing faith in faith and you had an opportunity to correct your friend gently, how would you explain the deficiency?

9. What is the risk to Christianity as a whole if faith or belief is defined only as mental agreement with certain "facts"?

10. Can you think of at least one practical way (a concrete action) to help yourself or another remember that when the Bible speaks of saving "belief" or "faith," more than mental agreement is intended?

2

LOYALTY AND THE FULL GOSPEL

Several months ago my wife and I were surprised by a mid-afternoon knock on our front door. Our shaggy beast leaped to his feet, his full-throated bark careening off the coffee table and chandelier. A middle-aged woman stood on our threshold, nondescript apart from a do-good demeanor. After exchanging a few awkward commonplaces with us, she explained the reason for her sudden appearance on our stoop. She was walking door-to-door to invite folks to a new church that was being launched in the neighborhood.

We expressed appropriate Christian enthusiasm for the venture but informed our visitor that we were already attached to a local church body. She was pleased to learn that we were churchgoers, but with the irrepressible doggedness of a politician, she still pressed a small tract upon us. Undoubtedly she was aware that church attendance is often nominal and that our participation did not guarantee that we had grasped the good news about Jesus. Now I am hesitant to say this, for it may forever encourage solicitors to stop at my door, but after she left, I did a rare thing—I began to read the tract.

Jesus Died for Me—the Truncated Gospel

As the door closed, I glanced at the title of the tract: "How to Be 100% Sure of Heaven."[1] Since I was currently drafting the first chapter of this book, I was compelled to see precisely what program was being offered for attaining

1. The tract is copyrighted by Rev. Jim L. Bray (2009) and directs the reader to www.thepower oftheword.com for ordering.

this certainty. The suggested procedure is unsurprising—indeed, it is the very procedure suggested in countless sermons throughout the world every week: to believe, repent, and then call on Christ to save. I was given a six-step program toward that end, after which I was instructed to repent and then to call on Christ in order to receive God's one-hundred-percent-certain promise. Regarding this calling upon the Lord, I was somewhat strangely directed to Psalm 55:16 and Psalm 116:13 and then more helpfully pointed to Romans 10:13: "For whosoever shall call upon the name of the Lord shall be saved" (KJV). The tract seemed particularly eager to remind me that "only the Lord can save you, not the Lord plus your own efforts to 'earn salvation' by your good deeds!" I was then invited to pray a certain prayer in my heart. If I had completed this final step, then I was joyfully informed, "Dear friend, if you prayed this prayer and meant it, you can be one hundred percent sure you're saved, based on God's promises in these verses!"

Now, I am not seeking to pick on this particular tract nor the kind woman who brought it to our front door. For even sophisticated books penned by excellent scholars occasionally contain similar infelicities.[2] Clearly the tract contains many truths that any sound Christian would be eager to affirm. Even if the message is slightly off the mark, many individuals can and do genuinely turn to the Christ through messages identical to the one that appears in this tract. Why then the fuss?

The errors in this tract are primarily a matter of framing, emphasis, definition, and aim, but the many small deviations compound, so that the result distorts both the gospel and the goal of salvation. In fact, rather than receiving the one-hundred-percent-certain promise of heaven, on the contrary, the tract's reader might actually be placing himself or herself at a heightened spiritual risk. The reader might be tempted to think, "Now that I've prayed this prayer, I have satisfied God and am on the road to glory—so now I can cross that off my bucket list and get back to life." Then, reflecting a little bit more, a reader might add, "I'll try to live a *little* better now, but my works don't really matter, and I certainly don't want to fall into the trap of trusting in my own righteousness, so I won't worry too much about it."

Perhaps the reader of the tract who has prayed this prayer will embrace a journey of Christian discipleship, or perhaps not. The gospel message presented in the tract, however, certainly implies that discipleship is optional. Other than feeling a vague regret over ongoing sins, any long-term behavior changes, inasmuch as these are "deeds," are not essential to the heavenly cake,

---

2. Such as including faith alone and our justification within the gospel's content; see discussion in "Jesus Proclaims the Gospel in the Gospels" in chap. 3.

but rather more like frosting. It might be rewardingly delicious to add some good deeds to the cake, but the cake is really terrific regardless—and so maybe it won't be worth the effort. Yet the full Christian gospel both demands and gives much more.

Toward the True Gospel

As we assess the truncated gospel and seek to replace it with the true gospel, it should first be noted that the former presupposes a skewed plot to the cosmic drama. The plot in the abbreviated gospel is self-centered: I have a problem (sin) and I am currently on the road to perdition, but Jesus died for my sins, so now I have the opportunity to change roads—to go to heaven. All that is required is my personal faith that Jesus's death completely saves me from my sins. But what if this gospel presentation were to begin not with me and my sin but with a story about Jesus? Or maybe something more primal like creation and new creation? Or perhaps with the fundamental human task of bearing God's image? How might this change the tenor of the whole narrative? Moreover, this truncated gospel assumes that the ultimate goal for humanity is spiritual bliss in heaven rather than, as we shall discuss further in chapter 6, *embodied participation in the new heavens and the new earth*. The difference has radical implications for what salvation actually means. In short, the story into which the truncated gospel has been made to fit needs to be rethought, and we will undertake that task together at the appropriate juncture.[3] Right now let's focus on the core gospel message.

The Gospel Proper

In general terms, the word *gospel* means "good news." It translates the Greek word *euangelion*, where the *eu-* prefix means "good" and *angelion* refers to a communicated message (it relates to the Greek word *angelos*, meaning "messenger," from which the English *angel* is derived). *Euangelion* refers to glad tidings heralded forth, a happy message publically announced and proclaimed. Imagine you are an ancient queen or king. Your generals are away fighting a battle upon which the fate of your kingdom hinges. Suddenly a runner dashes

---

3. For a like-minded analysis, see McKnight, *King Jesus Gospel*, 34–44. With regard to the gospel, McKnight shows that all too often in contemporary church culture the method of presenting the gospel (evangelistic persuasion) and the "plan of salvation" run roughshod over the gospel's true content—the story of Jesus framed by the story of Israel.

into the royal court: "Good news! Good news! We have triumphed, and the army is marching back with the enemies as captives!" Or, closer to the point for our purposes, imagine another ancient scene: everyone in the surrounding regions knows that because of political turmoil the royal throne has been temporarily vacant—but then a herald passes through the town crying out, "Good news! Prince Theodorus has now become king!" Something similar is intended by *euangelion* when used in the New Testament with reference to Jesus. In seeking a more precise understanding of the gospel, we will move from the center outward. In this chapter we will begin with the earliest and clearest statements in the New Testament about the gospel, examining the apostle Paul's descriptions, and then we will examine how these statements open wider contexts of meaning.

The most straightforward explanations of what the word "gospel" meant for the earliest Christians are found in three passages in Paul's Letters, Romans 1:1–5, 1:16–17, and 1 Corinthians 15:1–5 (cf. 2 Tim. 2:8). Another passage that does not use the word *euangelion* but aligns closely with the above mentioned is Philippians 2:6–11, which can help fill out our understanding. We begin with Paul because he is our earliest extant Christian writer—his letter writing began about fifteen years after Jesus's death—and also because there is evidence that Paul's explanations of the gospel were not idiosyncratic but common to the early apostolic church as a whole. Anticipating my conclusions, *the gospel is the power-releasing story of Jesus's life, death for sins, resurrection, and installation as king*, but that story only makes sense in the wider framework of the stories of Israel and creation. The gospel is not in the first instance a story about heaven, hell, making a decision, raising your hand after praying a certain prayer, justification by faith alone, trusting that Jesus's righteousness is sufficient, or any putative human tendencies toward self-salvation through good works.[4] It is, in the final analysis, most succinctly *good news about the enthronement of Jesus the atoning king* as he brings these wider stories to a climax.

Incarnation and Enthronement

The first gospel passage, Romans 1:1–5, fittingly stands at the head of Paul's most famous and lengthy letter. Paul opens his letter to the churches in

---

4. For a catalog of contemporary misapplications of the term "gospel," see Carson, "What Is the Gospel?—Revisited." Carson describes the root problem well when he states, "The Bible insists that there are both individual and communal *outcomes* to the preaching of the gospel, *neither of which is the gospel itself*" (159).

Rome—churches that he did not found but did desire to visit—by introducing himself and the gospel. And if Paul felt a summary of the gospel to be a suitable opening sally in seeking to win a hearing with the Romans, we already have good reason to suspect that this digest of the gospel would have been agreeable to the various Roman house churches.[5] Notice also that Paul does not say that this gospel is "my gospel," even though he is occasionally capable of that expression (Rom. 2:16; 16:25; 2 Tim. 2:8). Rather, since for Paul there is only one true gospel (cf. Gal. 1:6–7), he speaks in universal terms, calling it "the gospel of God":

> Paul, a slave of the Christ Jesus, a called apostle, having been set apart for the gospel of God—the gospel that he promised beforehand through his prophets in the holy Scriptures. (Rom. 1:1–2)

We discover an important truth about the nature of this one universal gospel. God has not merely *predicted* that this good news would emerge by sending prophets to declare it. God has done something more marvelous. This creator God, the only true God, the God whom not even the highest heavens can contain, has deliberately obligated himself to bring about the gospel through an advance *promise*. Even though he was under no compulsion, so Paul suggests, God chose to make himself beholden to his human creatures, and indeed to the whole creation, to accomplish a specific sort of good news in the future.

Continuing, Paul describes this good news in sparse but pregnant language for the Romans:

> [the gospel] concerning his Son, who as it pertains to the flesh came into existence by means of the seed of David; who as it pertains to the Spirit of Holiness was appointed Son-of-God-in-Power by means of the resurrection from among the dead ones—Jesus the Christ our Lord. (Rom. 1:3–4)[6]

In reading Paul's summary of the gospel, we quickly recognize that the gospel is not at its most basic level a tale about me and my quest for salvation (or even about "us" and "our" quest), but rather it is a grand, cosmic story about God's Son and what he has done.

---

5. Most scholars have determined (correctly in my judgment) that Rom. 1:3–4 consists of traditional material that Paul opted to incorporate into his letter. For scholarly discussion, see Jewett, "Early Christian Confession"; Jipp, "Interpretations of Romans 1:3–4."

6. For a full scholarly defense of this translation of Rom. 1:3–4 (which is my own) and of the interpretation subsequently offered in this subsection, see Bates, "Christology of Incarnation and Enthronement."

Fleshly Coming into Being

The first movement in this cosmic drama pertains to what later tradition would call the *incarnation*—the taking on of human flesh by Jesus. As the story opens, the Son preexists with God the Father, but *the good news, the gospel proper, begins when Jesus is sent by the Father to assume human flesh.*[7] Thus, as we shall see in chapter 6, the good news in its widest scope intimately connects to another person, Adam, who similarly came into existence and took on human flesh. Jesus as the paradigm for humanity, the truly human one, corresponds to and parallels Adam. As such, the full good news relates to Adam's role (and Eve's role) with respect to creation, and hence in the final analysis the gospel's associative context will prove to be as wide as creation itself. Yet the story of the "fall" of Adam and Eve in the garden and the resultant human plight is not part of the gospel proper; rather it is a necessary framing story without which the gospel cannot be fully understood. As will become increasingly clear as we continue, if we are to reframe faith, the gospel, and salvation accurately, precision about these details matters.

Given the compressed language Paul employs to outline the good news, it might be easy to pass by a second framing story: Jesus entered fleshly human existence not haphazardly, but his family line was carefully selected by God precisely to fulfill the promise God had made. Jesus, inasmuch as it pertains to the flesh, was not merely born into the family line of David but rather was brought into existence "by means of the seed of David." In other words, the gospel cannot be holistically comprehended without seeing the manner in which the incarnation fulfills God's promise to David, a promise God spoke shortly after David had secured the throne:

> When your days are fulfilled and you lie down with your ancestors, I will raise up your offspring after you, who shall come forth from your body, and I will establish his kingdom. He shall build a house for my name, and I will establish the throne of his kingdom forever. I will be a father to him, and he shall be a son to me. (2 Sam. 7:12–14 NRSV)

---

7. Jesus's preexistence in Rom. 1:3 is suggested (among other things) by the use of the verb *ginomai* to emphasize not just ordinary birth (in which case *gennaō* would typically be expected) but a change from a non-fleshly existence to a fleshly one (cf. Gal. 4:4; Phil. 2:7). Romans 8:3 reinforces this interpretation since God is described as "sending his own Son in the likeness of sinful flesh and for the sake of sin, in order to condemn sin in the flesh." It is presupposed that the Son is first with the Father in a non-fleshly state, but then he is sent, taking on something akin but not identical to *sinful* flesh, so that he might condemn sin in the flesh—all of which suggests that the Son took on real but *non-sinful* human flesh so that sin might be judged there (cf. Gal. 3:13; Rom. 3:25; 1 Pet. 2:24–25).

So David was promised an offspring, literally a "seed," who would be established as king over an unending kingdom. It is even stated that this king would enjoy a special filial relationship with God—metaphorical language that early Christians would see as anticipating a future reality: Jesus as the only begotten Son of God. This promissory language, however, echoes even earlier biblical narratives, that through Abraham and his seed "all nations on earth will be blessed" (Gen. 12:3; 22:18; cf. Gal. 3:16). And even earlier, that the serpent's head would be crushed through the seed of *the woman* (Gen. 3:15). So Paul's spartan "by means of the seed of David" evokes numerous images. It probably intends *Mary* as the seed of David, emphasizing her instrumental role in bringing the preexistent Son into fleshly existence.[8]

Yet the gospel is not just about the Davidic promise; it is also about the resurrection. The most compact yet explicit articulation of the gospel, as found in Paul's Second Letter to Timothy, makes this clear: "Remember Jesus the Christ, raised from among the dead ones, of the seed of David—that is my gospel" (2:8).[9] And as we shall see, the resurrection in turn is intimately connected with the coronation of Jesus.

Enthroned as Son-of-God-in-Power

In Romans 1:3–4, the second movement in this sweeping cosmic narrative is the *enthronement* of the Son. Paul states that after the incarnation something quite astonishing happened. The Son of God died (implied in Paul's description of the Christ's preresurrection state, "from among the dead ones"). Yet he was raised to new bodily life by God. On the basis of this resurrection, Jesus was then installed in a new position of authority: he "was appointed Son-of-God-in-Power," which is best construed as the informal description of the office into which the Son has been installed—a point that nearly all

8. Cf. *tou genomenou ek spermatos Dauid* ("who came into existence by means of the seed of David") in Rom. 1:3 with *genomenon ek gynaikos* in Gal. 4:4 ("having come into existence by means of a woman"). Note that an incarnational interpretation explains Paul's preference for *ginomai* rather than *gennaō* in Rom. 1:3 and Gal. 4:4 (cf. Phil. 2:7). Note further that an instrumental interpretation of *ek* in Rom. 1:3 preserves the parallelism with *ex* in Rom. 1:4, as the latter is clearly instrumental ("by means of his resurrection"). On Mary as an offspring of David, see Luke 3:23 (probably); Ign. *Eph.* 18.2; *Trall.* 9.1; Justin, *Dial.* 100.3; Irenaeus, *Epid.* 36; *Haer.* 3.16.3.

9. Some modern scholars do not believe that Paul really wrote 2 Timothy (and the authorship of five of Paul's other letters is disputed as well). Others, myself included, disagree for reasons discussed by Luke Timothy Johnson, *First and Second Letters to Timothy*, 55–90. Both because of my own scholarly convictions and because it has little bearing on the results of this study, I will refer to Paul as the author of the thirteen NT letters that make internal claims to his authorship.

contemporary English translations and most scholars miss when they offer the less likely translation: "declared with power to be the Son of God."[10]

The true thrust of Paul's line of thought is that the resurrection served to trigger the exaltation of Jesus from his lowly status among the dead, so that he came to be installed in a position of sovereign authority. Previously he was the Son of God; now he is the Son-of-God-in-Power, actively reigning until all his enemies are made a footstool for his feet (1 Cor. 15:25). In other words, in his earthly life Jesus was the anointed one, the one chosen as the royal Davidic Messiah (the Christ), but during his earthly sojourn he had not yet received his throne, he had not yet begun to reign as king. But the resurrection (and ascension) changed all this, as Jesus has now been enthroned at the right hand of God and is reigning as the Lord of heaven and earth. In fact, in summing up his presentation of the basic content of the gospel, Paul concludes by calling this Son-of-God-in-Power by slightly different titles that Paul prefers, "Jesus the *Christ* our *Lord*" (Rom. 1:4).

And what is this Jesus as Son-of-God-in-Power or Lord seeking to accomplish? Paul goes on to speak of the purpose of the gospel in the next verse. This Lord Jesus is the one who has commissioned Paul and the other apostles in order that they might bring about the "obedience of faith" (*hypakoēn pisteōs*) among the nations, all of which will bring glory to the name of Jesus (Rom. 1:5; cf. 16:26). We might wonder what is meant by this "obedience of *pistis*." If, as has traditionally been held by many since the Protestant Reformation, the gospel is all about faith alone, not faith plus works, then why doesn't Paul just say that the gospel is purposed toward *pistis*? Does Paul perhaps simply mean that the gospel will promote obedience *after* the "faith" decision has been made (that is, to use the terminology preferred by systematic theologians, after *justification* has transpired)?

We should be wary of quick answers that harmonize the multiple images pertaining to salvation (and their complex past, present, and future aspects) by offering a rigid order of salvation: first *justification*, being declared innocent by God; then *sanctification*, increasing in holiness through God's assistance; finally *glorification*, full transformation and attainment of heaven.[11] Such tidy contemporary systems offer convenient prepackaged descriptions alleging to describe how salvation works, but they do not cohere sufficiently to the

---

10. For evidence, see Bates, "Christology of Incarnation and Enthronement."

11. For a classic and sophisticated presentation of an order of salvation (going beyond merely justification, sanctification, glorification), consider Murray, *Redemption—Accomplished and Applied*. For a recent attempt to assess the degree to which we can describe Paul's vision of salvation in ordered terms, see Gaffin, *By Faith, Not by Sight*. For further discussion, see "Order of Salvation" in chap. 8 herein.

ancient thought structures on which such systems depend. I will have more to say about the relationship between obedience and *pistis* later.

The V Pattern

So, at the beginning of his most important letter, Romans, when Paul summarizes what he means by "the gospel," he tells a V-shaped story about Jesus.[12] Initially Jesus preexisted as Son of God, which seems to presuppose an exalted state, yet he moved downward, taking on human flesh and then reaching the very bottom—the abode of the dead. But once he reached bottom, the ascent began—he was raised from the dead and then installed in the heavenly sphere as Son-of-God-in-Power. Does this narrative sound suspiciously similar to several other famous passages in Paul's Letters? For those familiar with Scripture, it should. Although, unlike in Romans 1:1–5, Paul does not use the term "gospel" in describing the Jesus story in Philippians 2:6–11, the basic shapes of the narratives are identical—and several other passages have a similar shape even if we cannot examine them all here: Galatians 4:4–5; Romans 10:6–8; 2 Corinthians 8:9.

Down, Then Up

But we do have space to briefly explore Philippians 2:6–11.[13] In setting the context, Paul reminds his church, and hence all of us, that we are called to imitate the Messiah Jesus in our behavior. He then begins to narrate the V pattern, beginning with Jesus's descent:

> who, though he was in the form of God, did not consider equality with God a thing to be grasped, but made himself nothing, taking the form of a servant, coming into existence in the likeness of humans. And being found in human form, he humbled himself by becoming obedient to the point of death, even death on a cross. (Phil. 2:6–8)

The descent described here quite precisely parallels the movement downward in Romans 1:3, although it heightens the emphasis on Jesus's intentionality as well as his preexistence, incarnation, and descent to the realm of the dead. In the movement down Jesus is described as taking the initiative. So Jesus's

---

12. On the Christ story as a V pattern, credit goes to Ben Witherington III, *Paul's Narrative Thought World*, 95.

13. For a rich theological discussion of Phil. 2:6–11, see Gorman, *Inhabiting the Cruciform God*, 9–39.

personal agency even prior to his fleshly existence is stressed in this text. But then Paul tells the story of Jesus's movement upward. And in this next stage in the story God (the Father) takes the initiative rather than Jesus:

> Therefore God highly exalted him and granted to him the name that is above every name, so that at the name of Jesus every knee should bow, in heaven and on earth and under the earth, and every tongue confess that Jesus the Christ is Lord, unto the glory of God the Father. (Phil. 2:9–11)

The upward-movement elements in Philippians 2:9–11 do not precisely parallel those found in Romans 1:4 (e.g., Philippians does not mention the resurrection), but the overall shape of the two narratives is the same. In both Romans and Philippians, Jesus is granted a heavenly office and he is explicitly called *Lord*—even if that lordship is further described somewhat differently in Romans and Philippians. In Romans it is described with the informal title "Son-of-God-in-Power" and in Philippians as entailing the receipt of a name and of homage that is otherwise appropriate to Yahweh alone.[14]

A Common Pattern

Furthermore, not only is the basic structure of the narratives the same in each, but there are even some odd yet illuminating details that align. For example, in both Romans 1:3 and Philippians 2:9 the normal verb for birth, *gennaō*, is passed over in favor of *ginomai*, a term that can mean ordinary birth but much more often stresses change in status or existence. In Romans 1:3 Paul speaks of the Son who, as it pertains to the flesh, "*came into existence by means of the seed of David.*" Similarly in Philippians 2:9 the Christ Jesus is the preexistent one who nonetheless "*came into existence in the likeness of humans.*" In other words, in both passages Paul (and whatever sources he used) neglected the ordinary word for birth and selected instead *ginomai*, the best word to describe the coming into fleshly human existence of a preexistent divine being through birth (cf. also Gal. 4:4).

Another odd detail suggests correspondence between the stories. In both, Jesus starts with an almost unimaginably lofty status. In Romans he is the

---

14. Paul's allusion to Isaiah in Phil. 2:10–11 (see Isa. 45:22–23; cf. Rom. 14:11) shows that Paul was comfortable applying OT texts that refer exclusively to Yahweh to Jesus; see Capes, *Old Testament Yahweh Texts*. Bauckham (*Jesus and the God of Israel*, 197–210) would even say that in Phil. 2:10–11 Jesus and Yahweh have the same unique divine identity, so that for Paul the name Jesus receives is "Yahweh." Yet presently I would prefer to speak of a Christology of divine persons rather than a Christology of divine identity, for reasons discussed in Bates, *Birth of the Trinity*, 24–25.

"Son" of God (1:2), with it implied that he preexisted with the Father. Likewise in Philippians 2:6 he is described as "existing in the form of God" and as "equal to God." Yet, although one might be pardoned for thinking it impossible to attain to a higher status than Son of God, surprisingly in both texts Jesus does take on an even more exalted role. In Romans he moves from Son to "Son-of-God-in-Power" and "Lord." Meanwhile, in Philippians he is not just "exalted" so that he returns from his earthly sojourn to his prior heavenly status alongside God the Father; rather, as he returns he is "hyper-exalted" or "super-exalted" (*hyperupsoō*), so that he is stationed *even higher*—positioned to receive royal acclaim as the sovereign "Lord" both in heaven and on earth in a fashion that was previously unprecedented. The Son of God is now the enthroned and actively ruling Son of God, the cosmic Lord. Given the emphasis in both of these texts on Jesus's exercised sovereignty, it is safe to conclude that this new super-exalted status as cosmic Lord is not peripheral to the good news about Jesus. It is at the very heart and center—the climax of the gospel. Jesus has been enthroned as the king. To him allegiance is owed.

The Transmitted Christ Story

Another gospel passage is found in 1 Corinthians 15, and it stands at the head of Paul's justly famous defense and explanation of the resurrection of Jesus the Christ.[15] In it Paul explicitly gives the basic content of the gospel, and the details are noteworthy. Paul begins by reminding the Corinthians that the gospel he proclaims (or the gospel he "gospels") is something that he received from others. Not only had Paul received it in the past, but prior to penning 1 Corinthians he had already passed the gospel along to the Corinthians:

> Now, brothers and sisters, I bring to your attention the gospel [*euangelion*] that I gospeled [*euēngelisamēn*] to you, which you received, on which you stand, and through which also you are being saved—that is, if you hold fast to the word that I gospeled to you, unless you have *given pistis* in vain. (1 Cor. 15:1–2)

Notice that the gospel does indeed pertain to salvation, here depicted as an ongoing process ("being saved"). But Paul does not say anything about one-hundred-percent certitude—he seems to demand that the Corinthians must cling to this gospel, otherwise they will have *given pistis* to no avail.[16]

---

15. First Corinthians 15:1–11 is treated in a more technical fashion in Bates, *Hermeneutics of the Apostolic Proclamation*, 60–79.

16. In Greek the noun *pistis* has the same root as the verb *pisteuō* (traditionally, "I believe, have faith, trust"). But unfortunately there is no verb directly associated with "allegiance" in

Obviously more than intellectual assent or a one-time decision is required by this gospel; a certain amount of tenacity in adhering to the proclaimed message is also needed. But what is it about this proclaimed message that demands a holding fast? Paul goes on to spell out the content of the gospel, and we get some hints:

> For as a matter of primary import I handed over to you that which also I re-ceived: that the Christ died in behalf of our sins in accordance with the Scrip-tures, and that he was buried, and that he has been raised on the third day in accordance with the Scriptures, and that he appeared to Cephas [Peter], then the Twelve . . . then last of all, as if to a miscarried fetus, he appeared also to me. . . . Therefore whether I or those ones, thus we are preaching, and thus you believed. (1 Cor. 15:3–5, 8, 11)

Here Paul is extraordinarily clear about what the word "gospel" intends. Four matters pertaining to the gospel are especially noteworthy in this passage.

Unpacking the Transmitted Christ Story

First, much as in Romans 1:1–5, in 1 Corinthians 15 the gospel proper is not in the first instance a story about me and my need for salvation—that is not the correct starting place or framework. Rather, again it is a story about Jesus—namely, that Jesus died, was buried, rose on the third day, and then appeared to witnesses. Here, not surprisingly given the pastoral needs of the Corinthian congregation, Paul places the most emphasis on the validity of the resurrection as a real historical event (cf. 1 Cor. 15:19–20)—an event that Paul affirms has been validated by Jesus's postresurrection appearances to many witnesses (15:5–8). Yet it is important to observe that he does go on in the chapter to link the resurrection to Jesus's reign at the right hand of God, saying emphatically, "For he must reign until he has put all his enemies under his feet" (15:25). So here, much as in Romans 1:1–5 and Philippians 2:6–11, the gospel is intimately connected with Jesus's cosmic kingship.

Second, although we should not miss the Jesus-centered rather than self-centered starting point, the gospel does pertain to Jesus's death "in behalf of our sins" or "for the sake of our sins." The Greek phrase in question here, *hyper tōn hamartiōn hēmōn*, uses the preposition *hyper*, which in this type of context can range in meaning from notions of *comparative reference*

English, making my thesis more cumbersome to discuss in English than in Greek. So in this study, when appropriate, the verb *pisteuō* has been rendered "I give *pistis*" or "I give allegiance" (and the like) as a way of foregrounding *pistis* and the allegiance concept.

("with reference to" or "with respect to") to *benefit* ("for the sake of") to *representation* ("in behalf of") to *substitution* ("in place of"). Thus, taking both extremes, the idea could merely be that Jesus died with reference to our sins, or it could entail the theologically richer idea that Jesus died on the cross as a substitute in place of our sins. Some of Paul's more precise statements about Jesus's death elsewhere suggest that, at the very least, here Paul (using his source) intends *representation* and in all likelihood also *substitution* (see Rom. 3:25; 8:3; 2 Cor. 5:15; cf. 1 John 2:2).[17] Traditionally the latter has been termed "substitutionary atonement," meaning that Jesus took upon himself the death sentence that we merited (as expressed in the covenant curses), bore it in our place, and in so doing atoned (covered over) our sins (see Gal. 3:13).

That Jesus died for our sins and, as a portion of that "our," that he also died for *my* sins is truly part of the gospel—emphatically so!—but it is imperative to realize that it is only a small but vital portion of the gospel as properly understood, not the whole gospel. It is also critical to recognize that "faith" is not primarily aimed at trusting in the forgiveness-of-sins process. For Paul does not *primarily* call us to "faith" ("belief" or "trust") in some sort of atonement system in order to be saved (although mental affirmation that Jesus died for our sins is necessary), but rather to "faith" ("allegiance") unto Jesus as *Lord*. Abstracting this for-our-sins portion of the gospel from the full gospel and the larger narrative frameworks that control its meaning is risky, especially if over time this "Jesus died for our sins" portion is placed in a new, slightly different *me*-centered controlling narrative—as has happened in much of our contemporary Christian culture. For the wider narrative frameworks determine what "sins," "my need for salvation," and indeed what has traditionally been termed "faith" as it relates to the gospel might entail in the first place.

With respect to these wider narrative frameworks, third, Paul's description of certain Jesus events as "in accordance with the Scriptures" implies that the gospel proper involves the way Jesus's death for our sins and his resurrection on the third day have brought the Scriptures to a fulfilling climax. With regard to the meaning of "in accordance with the Scriptures," we can feel a certain measure of confidence that Paul intends not a couple Old Testament texts but a prominent scriptural pattern found in a wide variety of texts. This can be shown as probable on the basis of a combination of factors: the language choice here (*Scriptures* rather than *Scripture*), Paul's own wide-ranging use of Old Testament texts as evidence for the

17. For a nuanced defense of the substitutionary meaning of *hyper* here, see Gathercole, *Defending Substitution*, 55–79.

basic death-and-resurrection gospel pattern, and comparison with other early Christian interpreters.[18] Isaiah 52:13–53:12 and Psalms 16, 22, 69, and 116, with their pattern of suffering-unto-death followed by vindication, are the type of texts, collectively considered, that seem to be in view. Thus, just as in Romans 1:2, where Paul affirms that the gospel was "promised in advance by the prophets in the holy Scriptures," here Paul asserts that the gospel accords with the Old Testament. Thus, since this scriptural correlation is part and parcel of the gospel itself, the meaning of the gospel is both informed and constrained by the larger biblical story.

Fourth, the gospel that Paul received and delivered to the Corinthians is both universal and the common property of the apostolic church. Although Paul himself received the gospel from no human source but rather through divine revelation, as he is at pains to assert in his Letter to the Galatians (1:11–12), this is *not* to say that he received his *entire* gospel apart from the human-traditioning process. Paul was a witness to the resurrection and enthronement of Jesus, since the glorified Jesus had visually and audibly revealed himself to him (Acts 9:3–7; 22:6–10; 26:13–18; 1 Cor. 9:1; 2 Cor. 12:9; Gal. 1:16). Thus, Paul had received the cornerstone of the gospel, the reality of the resurrection and enthronement, from none other than the Christ himself. Yet he received other elements of the gospel, such as traditions about Jesus's life, death, and burial, from others, as he makes clear in 1 Corinthians 15:1–2 and intimates in Galatians 1:18.

A Single Gospel for the Apostles

That this gospel was not idiosyncratic to Paul but the common property of the apostolic church is made evident in several ways. First, Paul includes a summary of it at the beginning of his Letter to the Romans (he had neither founded nor previously visited the Roman churches). Second, Paul also asserts that the gospel outlined in 1 Corinthians 15:3–5 was preached not only by him but also by the apostles (including specifically Peter, James, and the Twelve) when he says, "Whether *I* or *those ones*, thus *we* are preaching, and thus you believed" (15:11). And Paul is clearly not stretching the truth in this regard, because the Corinthians—who had previously hosted numerous important Christian leaders (almost certainly including Peter), received letters, and sent out ambassadors—would have been in a very good position

18. See, e.g., Rom. 10:6–8 (Deut. 9:4; 30:12–14); 11:9–10 (Ps. 68:23–24 LXX); 15:3 (Ps. 68:10 LXX); 15:9 (Ps. 17:50 LXX); 2 Cor. 4:3 (Ps. 116:10). Regarding other early Christian interpreters that refer to a broader pattern of scriptural witness, compare Matt. 26:54–56; Mark 9:12; 14:21, 48–49; Luke 24:27, 32, 45; John 5:39; Acts 17:2.

to know if the facts were otherwise (Acts 18:18; 19:1; 1 Cor. 1:11–12; 3:6; 9:5; 16:17–19).

There is no evidence in the New Testament that any of those named as apostles—for example, Paul, James, or the Twelve—disagreed over any of the core constituent elements of the gospel that we have thus far explored (Jesus's preexistence, incarnation, life, death for sins, resurrection from the dead, and enthronement as Lord). Thus, when Paul is compelled to speak disparagingly of others who preach a different gospel (e.g., Gal. 1:6–9; 2 Cor. 11:4), he speaks out of the absolute conviction that there can only and ever be one true gospel, and that this gospel is shared by all genuine apostles of Jesus the Messiah.

Unleashing God's Saving Power

Now for the fourth and final gospel passage in Paul's Letters to be examined, Romans 1:16–17. The point that I want to make about the gospel with respect to this text could be developed in detail, but that is not necessary at this time. Yet what we learn about the gospel from this text is essential for a full picture of the gospel. The gospel is not just a story about Jesus; it is a *transformative story* because the gospel unleashes God's saving power for humanity. Paul describes this power-releasing feature of the gospel:

> For I am not ashamed of the gospel, for it is the power of God for salvation *for everyone who gives pistis*, to the Jew first and also to the Greek. For in it the righteousness of God is revealed by *pistis* for *pistis*, as it is written, "But the righteous shall live by *pistis*." (Rom. 1:16–17, citing Hab. 2:4)

If we were to look at some specific texts in detail, it could be shown that the saving power let loose by the gospel has both an objective (factual) component and a subjective (personal) component—but the point is not controversial, so I'll only say a brief word.[19]

The objective good news is that the power released through the cross was sufficient to decisively defeat sin, the covenant curses, death, and evil spiritual powers (Col. 2:13–15). The cross and resurrection are now in the past, and so the victory has already been won, but the effects of the victory are still being worked out, as Jesus must reign until all his defeated enemies are fully subjected (1 Cor. 15:20–28; Eph. 1:18–23). The world is genuinely different since Jesus defeated his enemies and started to rule actively. The subjective aspect

---

19. For further discussion, see Bird, *Saving Righteousness of God.*

of this good news is that for it to be personally effective, this saving power must be actualized by *pistis*—which is part of Paul's point in Romans 1:16–17.

So the main idea in Romans 1:16–17 is that the gospel is a transformative story because it reveals "the righteousness of God"—that is, the resurrection-effecting verdict that God rendered over Jesus the king and that resulted in our ability to share his resurrection life as a gift from God.[20] But notice that some things are difficult to understand about the passage. For instance, why does Paul say that the righteousness of God is revealed "by faith, for faith" (*ek pisteōs eis pistin*)? And why does he cite that brief text from Habakkuk 2:4, "But the righteous [one] will live by faith [*ek pisteōs*]"?

Allegiance unto Life

Tackling these questions in reverse order, the citation probably intends to refer to Jesus as the righteous one and to his fidelity to God, but beyond that also to all who give fidelity to Jesus as the Christ. In Habakkuk 2:4 the Hebrew form of the citation as found in the Old Testament reads, "But the righteous [man] will live by his *faithfulness*," where the Hebrew word *'emunah* means faithfulness, trustworthiness, steadiness, reliability, and so forth, not faith or belief. Paul's habit was to use Greek translations of the Hebrew, not the Hebrew itself. So the ancient Greek translations of the Hebrew Bible must be consulted as well in seeking after Paul's thoughts. The translator of Habakkuk 2:4, in casting the Hebrew into Greek, substituted *my* in place of *his* as follows: "But the righteous one will live by *my pistis*," referring to God's own faithfulness rather than human faith in God or the faithfulness of the human agent. So, although we are left uncertain as to Paul's exact meaning, *faithfulness* or *loyalty* rather than faith appears to be in view in any case.

The following seems most probable. Paul says, "The righteous one will live by *pistis*," because Jesus, who was both human and divine, *gave pistis* (he acted in loyal obedience) to God the Father in accomplishing the divine plan through the crucifixion; so in judging him, God declared Jesus to be what he clearly already was, the *righteous one* par excellence (cf. Rom. 5:18–19). And God proved the reality of Jesus's total innocence by raising him from the dead and seating him at his right hand, so now *he lives*. For Paul, Habakkuk had announced this future reality: "The *righteous* one, Jesus the Christ, will *live* by *pistis*"—that is, by his faithful loyalty to God.[21]

---

20. The meaning of "the righteousness of God" is extremely important and hotly contested. See "Reconsidering the Righteousness of God" in chap. 8.

21. On "the righteous one" as a reference to the Christ, see Acts 3:14; 7:52; 22:14; Gal. 3:11 (possibly); 1 Pet. 3:18; 1 John 2:1; Hays, "Apocalyptic Hermeneutic"; Young, "Romans 1.1–5."

But also for Paul, the prophet Habakkuk, in a like manner, announces the future reality of all who imitate the Christ pattern of faithful obedience to God through Jesus: "The righteous one will live by *pistis*." That is, the person who *gives pistis* (yields allegiance) unto Jesus as the king is declared *righteous* by God and *will live* (participate in eternal life by being raised from the dead). So: "The righteous person will live by faithful loyalty." How is this righteousness acquired? How this works for Paul will be spelled out later (see chap. 8), but in brief the righteous standing comes when we are declared righteous by *pistis* (allegiance) when we are found to be "in" Jesus the Messiah—that is, when we are joined to his righteousness by being incorporated into him.

Reconsidering "by Faith for Faith"

Notice that this solution helps explain the other riddle: Why, then, does Paul speak of the revelation of God's righteousness "by *pistis* for *pistis*" (Rom. 1:17)? Paul is explaining in an ultracompressed fashion how the saving power of the gospel is actualized: (1) "by *pistis*" and (2) "for *pistis*."[22] The following is a plausible suggestion that I would particularly invite other scholars to weigh: (1) "By *pistis*" is instrumental in a specific way. It means "by the fidelity of Jesus," as this fidelity was directed primarily to God. Jesus showed trusting allegiance to God and this ultimately resulted in his becoming the king of heaven and earth. (2) Meanwhile, "for *pistis*" means "for fidelity to Jesus as king." That is, Jesus's faithfulness to God was purposed toward facilitating our allegiance to Jesus as the king.

Rephrasing slightly, we might summarize Paul's "by *pistis* for *pistis*" in this way: in the gospel the righteousness of God is revealed (1) by Jesus's allegiance to God that ultimately led to his enthronement, and (2) in order to bring about our allegiance-yielding response to Jesus as the king. The saving power that the gospel unleashes must be tapped by allegiance to Jesus as the Christ, when this allegiance is pledged and lived out through the power of the Holy Spirit. In brief, my proposal is that we can summarize Paul's interpretation by paraphrasing as follows:

22. In Rom. 1:17 the translation "by *pistis*, for *pistis*" is to be preferred for *ek pisteōs eis pistin*, emphasizing instrumental means and purpose. Alternatives that stress progress or temporal shifts ("from faith until faith") or rhetorical entirety ("by faith from first to last") are not convincing because later Paul speaks of "the righteousness of God through [*dia*] the *pistis* of Jesus the Christ for [*eis*] all who give *pistis*" (Rom. 3:22). That is, since in 3:22 *dia* is instrumental and *eis* involves purpose, these are likely for Rom. 1:17. For discussion, see Watson, *Paul and the Hermeneutics of Faith*, 71. This suggests a subjective/objective flexibility in Paul's *pistis Christou* constructions, as the *faithfulness of Jesus* and *faith in Jesus* are both in view in Rom. 1:17 and 3:22.

For I am not ashamed of the gospel, for it is the power of God for salvation *for everyone who gives allegiance to Jesus as the Christ*, to the Jew first and also to the Greek. For in the gospel the righteousness of God is revealed by means of Jesus's *allegiance* to God; this righteousness becomes ours through our *allegiance* to Jesus the king. For both Jesus and us, all of this accords with the prophetic word, "But the righteous one shall live by *allegiance*." (Rom. 1:16–17)

In describing how God's saving power has been unleashed, Paul simultaneously stresses the allegiance of Jesus to God and our own allegiance to Jesus the king, connecting this with the "righteousness of God" and the attainment of life—topics that will be developed further in chapter 8.

In this chapter we have examined the most important descriptions of the gospel offered by the apostle Paul. We have noted that the gospel proper is not so much a story focused on "believing that Jesus died for my sins" or "trusting in Jesus's righteousness alone" as it is a power-releasing story about Jesus, the one who is now ruling as the allegiance-demanding Lord of heaven and earth. The gospel centers on Jesus the king. He provides the transformative power associated with the gospel by dying an atoning death and by sending the Spirit that unites us to him. But are there certain nonnegotiable portions of the Jesus story and others that are more peripheral? Can the gospel story be organized and compactly described? And did Jesus himself proclaim the gospel? If so, in what sense? These are some of the questions that will occupy our attention in the next chapter.

— FOR FURTHER THOUGHT —

1. Can you describe an occasion when you heard the gospel presented in a "me"-centered fashion? What are the pluses and minuses to such a presentation?
2. When presenting the good news about Jesus, do you think issuing warnings about hell is a valid technique of persuasion? What about encouragement to gain heaven? Why or why not?
3. Why might it be important to recognize that God didn't leave us just prophecies about a future Messiah, but also promises?
4. How does the gospel relate to the Old Testament? In what ways is it in continuity with the Old Testament story? How does it go beyond the Old Testament?

5. Why is it crucial to the gospel to recognize that although Jesus started out as the Son of God, after his resurrection and ascension he is now actively reigning as the Son of God?

6. What is the V pattern? Explain how several passages that we did not examine in detail (e.g., consider Rom. 10:6–8; 2 Cor. 8:9; Gal. 4:4–5) conform to the V pattern.

7. Why is it important to assess the degree to which the earliest church was in agreement regarding the origin and content of the gospel?

8. Which do you think is more important to grasp for those who are first hearing the good news: the content of the gospel or the power of the gospel? Why?

9. Paul says, "But the righteous [one] will live by *pistis*" (Rom. 1:17, citing Hab. 2:4). Can you explain how this was true for Jesus and how it could also be true for you?

10. If you were to combine Paul's various statements about the gospel into a single statement about Jesus's career, what elements would it contain?

3

JESUS PROCLAIMS THE GOSPEL

In the previous chapter we examined the earliest and the most forthright descriptions of the gospel in the New Testament—those found in Paul's Letters. Now I want to paint on a different canvas, using broad brushstrokes to examine the four ancient narratives accepted by the church that tell the story of Jesus. These are the four canonical Gospels: Matthew, Mark, Luke, and John. My point is simple: *there is only one gospel*, and just as in Paul's Letters, *it is the transformative story of how Jesus, who preexisted as Son of God, came to be enthroned as the universal king.* Jesus preached this gospel about himself by speaking about and enacting the kingdom of God. The four Gospels all tell this same story, leading our eyes upward to the enthronement of Jesus as the universal king.

The Gospels and Jesus's Kingship

Jesus preached the one gospel of God, and it aligns with the gospel as we find it in Paul's Letters. Yet if the gospel as correctly understood is about Jesus's entire career, and his career was only partially underway when he first began to preach the gospel, but not yet finished, then how can this be so?

Jesus as a Gospel Preacher

Jesus proclaimed the one gospel by announcing the inauguration of the kingdom of God as well as its anticipated culmination.[1] In fact, when Mark

---

1. On this whole topic of Jesus as a preacher of the gospel, see McKnight, *King Jesus Gospel*, 92–112.

summarizes Jesus's message, he makes it explicit that Jesus's fundamental task was to preach the kingdom of God as the gospel:

> Now after John was arrested, Jesus came into Galilee, proclaiming *the gospel of God*, and saying, "The time is fulfilled, and *the kingdom of God* is near; repent and believe in *the gospel*." (Mark 1:14–15; cf. Matt. 4:23)

Note that the gospel is placed in parallel and thus equated with the arrival of the kingdom of God. In comparison with Mark, Luke's summary of Jesus's ministry is even more emphatic in centering Jesus's ministry on the gospel. In Luke, after the crowds around Capernaum have had a brief taste of Jesus's healing power—a taste that leaves them craving more—they do not want him to leave. But in response Jesus says: "It is necessary for me to preach *the gospel of the kingdom of God* to the other towns as well, because for this reason I was sent" (4:43). That is, Luke attests that the very reason Jesus *was sent* in the first place was to preach *the gospel*. (The phrase "I was sent" is intriguing, speaking at the very least of Jesus's sense of his divine commissioning, but perhaps also hinting at Jesus's awareness of his own preexistence.)[2] And what is this gospel? Since it is called "the gospel of the kingdom of God," once again we are compelled to conclude that the gospel Jesus preached is intimately bound up with the kingdom of God.

That some of Jesus's contemporaries were eagerly awaiting the kingdom is witnessed both in the New Testament and in ancient literature outside the Bible. For instance, some Pharisees are reported to have asked Jesus when the kingdom of God would come (Luke 17:20). Also, Joseph of Arimathea is described as "a well-regarded councilman, who also himself was awaiting the kingdom of God" (Mark 15:43). Another group, which Josephus calls the Zealots, were known for believing that it is only right to serve God, and that this was incompatible with serving the Romans, their overlords, for "God alone is the true and righteous sole-ruler [*despotēs*] of humans."[3] In other words, the Zealots felt it was justifiable and necessary to use violence against the Romans to reinstitute God's reign—that is, they wanted to act to usher in the kingdom of God.

This did not mean that these various groups and individuals who were awaiting the kingdom thought that when it arrived, God alone would rule

---

2. On the "I have come" and the "I was sent" formulas and the possible implications for preexistence, see Gathercole, *Preexistent Son*, 83–189.

3. Josephus, *J.W.* 7.323; cf. Josephus, *Ant.* 18.23, where it is stated that the Zealots adhere to the notion "that God alone is their leader [*hēgemōn*] and sole-ruler [*despotēs*]." In this context in Josephus, the term *despotēs* (ruler, master) is being used in the autocratic sense of sole authoritative ruler. On these terms, see further Josephus, *Ant.* 4.223, 16.134; *J.W.* 1.202.

apart from any human government. Rather, God would act decisively by judging the wicked and ushering in a new era of fruitfulness, righteousness, and prosperity. All of this would almost certainly mean the ouster of the corrupt old regimes and the installation of appropriate priestly and kingly human leadership. In fact, a whole nexus of changes that were very much this-worldly were anticipated. As N. T. Wright puts it:

> "The kingdom of god," historically and theologically considered, is a slogan whose basic meaning is the hope that Israel's god is going to rule Israel (and the whole world), and that Caesar, or Herod, or anyone else of their ilk is not. It means that Torah [the law of Moses] will be fulfilled at last, that the Temple will be rebuilt and the Land cleansed. It does not necessarily mean a holy anarchy. . . . Rather, it means that Israel's god will rule her in the way he intends, through properly appointed persons and means. This will certainly mean (from the point of view of the Pharisees, Essenes, and anyone loosely described as Zealots) a change in the high priesthood. In some writings it also means a Messiah.[4]

Thus we see that for Jesus and his contemporaries the kingdom of God—or as it is characteristically called in Matthew, the kingdom of the heavens (here "heavens" is an oblique way of referring to the location of God's throne and hence refers also to God's sovereign reign [see Matt. 5:34 and 23:22])—was in the first instance concerned not with salvation of human souls in "heaven" after death but with real-world changes, the exercise of God's wise justice and benevolent rule through God-ordained human leadership.

The pinnacle of this human leadership was sometimes (but not always) expressly envisioned as a king, an anointed one, a royal Messiah from the family of David. *Messiah* is a Hebrew term that was translated into Greek as *Christos*, from which we get Jesus the *Christ*. Indeed, the ancient Israelite prophets had repeatedly fueled precisely these hopes of a national, even a cosmic, restoration through a Davidic offspring.[5] For example, we see the melding of this kingdom-of-God expectation and the royal-Davidic hope in Mark's Gospel. When Jesus rides down the Mount of Olives and enters the temple, the crowds, wild with enthusiasm over Jesus's messianic prospects, shout out, "Hosanna! Blessed is he who comes in the name of the Lord! Blessed is *the coming kingdom of our father David!* Hosanna in the highest!" (Mark 11:9–10). Here, for the crowds, the kingdom of God is the anticipation of the full display of God's rule as enacted through the Davidic Messiah.

4. Wright, *New Testament and the People of God*, 302.
5. Among the many texts that speak of a future Davidic restoration, consider Isa. 55:3; Jer. 23:5–6; 30:9; 33:14–22; Ezek. 34:23–24; 37:24–25; Hosea 3:5; Zech. 12:8–13:1.

So, given that Jesus's most characteristic teaching was the gospel of the nearness/arrival of the kingdom of God, and granted that this was typically understood to entail a turning of the ages such that God's reign was actualized through a Davidic king, then whenever Jesus put himself forward through word or action as the Davidic Messiah, he was preaching and effecting the gospel. Jesus was anointed (christened, "messiah-ed") by the Spirit and empowered as the Messiah when John baptized him at the beginning of his public ministry. So in one sense he was the Messiah even at the beginning of his public ministry.

But in another sense he was not the Messiah, the royal Davidic king, only the Messiah-designate, the Messiah-in-waiting, because he did not yet fully wield his sovereign authority.[6] He was akin to a crown prince, chosen as heir to the throne. A crown prince might wield considerable influence already by virtue of his relationship to his father but does not yet hold the complete sovereign authority that he will come to possess after the coronation. Jesus had been chosen as Messiah, but as of yet he did not have *a throne* from which to rule; he had not yet been *installed* as the reigning monarch. We can compare the mighty King David to Jesus in this regard. David was anointed by Samuel as the new king, so he was the *designated Messiah*, but he did not begin to rule as the *enthroned Messiah* until after his predecessor Saul committed suicide on the battlefield many years later (cf. 1 Sam. 16 with 2 Sam. 2).

Making a distinction between Jesus as designated Messiah and ruling Messiah helps us to see that Jesus was a herald of the one gospel. Note that Mark pointedly tells us that Jesus began preaching the gospel of the kingdom's nearness only *after* his baptism or "christening" (1:14; cf. Matt. 4:17; Luke 4:43)—that is, after hearing the heavenly voice that affirmed his preexistent messianic Sonship and after he had been anointed as king (see subsequent discussion of preexistence). Matthew, Mark, Luke, and John also all tell variations of the singular good news—the same basic gospel narrative that we have already found in Paul. It is the story of how Jesus the Son, who was chosen far in advance by God as the *appointed Messiah*, was anointed by God at his baptism as the *designated Messiah*, and then came to be the *enthroned Messiah* after his resurrection from the dead—the story of how the kingdom of God was made a concrete this-world reality when Jesus was installed as king and given authority to rule, uniting heaven and earth.

The Titles of the Four Gospels

The idea that there is only one gospel, but that the one gospel receives various articulations, is supported by ancient manuscript evidence regarding

6. This point is owed especially to Allison, *Constructing Jesus*, 279–93.

the four canonical Gospels. The earliest physical manuscripts we possess today indicate that originally the titles of these books, at least as soon as they came to be collected, were not "The Gospel *of* Matthew," "The Gospel *of* Mark," but rather "The gospel *according to* Matthew," "The gospel *according to* Mark," and so on.[7] How should we assess this subtle difference?

For us today the former implies a fixed literary genre authored by a certain person—that is, for us *The Gospel of Mark* equates to *The Gospel-type-of-literature written by Mark*. We know what a "Gospel" is, just like we know what a mystery novel or a modern biography is. It is a certain stereotyped kind of ancient biography or history writing, usually about Jesus. But there is no clear pre-Christian use of the term *euangelion* ("gospel") in antiquity to designate a literary genre. Rather, the Greek preposition *kata* ("according to") was primarily meant not as a claim to authorship (although it may have entailed that as well) but as a way to differentiate one gospel account from another. What's the point?

The earliest Christians spoke about the story of the life, death, and resurrection of Jesus as one thing, one story, one message of "good news," while acknowledging that this one message was attested by different tellers of that single story—Matthew, Mark, Luke, and John. So the title most frequently evidenced in ancient copies of the earliest Gospel is *The Gospel according to Mark*. And this title equates not to the Gospel-type of literature written by Mark but rather to *the version of the singular good news attested by Mark*. The same can be said with regard to the ancient titles of Matthew, Luke, and John. This reinforces the basic point: the gospel proper is not in the first instance a story about human need for salvation but a story about Jesus's career, a career that culminates in his attainment of heavenly authority. The gospel story integrally involves Jesus's death for sins, but that is only part of the story, and the gospel narrative draws our eyes above all to Jesus's kingship.

Jesus Proclaims the Gospel in the Gospels

In continuing to spell out how Jesus and the Gospel writers preached the one gospel, it will be helpful to trace out the story of Jesus's career. I want to show that each of the following eight movements that form the full gospel are present in Jesus's preaching about himself as depicted in the four Gospels. Where does my list of eight come from? These eight stages expand on the content

7. On the ancient manuscript evidence, see Trobisch, *First Edition of the New Testament*, 38.

of the gospel as we reconstructed it in the previous chapter with respect to Paul. But the stages can also be extracted from the sermons that the apostles are reported as having preached in the book of Acts.

It is worth pondering: if there is a common pattern of early gospel preaching about Jesus, and if these elements are what the first apostles felt were the most essential pieces of information to communicate to the audiences they were seeking to persuade, then perhaps they should be regarded as *totally nonnegotiable*, as the most basic and central facts that *must* be upheld by any who would receive salvation through Jesus the Christ. In other words, the apostolic proclamation is *the complete content of the gospel*, albeit in outline form. Nor is it a coincidence that the elements within the apostolic proclamation are very close to the Apostles' Creed, which originated in the second century but has even earlier roots (for more on this creed, see chap. 9).

In a famous study, C. H. Dodd identified seven elements in the apostolic preaching, which can be slightly modified to the following eight:[8]

The Gospel: An Outline

Jesus the king

1. preexisted with the Father,
2. took on human flesh, fulfilling God's promises to David,
3. died for sins in accordance with the Scriptures,
4. was buried,
5. was raised on the third day in accordance with the Scriptures,
6. appeared to many,
7. *is seated at the right hand of God as Lord*, and
8. will come again as judge.

It would be easy to demonstrate from Peter's and Paul's sermons in Acts that these eight events are often presupposed or mentioned. But notice in particular how frequently the proclamations of the gospel in Acts reach their apex with the assertion of Jesus's sovereign rule: "Therefore let the entire house of Israel know with certainty that *God has made* this Jesus whom you crucified *both Lord and Christ*" (Acts 2:36); "Therefore repent and turn back, . . . that he may send *the one* appointed for you, the Christ, Jesus, *whom it is necessary for heaven to receive until the time of the restoration of all things*" (Acts 3:19–21). In other places the entire gospel proclamation

---

8. See Dodd, *Apostolic Preaching*, esp. 17.

is framed for the audience by an assertion that Jesus has become *Lord* of all (Acts 9:36) or that the resurrection of Jesus is the fulfillment of the *kingly* promises made to David (Acts 13:22–24, 32–39). Because Jesus's enthronement at the right hand of God as king is the climax of the gospel, but is frequently not felt to be part of the gospel proper, this element is italicized in the gospel outline above.

Anyone who desires further evidence that Acts presupposes these eight stages in its gospel proclamation is welcome to work through the texts personally or to read Dodd's *Apostolic Preaching*. Meanwhile, with the exception of the final element, which is very well attested elsewhere in Paul's Letters (e.g., Rom. 2:16; 1 Cor. 15:23; 1 Thess. 4:15; 5:23; 2 Thess. 2:1, 8), it has already been shown in chapter 2 that the other seven are present when Paul describes the content of the gospel in his letters. Let's go further.

I want to demonstrate in sufficient detail that both Jesus and the four Evangelists, collectively considered, also proclaim this single gospel message. This will have the added benefit of helping us to readjust the images that perhaps float into our minds when we hear the phrase "the gospel"—images such as all-have-sinned altar calls, emotion-laden persuasive appeals, faith-versus-works polemics, phrases such as "trusting in Jesus's righteousness alone," hellfire warnings, depictions of heavenly bliss—so that we can replace them with images truer to the gospel. Notice that the *content* of the gospel proper says nothing about either "faith" or "our righteousness," but rather these concepts interface with the gospel (as, respectively, the means by which the gospel power is tapped and the results). It is, however, a very common misstep to include them in the gospel—a misstep made even by otherwise outstanding scholars.

For example, R. C. Sproul is typical inasmuch as he includes faith alone (or trust in Jesus's imputed righteousness alone) over against meritorious works as part of the essential *content* of the gospel that must be believed for salvation.[9] John Piper does the same.[10] Meanwhile, Thomas Schreiner is more nuanced since he acknowledges that "faith alone" is not the gospel, but then he muddies things by saying it is "one element or entailment of the gospel" and then proceeds to speak occasionally as if the gospel really is faith alone.[11] While I agree with much that Piper and Schreiner have to say about righteousness in salvation (see chap. 8), I submit that some of these statements are imprecise, promoting confusion.

9. Sproul, *Getting the Gospel Right*, 100–103.
10. Piper, *Future of Justification*, 83–85.
11. Schreiner, *Faith Alone*, e.g., 18, 25, 223–24.

Properly speaking, *pistis* is not part of the gospel but the fitting *response* to the gospel. Moreover, our justification is not part of the *content* of the gospel proper either; only Jesus's justification is, inasmuch as the resurrection is the effect of his being declared righteous. Our justification is a *result* of the gospel when we are united by *pistis* to Jesus the atonement-making king. Full clarity can only be achieved if precision about these matters is maintained. So let's walk through the eight elements of the true gospel one by one as presented in the four Gospels and by their descriptions of Jesus's teachings.

1. Jesus Preexisted with the Father

Is Jesus presented as attesting to his own preexistence in the Gospels? Yes. Many obvious examples are found in the Gospel of John, but we find hints in this direction in Matthew, Mark, and Luke as well.

PREEXISTENCE IN THE GOSPEL OF JOHN

In John 8, Jesus is disputing with his opponents, who have accused him of being a Samaritan and demon-possessed. The long-dead patriarch Abraham becomes the center of extended discussion. When Jesus asserts that Abraham "rejoiced that he would see my day, saw it, and was glad" (John 8:56), his opponents are both incredulous and offended. But Jesus replies to them, "Truly, truly, I say to you, before Abraham was, *I am*" (John 8:58). Jesus's enemies are not slow in discerning the implications, for not only has Jesus asserted his preexistence, but he has also made a divine claim—as Yahweh, the one true God, had famously revealed himself to Moses at the burning bush, saying, "*I am* who *I am*" (Exod. 3:14) or "*I am* the one who is" (Exod. 3:14 LXX). Accordingly, Jesus's opponents pick up stones to execute him for blasphemy, but Jesus manages to hide himself, escaping to the temple.[12]

Elsewhere in John, Jesus self-attests his heavenly preexistence alongside the Father. He asserts that he is the bread of life, saying, "For the bread of God is he who descends from heaven and gives life to the world" (John 6:33). At the Last Supper, Jesus no longer speaks obliquely but makes it as crystalline as possible, saying to his closest followers, "I went forth from the Father and have come into the world; now I am leaving the world and going to the Father" (16:28).

Meanwhile, many other passages in John speak of Jesus's prior existence as well. The Gospel opens with the assertion not only that Jesus was present "with

---

12. For some other interesting "I am" (*egō eimi*) statements in John, in which Jesus is presented as making a veiled divine claim, consider 6:20; 8:24, 28; 13:19; 18:5–8.

God" in the beginning (prior to creation) as the Word (*Logos*) but also that Jesus as the Word was in fact *God* (John 1:1; cf. 1:18). Then, as Jesus's public ministry is just about to begin, John the Baptist declares, "After me comes a man who ranks before me, because he was before me" (1:30). Finally, as the end of Jesus's ministry is approaching and Jesus has made himself clearly known, the disciples are able to exclaim, "We believe that you came from God!" (16:30).

PREEXISTENCE IN MATTHEW, MARK, AND LUKE

When we come to consider preexistence in Matthew, Mark, and Luke (collectively called the Synoptic Gospels), the evidence is more subtle. So subtle, in fact, that some scholars altogether deny that these three Gospels ever affirm Jesus's preexistence.[13] Other scholars, such as Simon Gathercole, Aquila H. I. Lee, and Douglas McCready disagree.[14] I have sought to contribute to this discussion by assessing moments when New Testament authors such as Matthew, Mark, and Luke seem to have felt that an ancient prophet had spoken in the guise of the future Messiah hundreds of years before his actual birth. The technical term for this is *prosopological exegesis*—more simply, person-centered interpretation.

I think the cumulative evidence shows that these Gospel writers probably believed not only that Jesus was a preexistent divine being but also that the historical Jesus had come to believe in his own preexistence.[15] This is made probable not just by the "I was sent" formulas (e.g., Luke 4:43; Matt. 15:24; Mark 12:6; and parr.) and the suggestive nature of the virgin birth that hints at preexistence, but also by other texts.[16] A full scholarly case for this view cannot be made here (the interested reader is encouraged to pursue the matter further by examining the scholarship just mentioned), but a couple examples might prove helpful.

Jesus's baptism. At his baptism Jesus is reported to have heard the following words spoken from heaven: "You are my Son, the beloved one, with you I am well pleased" (Mark 1:11; Luke 3:22; cf. Matt. 3:17).[17] These words allude to

13. Collins and Collins, *King and Messiah*, 123–48, 209.

14. Gathercole, *Preexistent Son*; Lee, *From Messiah to Preexistent Son*; McCready, *He Came Down from Heaven*.

15. Bates, *Birth of the Trinity*, 41–80, esp. 64–67.

16. For example, when his parents find the boy Jesus, Mary says, "Behold, *your* father and I have been searching for you in great distress," and Jesus replies, "Did you not know that I had to be in *my* father's house?" (Luke 2:48–49). Bovon (*Gospel of Luke*, 1:109–10) gives the fair-minded judgment that Luke's depiction here is not legend but "traditional material" with "biographical interest."

17. The historicity of Jesus's baptism by John is almost universally affirmed. It is unlikely that early Christians would have created a scene in which John the Baptist takes the lead over

Psalm 2, in which the person identified as the Messiah (Ps. 2:2) and as Son (Ps. 2:12) *reports a prior conversation*, at which time God said to this Son, "You are my Son; today I have begotten you" (Ps. 2:7). We have good reason to suspect (on the basis of other readings of this psalm in early Christian documents) that Jesus would have reflected on the meaning of these psalm-steeped words spoken to him at the baptism.[18] For if David, many hundreds of years prior to Jesus, was able to speak in the person of the Son in this psalm, and to report a *previous conversation* that God and the Son enjoyed, then could it be that this Son mentioned in the psalm preexisted alongside God (the Father)? Accordingly, Jesus may have taken the "You are my Son" words spoken at the baptism as indicative of his preexistent status alongside God (the Father).[19]

The transfiguration amplifies the preexistence tradition associated with the baptism. The disciples are addressed (with Jesus present) with very similar heavenly words: "This is my beloved Son! Listen to him!" (Mark 9:7; cf. Matt. 17:5; Luke 9:35). Furthermore, these words are connected with the unveiling of Jesus's glory on the mountain, all of which suggests his heavenly origin. The suggestion that Jesus would have reflected on the meaning of Old Testament passages such as Psalm 2:7 in considering his self-identity is strengthened by an episode of controversy that occurred much later in Jesus's life, as reported in Matthew, Mark, and Luke.

"The Lord said to my Lord." During the final week of Jesus's life, as the hostility increases, Jesus is interrogated by his opponents. Having successfully avoided their attempts to trap him, Jesus spins on them, asking the following question:

> How is it that the scribes are saying that the Christ is the son of David? David himself said while speaking by means of the Holy Spirit, "The Lord said to my Lord, 'Sit at my right hand until I place your enemies as a footstool for your feet.'" David himself calls him "Lord," and so how is he his son? (Mark 12:35–37; cf. Matt. 22:41–46; Luke 20:41–44)

Jesus, especially because the baptism is for the forgiveness of sins (creating potential difficulties regarding Jesus's sinless status). Yet the historicity of the heavenly words is more difficult to assess, so invariably worldview-level assumptions inform scholarly judgments. On speeches in antiquity, see Keener, *Acts*, 1:258–319.

18. For an assessment of Jesus's baptism and preexistence with regard to Ps. 2:7, see Lee, *From Messiah to Preexistent Son*, 240–83; Bates, *Birth of the Trinity*, 62–80.

19. What sort of view could the historical Jesus have held regarding his own preexistence? It is best to propose as a minimum a visionary or oracular ontology of personhood. That is, Jesus is portrayed as believing that he at least preexisted such that a prophet could converse with God *from the person* of the Messiah during the time period of the OT (and even earlier)—and that Jesus had identified himself as that Messiah. For discussion, see Bates, *Birth of the Trinity*, 34–36. On types of preexistence, see McCready, *He Came Down from Heaven*, 15–19.

The passage of Scripture from which Jesus has quoted is Psalm 110:1. The best explanation is that Jesus is pointing out a puzzle in the text, encouraging his opponents and the crowds to correctly identify the speaker and the person being addressed.[20] We might paraphrase the interpretation of Psalm 110:1 that Jesus seems to have arrived at as follows:

> DAVID *himself* (reporting the setting, a conversation between GOD and a person whom David can call "*MY LORD*"): "The Lord God said to my Lord . . ."

> *David in the person of* GOD *(spoken to* MY LORD, THE CHRIST*):* . . . "Sit at my right hand, O Christ, Lord of David, until I make your enemies a footstool for your feet."[21]

So Jesus has invited his audience to identify God as the speaker and the Christ (that is, his very self) as the person addressed—with this conversation spoken initially long ago by the prophet David. Since we have no reason to doubt the historicity of this episode of scribal debate,[22] this already suggests that the historical Jesus believed that he in some fashion preexisted alongside God the Father.[23] But as the psalm continues, the evidence becomes even clearer that Jesus's own preexistence and divine begottenness are in view. Since Jesus has invited his audience to solve a riddle about the speaker and addressee in the first verse of the psalm, it is fair to suppose that Jesus would have expected his audience to think not just about Psalm 110:1 but also about the verses that follow in the psalm. That is how scribal debate—and the context in the Gospels is precisely a scribal debate—went forward in Jesus's day: reference to part of a passage could evoke the whole (as well as other associative frameworks).[24] Again paraphrasing, I suggest that Jesus was reading the next couple verses in the psalm (110:2–3) in approximately the following way when he set forth his riddle:

> DAVID *himself* (reporting the setting to "*MY LORD*"): "The Lord God will send forth your rod of power, O my Lord, from Zion . . ."

20. What follows on Mark 12:35–37 and preexistence is developed with more supporting evidence in Bates, *Birth of the Trinity*, 44–62.

21. Since the Gospel writers generally used Greek versions of the OT (the Septuagint) in describing Jesus's interpretation of Ps. 110, my translation and explanations follow the Greek as well.

22. Even those who are skeptical about the historical reliability of the Gospels generally grant the value of this episode. For example, Crossan, *Historical Jesus*, 236, 429, places this saying in the first stratum ("2Q" is his classification for the earliest apocalyptic Jesus material).

23. On what is meant by preexistence here, see note 19 above.

24. For overviews, see Longenecker, *Biblical Exegesis*; Beale, *Handbook*. On the invocation of associative frameworks of meaning in early scriptural interpretation, see Hays, *Echoes of Scripture*, 10–21; Kugel, *In Potiphar's House*, 247–70.

David in the person of GOD (spoken to MY LORD, THE CHRIST): . . . "Rule in the
midst of your enemies! With you is the sovereign authority on the day of your
power in the midst of the bright splendors of the holy ones; from the womb,
before the dawn-bearing morning star appeared, I begot you."

And what is it that we learn from these verses? We find that "before the
dawn-bearing morning star appeared," the Christ was begotten by God ("I
begot you").[25] Thus, God begot the Christ before creation itself. Furthermore, this begetting is described as "from the womb." The language is quite
picturesque while still remaining precise. This Lord is begotten, not created
or made. So the phrase "from the womb, before the dawn-bearing morning
star appeared" suggested to many early Christian readers that the hoped-
for Davidic Christ preexisted as a person capable of conversing with God,
and that God had prophetically announced that the Christ's birth "from the
womb" would be unusual. And all of this would find fulfillment when Jesus
the Messiah would come forth "from the womb" of a virgin as the Son of
God.

Thus we see that the seemingly innocuous riddle advanced by Jesus with
respect to Psalm 110, "The Lord said to my Lord, 'Sit at my right hand until
I make your enemies a footstool for your feet,'" is pregnant with meaning.
Jesus's use of it shows that he had deduced that he was the one addressed by
God in the psalm. But this person addressed in the psalm is not just anyone;
he is a preexistent being. For if not, then David as a prophet could not have
spoken in the person of God to him. Moreover, within that Old Testament
conversation in the psalm, it was further revealed that this preexistent Christ
was begotten by God before creation and "from the womb." Although more
texts pertaining to preexistence could be discussed, this from-the-womb reference brings us conveniently to the next stage, the incarnation, as we seek to
explore together the gospel in the four Gospels.

2. Jesus Took on Human Flesh, Fulfilling God's Promises to David

All four of the canonical Gospels affirm that Jesus was born into the family of David. John, however, merely alludes to Jesus's Davidic origin (7:42),

25. The Hebrew text of Ps. 110:3 is famously difficult: "Your people [will be] willing on the
day of your power, in holy attire; from the womb of the dawn, unto you [is] the dew of your
youth." Greek manuscript evidence (and comparison with Ps. 2:7) suggests that the Hebrew was
intended as a verb *yĕlidtîkā* ("I begot you") rather than as a possessive noun *yaldūtêkā* ("your
youth"). Thus, the person-centered reading advanced here on the basis of the Greek—"before
the dawn-bearing morning star appeared, I begot you"—corresponds closely to the most likely
reading of the Hebrew in the time of Jesus. See Bates, *Birth of the Trinity*, 44–62, esp. 54n25;
Lee, *From Messiah to Preexistent Son*, 111–14, 225–38.

preferring to focus on the incarnation instead. Yet, John goes on to attest both Jesus's preexistence and the incarnation when he affirms the transition of the Word (*Logos*) from a heavenly abode in the presence of God ("and the Word was with God" [1:1]) to earthly embodiment. John famously speaks of the moment of incarnation: "And the Word *became flesh* and made his dwelling among us" (1:14).

The testimony from Mark is somewhat like that of John, with the crowds affirming that the Christ will come from David's line (Mark 11:10). Mark is not quite so spare, however, because he reports Bartimaeus's acknowledgment of Jesus as a son of David (10:47–48). Finally, Mark 12:35–37 (the passage examined in the last section) indicates that Jesus himself had determined that the Christ would be both David's son and Lord. Mark ultimately shows that Jesus accepts the messianic vocation as an offspring of David.

Matthew and Luke are more explicit than Mark about Jesus's Davidic origins and the miraculous circumstances surrounding his enfleshment. In fact, both Matthew and Luke offer firm evidence of Jesus's Davidic credentials by presenting genealogies that trace Jesus's lineage through David (Matt. 1:1, 6, 17; Luke 3:31). Although the matter is not really clear, some scholars believe that Matthew gives Jesus's legal lineage through his adoptive father Joseph, but Luke presents it through Mary, his natural mother, as is signaled by Luke's "as was supposed" when he writes, "Jesus . . . who was the son (*as was supposed*) of Joseph" (3:23). Be that as it may, individually considered, Joseph and Mary were *both* certainly remembered as direct descendants of David by the earliest Christians.[26] That Jesus was born in the line of David, fulfilling God's promise to David, is integral to the good news in all four Gospels.

Regarding the virgin birth, Matthew and Luke narrate the story of the circumstances surrounding Jesus's conception and birth. Mary was betrothed to Joseph, but they had not had any physical union. Jesus was conceived "from the Holy Spirit" (Matt. 1:18, 20), for Mary was still a virgin when the Holy Spirit came upon her and "overshadowed" her (Luke 1:35). Matthew links this event to the famous yet complex ancient prophecy made by Isaiah, "The virgin will conceive and give birth to a son, and they shall name him 'Immanuel'" (Matt. 1:23, citing Isa. 7:14). In short, the virgin birth complements both of the first two elements of the gospel, Jesus's preexistence with God the Father and his taking on human flesh in the line of David.

---

26. On Joseph as a Davidic offspring, see among other texts Matt. 1:20; Luke 1:27; 2:4; on Mary, see Luke 3:23 (probably); Ign. *Eph.* 18.2; *Trall.* 9.1; Justin, *Dial.* 100.3; Irenaeus, *Epid.* 36; *Haer.* 3.16.3.

3. Jesus Died for Sins in Accordance with the Scriptures

Thus far in our exploration of the way in which Jesus and the Gospel writers take up the same gospel as is found in Paul's Letters and in the sermons in Acts, we have looked at Jesus's preexistence and incarnation into the line of David. The next element involves Jesus's death for sins, a topic that was treated already with respect to 1 Corinthians 15:3 in the previous chapter. It was concluded that Paul's most likely meaning shades toward substitution—"Jesus died in our place." In two especially important episodes in the Gospels, Jesus is described as explaining the significance of his own death in a similar fashion.

The ransom saying. The most vital statement made by Jesus in this regard is his so-called ransom saying as reported in Mark and Matthew. Two of Jesus's disciples, James and John (with the assistance of their mother as reported by Matthew), are jockeying for prime seating in Jesus's kingdom—that is, once it has fully arrived. Jesus asks them if they are able to drink the cup (of suffering) that he is about to drain to the dregs. They reply in the affirmative, and Jesus indicates that they will indeed drink the cup but it is not his prerogative to grant special kingdom seating arrangements. The other ten are indignant when they hear about all of this, for they all are coveting such trappings of power and privilege. Jesus takes the opportunity to tell his disciples that they must not behave like the rulers among the nations, but rather that whoever wants to be the greatest must be a servant of all.

It is in this context that we find the famous ransom saying, as Jesus adds, "For the Son of Man also came not to be served, but to serve, and to give his life as a ransom for many" (Mark 10:45; cf. Matt. 20:28). The "ransom for many" (*lytron anti pollōn*) carries a substitutionary meaning. Jesus says that the reason he *came* (notice the similarity to the "I was sent" sayings and the possible implications again for preexistence) was so that he could give his life as a ransom. Our own common usage today reflects well the underlying idea in Greek. Today a ransom is money that is paid, perhaps to a kidnapper, in order to secure the release of a child or an adult that has been unlawfully seized. The money is offered as a substitute for the person. Similarly the Greek word *lytron* ("ransom") was used during Jesus's era to describe the money paid to set slaves free (e.g., Lev. 19:20; Josephus, *Ant.* 12.46). It was also used to redeem sacrificial victims, so that the victims might not be offered but rather be released (e.g., Num. 18:15).

Meanwhile, unlike the similar Greek preposition *hyper* that has a broad range of meaning but can entail substitution (as discussed in chap. 2), *anti* has a narrower range of meaning, virtually always intending a substitutionary idea. For example, in the New Testament, the ruler Archelaus is said to reign "*anti* his father Herod"—that is, "in place of his father Herod" (Matt. 2:22). Likewise Jesus says, "You have heard that it was said, 'Eye *anti* eye'" (Matt. 5:38), which is usually translated "an eye for an eye" but means "an eye in place of an eye"—that is, an eye removed as a penalty from one person to compensate for the eye wrongly removed from another person.

Intriguingly, we can even find the exact same words that are present in the ransom saying, *lytron* ("ransom") and *anti* ("in place of"), used together to describe the idea of substitution in ancient literature contemporaneous with the New Testament. For example, Josephus describes the action taken by a certain priest named Eleazar to secure the golden temple vessels that a certain Crassus was in the process of plundering. Eleazar gave him a bar of gold as *a ransom for all of them* (i.e., all of the temple vessels). That is, the gold bar was offered as a substitute so that Crassus would relinquish his claimed rights over the vessels and would take the gold bar in their stead (*Ant.* 14.107; the expression in Greek is *lytron anti pantōn*).

So when Jesus says that he has come in order to give his life as "a ransom *anti* many," the substitutionary idea is foregrounded—"a ransom *in place of* many." Notice here that the payment Jesus is going to offer is not money but his own life. These captives' lives are forfeit since they owe a debt that they cannot pay to secure their own release. But Jesus's own life is not forfeit. His life is of such tremendous value that by substitution it can secure the purchase of *the many* who are bound.

How can this notion of Jesus offering his life as a ransom for many be said to be "in accordance with the Scriptures"—that is, in alignment with the Old Testament? The idea of giving a life in place of a life is so foundational to the Old Testament sacrificial system that it is not strictly necessary to identify specific texts (but on life-for-life atonement see in particular Lev. 17:11). Indeed, we even see the principle narrated in texts such as Genesis 22 (the ram in place of Isaac) and Exodus 12 (the lamb in place of the firstborn). So, for instance, when John the Baptist says with reference to Jesus, "Look! The lamb of God who takes away the sin of the world!" (John 1:29), we are in touch with a theological tradition like unto the ransom saying in Mark and Matthew. The most obvious historical bridge between the ransom saying and the lamb-of-God tradition is the Last Supper that Jesus celebrated with his disciples in association with the Passover just prior to his death.[27]

---

27. Famously there is a difficulty regarding the timing of the Last Supper with respect to the Passover meal. Matthew, Mark, and Luke indicate that the meal was a Passover celebration on Thursday (see Mark 14:12–16 and parr.). But in John the Last Supper seems to occur prior to the Passover (see John 13:2; 18:28). Many think that John moved it so that Jesus, the true

The Last Supper. Luke gives the fullest explanation of the meaning of the Last Supper when he reports that Jesus said, "I have earnestly desired to eat this Passover with you before I suffer; for I tell you I shall not eat *it* [the Passover meal] until *it* [probably the meal] is fulfilled in the kingdom of God" (22:15–16). Jesus states that the Paschal meal itself is about to find fulfillment in the kingdom of God. Jesus hereby indicates that the Passover meal as given in the Old Testament had an end toward which it was aimed within God's purposes, but that this end had not yet been reached prior to Jesus. But this end, Jesus was saying, was soon to be reached.

Meanwhile, all the Evangelists, as well as the apostle Paul, report that Jesus took bread and a cup and provided interpretative words in association with the bread and the wine. Jesus calls the bread "my body," and Luke and Paul add that Jesus told his disciples that it is given "for you." In Mark the cup of wine is described by Jesus as "my blood of the covenant, which is poured out *in behalf of many*" (14:24). Matthew is nearly identical to Mark but also reports that Jesus said something more: "poured out *for many for the forgiveness of sins*" (26:28). Paul is probably even earlier than Mark, and he, in agreement with Luke, gives a slight variation, indicating that Jesus described the cup not just as "my blood of the covenant" but as "the *new* covenant in my blood" (1 Cor. 11:25; Luke 22:20). Luke also makes the substitutionary function of the cup explicit, saying that the cup is poured out "in your behalf" (22:20). How is all of this according to Scripture? Obviously, the Passover is an Old Testament institution (see esp. Exod. 12), but also this "covenant" language evokes the numerous Old Testament covenants (e.g., with Noah, Abraham, all the people at Mount Sinai, and David). Moreover, the "new covenant" terminology directly corresponds to the promised future "new covenant" described in Jeremiah 31:31–34, to which we might also compare the anticipated time of the "new heart" and "new spirit" described in Ezekiel 36:22–32 (esp. v. 26) and other texts.

We can see other links between Jesus's death for our sins and the Old Testament, especially the atoning work of the suffering servant described in Isaiah:

> He was wounded for our transgressions; he was crushed for our iniquities; upon him was the chastisement that brought us peace, and with his stripes we are healed. All we like sheep have gone astray; we have turned every one to our own way; and the LORD has laid on him the iniquity of us all. . . . He poured out his soul to death and was numbered with the transgressors; yet

---

Passover lamb, is offered at the same time as the slaughtering of the Passover lambs (cf. John 1:29; 19:14, 31, 42). See Stein, "Last Supper"; for a comprehensive treatment, see Pitre, *Jesus and the Last Supper.*

he bore the sin of many, and makes intercession for the transgressors. (Isa. 53:5–6, 12)

Not only is the atoning function of the servant explicit in this passage, Gospel texts such as Luke 22:37 (citing Isa. 53:12; cf. Matt. 8:17; John 12:38) make it all but certain that Jesus was remembered as interpreting his mission in terms of the suffering servant of Isaiah. In short, through the ransom saying, the Last Supper, and other texts, Jesus and the Evangelists both stress that Jesus died for our sins in accordance with the Scriptures.

4. Jesus Was Buried

Jesus's burial as a genuine historical event is an integral part of the gospel. Jesus's burial is detailed in all four Gospels. All state that Joseph of Arimathea was the principle actor in facilitating the burial, while John also mentions Nicodemus. All indicate that Jesus was wrapped in linen and placed in a new tomb (see Matt. 27:57–61; Mark 15:42–47; Luke 23:50–56; John 19:38–42). Meanwhile, when outlining the gospel, Paul emphasizes that Jesus died for our sins in accordance with the Scriptures, *that he was buried*, and that he was raised in accordance with the Scriptures (1 Cor. 15:3–5). Seen in this light, for Paul, Jesus's burial itself, unlike his death and resurrection, is not something that is strictly speaking "in accordance with the Scriptures." But the burial does serve to confirm the reality of the previous stage in the gospel narrative, Jesus's death. It also paves the way for the next stage, Jesus's resurrection. And both of these other stages are said to be "in accordance with the Scriptures."

Not only is the reality of the burial emphasized in the Gospels; Jesus is also reported to have predicted not only his death but, more specifically, the three-day duration of his burial. For instance, after Peter's confession that Jesus is the Messiah, Jesus explains that the path of discipleship is the path of the cross, and also "that the Son of Man must suffer many things, be rejected by the elders and the chief priests and the scribes, and be killed—and *after three days* rise again" (Mark 8:31; cf. 9:31). Perhaps the most memorable of these predictions is made in response to the scribes and Pharisees when they approach Jesus, seeking that Jesus offer a miraculous sign to validate himself. Jesus replies:

> An evil and adulterous generation seeks a sign—and a sign will not be given to it except the sign of the prophet Jonah. For just as Jonah was in the belly of the sea creature for three days and three nights, *so the Son of Man will be in the heart of the earth for three days and three nights.* (Matt. 12:39–40; cf. 16:4)

Jesus compares himself to the prophet Jonah, who had preached an ambiguously terse message to the wicked Ninevites, demanding repentance. And lo and behold, when Jonah went, these gentiles were surprisingly stimulated to repentance by his halfhearted preaching. Now, then, since Jesus has arrived as "one greater than Jonah" and has preached an unambiguous message of repentance, how much more readily should Jesus's Jewish compatriots repent! Yet they are instead delaying repentance and demanding miraculous signs. Here Jesus indicates that they will indeed get the miraculous sign that they crave—the Son of Man will be in the heart of the earth for three days and nights. But the contrary nature of the sign (the burial of the Son of Man with all the defeat and weakness that such an event entails) means that its significance will be missed by the majority.

At the time of Jesus's puzzling actions in the temple, when he overturned the tables of the money changers, Jesus is remembered in John's Gospel as predicting a three-day burial in a very cryptic fashion: "Destroy this temple and in three days I will raise it" (2:19). Jesus's opponents are puzzled, since it has taken forty-six years to build the current temple, but John, breaking into the scene as the author, clarifies Jesus's intent: "But he was speaking about the temple of his body" (2:21), a point which would only become clear to the disciples after Jesus was raised from the dead (2:22). It may be that we find vestiges of this tradition not only in John but also in Matthew and Mark. During Jesus's trial, when false accusations are brought by the witnesses against Jesus, they say, "We heard him say, 'I will destroy this man-made temple and in three days I will build a different one, not made by man'" (Mark 14:58; cf. 15:29–30; Matt. 26:12; 27:40; 27:63). So Jesus's burial is certainly part of the good news—indeed, there are numerous reports that Jesus himself had prophesied a three-day burial. This "on the third day" tradition is even something that Paul indicates was anticipated as part of the gospel in the Old Testament in connection with the resurrection.

5. Jesus Was Raised on the Third Day in Accordance with the Scriptures

Jesus's resurrection, his movement from death to physically embodied new life, is central to the good news. Obviously both Jesus and the Gospels affirm the resurrection. Jesus makes numerous predictions concerning the resurrection—indeed, we have just had occasion to explore the "on the third day" tradition in some detail in connection with his burial. Some have sought to figure out precisely what passage (or passages) Paul might have had in mind in the Old Testament that anticipates the resurrection specifically *on the third day*—with Hosea 6:2, Jonah 1:17, and 2 Kings 20:5 being suggested.

But inasmuch as Paul here (1 Cor. 15:4) uses the plural *Scriptures* rather than the singular *Scripture*, as is his custom when generalizing rather than discussing the meaning of a specific text, it is unlikely that Paul has a specific text in view. Rather, in speaking of the resurrection as "in accordance with the Scriptures," he is probably referring to the general pattern of the vindication of the righteous after suffering and death rather than to a specific text or two.

In describing the resurrection in the Gospels, I do not want to belabor the obvious, so just the basics will be sketched. The Gospels all agree with regard to the main story line: after his death Jesus is buried on Friday, women (including Mary Magdalene) appear at the tomb on Sunday morning, but the stone has already been rolled away and the tomb is empty. Most of the accounts add the appearance of an angel or angels announcing the resurrection. Then in all the Gospels, except in the complex case of Mark's Gospel (which has multiple endings attested in ancient manuscripts),[28] the disciples are informed, but some or all of them do not believe at first. Subsequently, Jesus appears to various disciples at numerous times, including the eleven apostles.

Yet the stories in the four Gospels differ with regard to some of the details. And at least to my mind the small differences in detail and emphasis show we are dealing with authentic remembrances rather than a doctored-up, tightly coordinated "official story" created by the later church. For instance, Matthew adds that the tomb was guarded and sealed prior to the resurrection (27:62–66) and that after the resurrection a bribe was given to some of the guards to report that the disciples stole the body (28:11–15). Luke tells us that Peter ran to the tomb after receiving the report from the women, inspected the state of the grave clothes, and departed puzzled (24:12). John adds that not only Peter but also the disciple whom Jesus loved (probably John himself) ran to the tomb, giving more details about the unusual positioning of the grave linens (20:3–9). John also adds that after that time, Peter and the beloved disciple returned home, but while they were returning Mary Magdalene remained at the tomb weeping (20:10–18). Mary Magdalene is honored as the first named disciple to see the resurrected Jesus.

28. The earliest manuscripts of Mark end after 16:8, which reads, "And they [the women] went out and fled from the tomb, for trembling and astonishment had come upon them; and they said nothing to anyone, for they were afraid." Many scholars today regard this as the original ending, although others judge that Mark's original ending was akin to Matthew's and has been lost. Some manuscripts add a short ending, "But they reported briefly to Peter and those with him all that they had been told. And after this, Jesus himself sent out by means of them, from east to west, the sacred and imperishable proclamation of eternal salvation." An even longer ending became traditional, comprising Mark 16:9–20, but in modern editions of the Bible its unoriginality is almost always marked.

6. Jesus Appeared to Many

Just as there is considerable variety in detail in the recounting of the resurrection in the four Gospels, so also are there diverse but largely complementary traditions pertaining to the subsequent appearances. Given the diversity of witnesses and the complex sequencing, it is easy to miss how much evidence for the postresurrection appearances is given in the Bible. In fact, at least thirteen distinct postresurrection appearances are reported, while there is also evidence that Jesus, after being raised, spent considerable time instructing his disciples, appearing many more times over a forty-day period (Acts 1:3). The centrality of the resurrection to the gospel, indeed to all of Christianity, makes it worth noting these thirteen distinct appearances:

1. To the women (including Mary Magdalene) (Matt. 28:9–10)
2. To Mary Magdalene specifically (John 20:14–17; cf. Mark 16:9)
3. To two travelers (Luke 24:13–32; cf. Mark 16:12–13)
4. To Peter (Luke 24:33–34; 1 Cor. 15:5)
5. To the eleven and others minus Thomas (John 20:19–25; cf. Luke 24:36–49)
6. To the eleven including Thomas (John 20:26–28)
7. At the Sea of Tiberius (John 21)
8. On a mountain in Galilee (Matt. 28:16–20; cf. Mark 16:7)
9. To the five hundred brothers (1 Cor. 15:6)
10. To James, the Lord's brother (1 Cor. 15:7)
11. To the other apostles (1 Cor. 15:7)
12. On the Mount of Olives (Acts 1:6–12)
13. To the apostle Paul (Acts 9:3–9; 22:6–11; 26:12–18)

In short, Scripture attests that Jesus appeared to a great variety of witnesses in diverse geographical locales over the course of some forty days. These appearances are a core constituent of the good news. Last of all Jesus appeared to Paul, as he so memorably puts it, "as if unto a miscarried fetus" (1 Cor. 15:8). Paul means that he saw Jesus when he was in a state of utter spiritual death. And as the last in the chain of witnesses, his viewing was fundamentally different than the rest of the apostles, all of whom had seen Jesus prior to his ascension. It is this ascension, however, together with the events surrounding it, that is the most critical yet most neglected component of the gospel today.

7. *Jesus Is Seated at the Right Hand of God as Lord*

In our exploration of the degree to which Jesus and the four Gospel writers proclaimed the same message of good news as Paul, we have already examined Jesus's preexistence, birth into the line of David, death for sins, burial, resurrection on the third day, and appearances—as well as the way many of these stages connect to the Old Testament. Now we come to the most important part of the gospel for us today, Jesus's reign at the right hand of God. This is the most important stage not because it is inherently more vital than the other stages—they are all equally crucial and irreducibly part of the one true gospel—but instead the most important for two reasons.

Jesus's reign is a nonnegotiable portion of the good news. First, when the gospel is presented today by a preacher or teacher, most of the time this "Jesus reigns" portion of the gospel is either entirely absent or mentioned as an aside. The cross and resurrection get central billing, but Jesus's kingship is tucked away offstage.[29] We need to recover Jesus's kingship as a central, nonnegotiable constituent of the gospel. Jesus's reign as Lord of heaven and earth fundamentally determines the meaning of "faith" (*pistis*) as "allegiance" in relation to salvation. Jesus as *king* is the primary object toward which our saving "faith"—that is, our saving allegiance—is directed.

Jesus reigns right now. Second, Jesus's reign corresponds to the *present* epoch of world history that we find ourselves in now. The first six stages of the gospel refer to events in the *past* with respect to Jesus's life story—for example, he has already taken on human flesh, died for our sins, and been raised from the dead. But if Jesus has been raised from the dead, then where is he now? And what is he doing? It shouldn't surprise us if the answer proves to be fundamental to all aspects of Christian life today. Jesus *is* currently the enthroned king, Lord of heaven and earth, and he *is* actively ruling until, as Paul puts it in 1 Corinthians, "he has put all his enemies under his feet" (15:25). He *is* also serving in heaven as the great high priest who has offered his own blood as a redemption for our sins, so he is busy interceding on our behalf (Heb. 8:1–2; 9:11–12). Satan may be called "the god of this age" (2 Cor. 4:4), but his power is limited because it has been decisively broken through the cross and resurrection; the new age of Jesus's kingly rule is currently overwhelming the old age (Col. 1:13–14).

---

29. Even as careful a scholar as D. A. Carson ("What Is the Gospel?—Revisited"), who is well aware that the enthronement is part of the gospel (see his mention of Jesus's "session" and "reign" on p. 162), may be guilty of slightly marginalizing it in favor of the cross and resurrection. For example, he emphatically declares: "The heart of the gospel is what God has done in Jesus, supremely in his death and resurrection. Period" (162).

Although all the elements of the gospel remain irreducibly vital, Jesus's reign is the most important stage for us today. The church age—the age we find ourselves in now—is defined by the Christ's dynamic rule as he serves as king of heaven and earth at the right hand of God the Father while his enemies are being subdued. Moreover, the reign of Jesus *as king or Lord* is consistently presupposed when Scripture promises that *pistis* unto Jesus the Christ will result in salvation or eternal life. This theme will be developed later, but at the moment it needs to be shown that Jesus, as a preacher of the good news, is portrayed by the four Gospel writers as announcing his forthcoming enthronement and rule.

Jesus heralds his forthcoming reign. Does Jesus as portrayed by Matthew, Mark, Luke, and John announce that he will in fact be installed as the ruler of heaven and earth? In short, yes. Indeed, to such a degree that one might even argue that the story of how Jesus, through the paradoxical victory of the cross, came to be enthroned at the right hand of God encapsulates the basic plot of the fourfold Gospels. In fact, this is precisely the argument advanced by N. T. Wright in his recent book *How God Became King*. That the four Gospels are intended to draw our eyes to the reign of God as accomplished through Jesus's enthronement is not an ordinary way of thinking about the Gospels today. They are usually read by the pious primarily through the *imitatio Christi* lens—that is, as fuel to foster the imitation of Jesus in daily life. But Wright makes a cogent and compelling case that all four Gospels, despite their various differences, in their own unique way contribute to this "how God became king" chorus.

Jesus's resurrection from the dead in the Gospels is the moment when God decisively proves Jesus's innocence—and predicated within it is the promise of a jubilant return to heavenly glory alongside God the Father. That the ascension is already latent in the resurrection is made clear by Jesus's own explanation of his resurrected state in his words to Mary Magdalene when she encounters him near the empty tomb. The freshly raised Jesus tells Mary, "Do not hold on to me, for I have not yet ascended to the Father; but go to my brothers and say to them, 'I am ascending to my Father and your Father, to my God and your God'" (John 20:17). In other words, for Jesus the resurrection inevitably entailed the ascension. As Wright puts it, "The resurrection, in short, is presented by the evangelists not as a 'happy ending' after an increasingly sad and gloomy tale, but as the event that demonstrated that Jesus's execution really had dealt the deathblow to the dark forces that had stood in the way of God's new world, God's 'kingdom' of powerfully creative and restorative love, arriving 'on earth as in heaven.'"[30] That is, the

30. Wright, *How God Became King*, 246.

resurrection necessitates the ascension and thus the ultimate defeat of the evil forces that oppose God, as Jesus, fully human and fully divine, the union of heaven and earth, is now exercising God's royal rule at the helm of the universe. The kingdom of God, the reign of God on earth as in heaven, has been effected through God's chosen agent, Jesus the Messiah, the Christ, the king—God's very own Son.

Even prior to the resurrection, during the earthly ministry of Jesus, we find many statements affirming that Jesus as the Son of Man (Jesus's favorite title for himself) anticipated personally bringing to fulfillment the reign of God in the future. Just a few examples among the (at least) twenty-six unique sayings in the Synoptic Gospels that entail such ideas are offered here.[31]

> And James and John, the sons of Zebedee, approached him and said to him, "Teacher, we want you to do for us whatever we might ask." And he said to them, "What do you want me to do for you?" And they said to him, "*Grant us that we might be seated, one at your right and one at your left, in your glory.*" Then Jesus said to them, ". . . to sit at my right or at my left is not mine to grant, but it is for those for whom it has been prepared." (Mark 10:35–38, 40)

> Jesus said to them, "Truly I say to you, in *the renewed world, when the Son of Man sits on his glorious throne*, you who have followed me will also sit on twelve thrones, judging the twelve tribes of Israel." (Matt. 19:28; cf. Luke 22:28–30)

> [Jesus said,] "*Whenever the Son of Man comes in his glory, and all the angels with him, then he will sit upon his glorious throne.* All the nations will be gathered before him, and he will separate them from one another, just as a shepherd separates the sheep from the goats." (Matt. 25:31–32)

> [Jesus said,] "Now is the judgment of this world; now the ruler of this world will be thrown out. *And when I am lifted up from the earth, I will draw all people to myself.*" Now, he said this to indicate the kind of death he was about to die. (John 12:31–33)

Collectively considered, these sayings feature a definite expectation that Jesus as the Son of Man, a title that suggests Jesus's essential and paradigmatic humanity (but is further invested with meaning through Daniel 7:13–14 as is discussed in the next subsection), will reign in a glorified state. Several of the texts emphasize the receipt of a kingly throne.

---

31. For a sophisticated analysis of Jesus's eschatological statements and how these relate to his self-conception, see Allison, *Constructing Jesus*, 31–304, esp. the sayings listed on pp. 227–30.

Jesus announces his enthronement while on trial. But do our Gospel writers show that Jesus connected this receipt of a throne with divine vindication after death? Jesus's trial before the Jewish high priest contains a clear affirmation. In short, although Jesus knew that a human verdict was about to be rendered against him, nonetheless he expressed confident assurance that God would judge in his favor, granting him a share of the divine throne itself:

> But he was silent and did not answer anything. Again the high priest questioned him, "Are you the Christ, the Son of the Blessed One?" And Jesus said, "I am, and you will see the Son of Man seated at the right hand of the Power, and coming with the clouds of heaven." (Mark 14:61–62)

Jesus had explosively combined imagery drawn from two powerful Old Testament texts—Psalm 110 and Daniel 7—making them mutually interpretative.[32] And in so doing he was claiming that his death would result in exaltation and the gift of a heavenly throne.

The first text, Psalm 110, has already captured our attention earlier in this chapter. Jesus had already riddled his audience by referencing Psalm 110:1, "The Lord said to my Lord, 'Sit at my right hand until I make your enemies a footstool for your feet'" (Mark 12:36). He asked them how, if the Messiah was expected to be David's son, that David could call him "my Lord"? The solution to the riddle, of course, is that the Messiah is David's son but is much greater than David—so great in fact that God had spoken to this Messiah, this "my Lord," inviting him to sit at God's own right hand, that is, to participate in God's royal heavenly rule. In both Mark 12:35–37 and this passage, Mark 14:61–62, in which Jesus speaks during his trial before the high priest, Jesus has asserted that he is ultimately the person to whom God is speaking in Psalm 110, and therefore that God has invited him to sit (be enthroned) at his right hand.

The second text, Daniel 7, provides an image of "one like a son of man" sharing in God's sovereign reign, but introduces elements of judgment and vindication that are subversive yet appropriate to Jesus's trial scene. In Daniel's vision four monstrous beasts emerge out of the sea. Later we are explicitly told that the four beasts represent four kings and their respective kingdoms (see Dan. 7:17, 23). We are further told in the interpretation that the fourth beast, in particular one of its odious horns, "made war with the saints and prevailed over them, until the Ancient of Days came, and judgment was given for the saints of the Most High, and the time came when the saints possessed the kingdom" (7:21–22 ESV). It is in response to the fourth beast that God

---

32. What follows pertaining to Jesus's trial depends esp. on Wright, *Jesus and the Victory of God*, 519–28.

acts decisively to judge the beasts and render judgment in favor of a decidedly non-beastly character, "one like a son of man." A courtroom scene unfolds, and the Ancient of Days, clearly God himself, sits in judgment, attended by myriads and myriads of servants (7:9–10). Books are opened. The fourth beast is killed, and the authority of the other beasts is removed, albeit only for a time.

Then comes the most crucial and astonishing part—the gift of an eternal kingdom to the one like a son of man. Daniel describes what happens next in this courtroom scene:

> I saw in the night visions, and behold, with the clouds of heaven there came *one like a son of man*, and he came to the Ancient of Days and was presented before him. *And to him was given dominion and glory and a kingdom*, that all peoples, nations, and languages should serve him; his dominion is *an everlasting dominion*, which shall not pass away, and his kingdom one that shall not be destroyed. (Dan. 7:13–14 ESV)

Two things are particularly noteworthy here. First, not only is this "one like a son of man" given glory and an eternal kingdom; the scope of his rule is also universal, "that all peoples, nations, and languages should serve him." Second, Jesus has deliberately alluded to this particular vision from Daniel 7 with his provocative words "and you will see *the Son of Man coming on the clouds of heaven*." The images evoked—a trial scene, the coming of the Son of Man, the clouds of heaven, and receipt of heavenly authority to rule—are far too specific to suggest anything otherwise.

So Jesus, before a human tribunal, makes the outrageous statement that he indeed is "the Christ, the Son of the Blessed," implying that even if he is falsely judged by a human court, he will be vindicated by God, seated at God's right hand, and given an everlasting kingdom over which he will rule. And in so doing, Jesus once again has subversively turned the tables on his accusers, bringing out the deep irony of the entire trial scene. For if those who are trying Jesus—the Jewish high priest, ruling council, and their lackeys—find him guilty, then Jesus has insinuated that they will in fact be acting *not* as the Ancient of Days would desire, but rather in collusion with the fourth beast and its arrogant horn by attacking Jesus. And these are the very ones who fancy themselves to be standing in the legitimate place of the God of Israel in giving a verdict, especially the high priest! Jesus's words have turned the entire trial scene upside down, for Jesus has asserted that this earthly trial is an inversion of the heavenly reality. It is in fact, as Jesus has painted the picture, the high priest and his minions who are really on trial in association with the fourth beast's hostile activities, and they will be condemned and ultimately destroyed by God! Meanwhile, Jesus is about to be declared innocent and installed as king, sharing in God's very throne.

Is it any wonder, then, that upon hearing Jesus's shocking allusion to Psalm 110 and Daniel 7, the high priest tore his garments, exclaiming, "Why do we need any more witnesses? You have heard the blasphemy. What is your decision?" And then we find it summarily reported, "They all condemned him as deserving of death" (Mark 14:63–64). Knowing full well that he was going to die, Jesus had claimed that he was nonetheless about to be installed as the king at God's own right hand, as the ruler over a universal and everlasting kingdom, and that his accusers would soon be condemned by God. *Jesus anticipated that his death and resurrection were in the final analysis purposed toward his enthronement as the king of heaven and earth.* In other words, in the Gospels Jesus is described as proclaiming the good news that he would be seated at the right hand of God as the cosmic king or universal lord.

8. *Jesus Will Come Again as Judge*

As we continue to explore how Jesus and the four Gospel writers proclaim the one true gospel of God, we have a final stage left to examine—Jesus's anticipated second coming. Our most magnificent descriptions of this long-awaited public return are given outside the Gospels, in Revelation 19:11–21 and 1 Thessalonians 4:13–17. But again, there are an overwhelming number of texts in the Gospels in which Jesus announces that he will come, especially as judge. However, the complicating question in these Gospel texts is, what does this "coming" involve? We have already seen in the last subsection that Jesus, in his trial before the high priest and Sanhedrin, said that his enemies would soon see him "coming on the clouds of heaven," and that this referred not to his coming from heaven down to earth but rather the other way around—it evoked the imagery of the Son of Man leaving earth and arriving on the clouds to appear before the Ancient of Days in heaven.[33] In other words, this particular "coming" involves Jesus's arrival in heaven to be enthroned, much as Jesus is described in Acts as ascending in the presence of the apostles until "a cloud took him out of their sight" (1:9), not his return for his people.

Meanwhile, other passages suggest that the "coming" of Jesus will specifically be directed at executing judgment on his recalcitrant compatriots, those who were his contemporaries during his earthly life but who rejected his claims and manner of life. For example, Jesus, after giving instructions to his apostles when sending them out on an early mission, states, "Whenever

33. See Wright, *Jesus and the Victory of God*, 524.

they persecute you in one town, flee to another; for truly I say to you, *you will not have finished [visiting] the towns of Israel before the Son of Man comes*" (Matt. 10:23). Also, near the end of his ministry as described in the Gospel of Matthew, after pronouncing seven dreadful woes on the scribes, Pharisees, and hypocrites, Jesus brings his discourse to a terrifying climax, saying:

> Fill up, then, the measure of your fathers. Serpents! Brood of vipers! How are you to escape being sentenced to hell? For this reason, look, I am sending you prophets and wise men and scribes. Some you will kill and crucify, some you will whip in your synagogues and persecute from town to town. In this manner all the righteous blood shed on earth might come upon you, from the blood of innocent Abel to the blood of Zechariah the son of Barachiah, whom you murdered between the sanctuary and the altar. Truly I tell you, *all these things will come upon this generation.* (Matt. 23:32–36)

Jesus states that the woes will be brought to bear on this generation, and the immediate context makes it clear that a near-range judgment is coming, as Jesus immediately moves to a lament over Jerusalem:

> O Jerusalem, Jerusalem, the city that kills the prophets and stones those sent to her! How often I have wanted to gather your children as a hen gathers her chicks under her wings—and you did not want it! Look, *your house is left to you desolate.* For I tell you, *you will not see me again, until* you say, "Blessed is he who comes in the name of the Lord." (Matt. 23:37–39)

Could at least some of these passages envision a short-range "coming" in order to execute immediate judgment rather than a long-range return for the church (cf. Rev. 2:5)? It is beyond dispute that here Jesus is at the very least proclaiming that Jerusalem, and especially the temple system, is about to be radically judged by God. For in the very next passage Jesus tells his inquiring disciples, who are impressed by the temple complex, "Truly, I say to you, there will not be left here one stone upon another that will not be thrown down" (Matt. 24:2 ESV). And historically we know that this in fact happened. The Romans leveled the temple in the Jewish uprising of AD 66–70.

Even if it is not always straightforward to separate out precisely which "coming" is intended by Jesus, nevertheless in a number of passages Jesus clearly announces that ultimately his return will have not merely a local but a universal scope:

> Whenever the Son of Man comes in his glory, and all the angels with him, then he will sit upon his glorious throne. All the nations will be gathered before him,

and he will separate them from one another, just as a shepherd separates the
sheep from the goats. (Matt. 25:31–32)

And then they will see the Son of Man coming in clouds with much power and glory.
And then he will send out the angels and gather his elect from the four winds, *from
the end of the earth to the end of heaven.* (Mark 13:26–27; cf. 1 Thess. 4:13–18)

And of course, the universal scope of Jesus's sovereignty quite naturally entails
his universal function as the judge who will return to effect fully his sovereign
will—as he renders judgment not just for his people but for the nations, the
gentiles, as well.

Having at first presented a bare-bones outline of the one gospel—that is, the
saving message that the apostles proclaimed and that Paul also sketches—we
have now laid flesh on it. Not only do the titles of the four canonical Gospels
indicate that there is only one gospel, albeit witnessed from a variety of perspectives (the Gospel *according to* Matthew, etc.), but the four Evangelists
also present Jesus as a herald of this singular gospel. An eight-part story of
Jesus has been offered as a concise summation of this gospel:

The Gospel: An Outline
Jesus the king

1. preexisted with the Father,
2. took on human flesh, fulfilling God's promises to David,
3. died for sins in accordance with the Scriptures,
4. was buried,
5. was raised on the third day in accordance with the Scriptures,
6. appeared to many,
7. *is seated at the right hand of God as Lord*, and
8. will come again as judge.

This chapter has sought to demonstrate that Jesus's proclamation of the
kingdom of God was a heralding of this one gospel. Jesus's most central message as reported by the Gospel writers was that the kingdom of God had drawn
near, meaning the concrete, active rule of God as instituted through God's
appropriate human agents. Jesus came to identify himself as the anointed one,
the Messiah, the king. In the Gospels Jesus is anointed as king at his baptism,
becoming the king in waiting. Meanwhile, his resurrection entails his ascension

to kingship at the right hand of God, at which time he begins his formal rule. With his ascension, the kingdom of God has been fully launched. But if this eight-stage narrative about Jesus is the gospel, what does this suggest about the meaning of "faith" with respect to Jesus and the gospel? We will explore this question in the next chapter.

FOR FURTHER THOUGHT

1. Why is it important to establish whether or not Jesus preached the gospel?

2. Can you explain in your own words why the "according to" part of the original titles of the four Gospels is significant?

3. Do you think an individual could legitimately claim to be a Christian but fail to believe in the preexistence of Jesus alongside God the Father? Why or why not?

4. Why did Jesus have to take on human flesh?

5. To fully understand the Lord's Supper (or the Eucharist or the Mass), why is it vital to recognize that the original setting was during the Passover festival?

6. Do you think God places signs around us that point to God's reality and truths? Why are these signs, assuming they exist, capable of multiple interpretations?

7. It is easy for many to recognize that Jesus needed to die for our sins. But why do you think it was necessary for us that he be brought back to life after his death?

8. Why is it significant to our understanding of the whole Christian story that Jesus appeared bodily, that he was not merely a spirit or ghost?

9. What, in comparison with the other gospel elements about Jesus, is unique about the one saying that he "is seated at the right hand of God as Lord"?

10. How are Jesus's words "And you will see the Son of Man coming with the clouds of heaven" absolutely central to the gospel? Why did the religious leaders find these words blasphemous?

11. How do you think the destruction of Jerusalem by the Romans in AD 70 relates to the future return of Jesus the Christ?

12. What makes some elements that appear in all four Gospels, such as Jesus's death and burial, essential to the gospel, but other elements, such as the feeding of the five thousand, more peripheral?

4

Faith as Allegiance

What is saving "faith"? And how does it interface with the gospel? The first chapter was a ground-clearing exercise, indicating what faith is *not*. But after the first chapter we were not quite ready to answer questions about what faith *is*. For in light of widespread confusion about the gospel, especially a tendency to reduce it to a "me"-centered story about forgiveness, we first needed to recover a crisper articulation of the gospel as it is presented in the Bible. Accordingly, in chapter 2 we examined Paul's most precise statements about the gospel. Chapter 3 explored the way in which Jesus and the four Gospels also herald the same outline of the gospel. Despite the many differences between all the portraitures of Jesus's life explored thus far, nevertheless all our witnesses individually and collectively affirm one basic gospel. It has been argued that this singular gospel is best described as consisting of an eight-part narrative. The key result? The gospel climaxes with the enthronement of Jesus as the cosmic king, the Lord of heaven and earth, even though all too often this portion of the gospel is entirely omitted when it is proclaimed today. As such, the gospel cannot be reduced to statements pertaining to how salvation has been wrought through Jesus's death for our sins, or to his resurrection.

In this chapter, having reframed the gospel so that its climax has properly been identified—Jesus's reign as king—we are now in a stronger position to discuss what faith *is*. The gospel reaches its zenith with Jesus's installation and sovereign rule as the Christ, the king. As such, *faith* in Jesus is best described as *allegiance* to him as king.

Evidence for Allegiance

I have made the claim that *pistis*, which has traditionally been translated as "faith" in Paul's Letters, is better understood as allegiance when speaking of how the gospel of Jesus unleashes God's power for salvation. This is not to say that all occurrences of the noun *pistis* (and associated words) should be uniformly translated this way—in fact, they manifestly should not. There is no one-to-one correspondence between *pistis* and *allegiance* even though these terms overlap appreciably. The word *pistis* in Greek has a much wider range of possible definitions than the English *allegiance*. (Put more technically, scholars speak of its large semantic domain.)[1] My intention is not to flatten the rich multiple meanings and nuances of *pistis* into a bland singleness. Rather it is to claim that, when discussing salvation in generalized terms, *allegiance* is a better overarching English-language term for what Paul intends with his use of the *pistis* word group than the more customary *faith*, *belief*, and *trust*.

Now for four specific arguments in favor of allegiance. First, although *pistis* does not always mean allegiance, it certainly does carry this exact meaning sometimes in literature relevant to Paul's Letters and the rest of the New Testament. Second, since Paul regards Jesus above all else as the king (the Christ) or the Lord, this is the most natural way for Paul to speak of how the people of God should relate to Jesus. Third, allegiance makes better sense of several otherwise puzzling matters in Paul's Letters. Fourth, the proclamation "Jesus is Lord" resonated with Greco-Roman imperial propaganda, so that *pistis* as allegiance fits into the broader cultural milieu of the New Testament world.

Allegiance in the New Testament Era

I want to show, briefly, how allegiance to Jesus can help make sense of some important texts pertaining to justification and righteousness in Paul's Letters. But first it needs to be demonstrated that it is beyond dispute that *pistis* (and related terms) can and does sometimes mean faithfulness, fidelity, or loyalty—that is, terms synonymous with the English word *allegiance*. In fact, the most authoritative Greek dictionary of the New Testament time period (BDAG, edited by Danker) gives dozens of references in literature relevant to (or inclusive of) the New Testament where something akin to "faithfulness"

---

1. On contemporary English-language biases regarding what *faith* means and the range of *pistis* in the NT time period, see D. Campbell, *Quest for Paul's Gospel*, 178–207. Campbell proposes (esp. pp. 189–90) that when translating *pistis*, the term *faith* should either be abandoned or put in scare quotes as "faith."

is the best definition of *pistis* (e.g., consider Matt. 23:23; Rom. 3:3; Gal. 5:22; 2 Thess. 1:4; Titus 2:10).[2] On the basis of my own analysis of the relevant literature, I will give a couple examples where *pistis* must carry the precise meaning of allegiance.[3]

In 3 Maccabees, written sometime between 30 BC and AD 70 (so contemporaneous with the writing of the New Testament), King Ptolemy becomes extraordinarily angry at the Jewish people. As the story goes, after being thwarted by God in his desire to enter forbidden spaces in the Jewish temple, Ptolemy became enraged at the Jews and sought to disgrace them by forcing them to worship inappropriately, pay a poll tax, and accept enslavement. The majority of the Jews did not obey the king, after which even more hostilities were planned. Yet we find this report about the demeanor of the Jews:

> While these matters were being arranged, a hostile rumor was circulated against the Jewish nation by some who conspired to do them ill, a pretext being given by a report that they hindered others from the observance of their customs. The Jews, however, continued to maintain goodwill and unswerving loyalty [*pistis*] toward the dynasty; but because they worshiped God and conducted themselves by his law, they kept their separateness with respect to foods. For this reason they appeared hateful to some. (3 Macc. 3:2–4 NRSV)

In this text it is certain that *pistis* intends loyalty or allegiance, for what is stressed is the faithful behavior of the Jews toward the king despite his gross mistreatment of them. The allegiance of the Jews to the Ptolemaic dynasty is again stressed in 3 Maccabees 5:31, where the king, in a surprising reversal in light of the accusations lodged by the king's friends, states that the Jews have given him no personal cause for complaint and have showed "a full and firm loyalty [*pistis*] to my ancestors" (NRSV). Once again, *pistis* means loyalty or allegiance to the king and his dynastic forefathers.

Consider further a likeminded example found in one of the Greek expansions to the book of Esther, which was composed sometime prior to AD 93. Like the other examples presented, regardless of whether the reader considers the text itself to be an authoritative portion of the Bible, the Greek expansion does show how the word *pistis* was being used during the New Testament era. The expansion purports to be a letter sent out by the Persian king Artaxerxes at the request of the wicked Haman, who had convinced the king to destroy the Jewish people on a single day. Part of the letter reads:

2. BDAG, s.v. *pistis*, def. 1 (p. 818).
3. See also 1 Macc. 10:25–27 as cited in this book's introduction.

> When I [Artaxerxes] asked my counselors how this [destruction of the Jews] might be accomplished, Haman—who excels among us in sound judgment, and is distinguished for his unchanging goodwill and steadfast fidelity [*pistis*], and has attained the second place in the kingdom—pointed out to us . . . (Add. Esth. 13:3–4 NRSV; this is from Addition B, inserted after Esther 3:13)

At this point in the story, King Artaxerxes is still enamored with Haman, seeing him as his most loyal and faithful official. In fact, the king is so confident of Haman's fidelity that he has appointed him second rank in the entire kingdom. Thus, it is clear that *pistis* in the passage above should be translated as fidelity, loyalty, or allegiance.

Meanwhile, the Jewish historian Josephus, who wrote in approximately AD 75–100, uses *pistis* as allegiance or loyalty so frequently that I will just take a few examples almost at random.[4] In a letter, King Ptolemy speaks of Jews installed in positions requiring *pistis* in the royal court (*Ant.* 12.47); King Antiochus praises the *pistis* of the Jews for their allegiance to him during a time of revolt (*Ant.* 12.147); *pistis* and the related verb *pisteuō* are used with reference to matters of sworn allegiance, loyal commitment, and treason in battle (*Ant.* 12.396); Antipater is described as having initially shown *pistis* to Hyrcanus as the one with the claim to the Hasmonean throne, even though he would ultimately seek to use Hyrcanus to gain more for himself (*J.W.* 1.207); the tribune Neapolitanus, after a tour of Jerusalem, commends the citizens for their *pistis*—that is, their loyalty to Romans (*J.W.* 2.341). In brief, the *pistis* word group has a large range of meanings during the New Testament era, but it does frequently mean allegiance.

Allegiance in Paul's Letters

Thus, when we find the apostle Paul saying that we have a right relationship with God through *pistis*, we need to recognize that *pistis* frequently entails allegiance. That is, we cannot arbitrarily block out the allegiance-demanding portion of the range of meaning of *pistis* without warrant. How might this work contextually in Paul's Letters?[5] In Romans 3:3, which contains the final reference to *pistis* prior to Paul's great "justification by faith" passage in Romans 3:21 and following, notice how *pistis* must be translated. Paul says with reference to the Jews, "What if some did *not evidence pistis* [*ēpistēsan*], will their *lack of pistis* nullify God's *pistis*?" (Rom. 3:3). Notice that, as

4. For further evidence, see Lindsay, *Josephus and Faith*, esp. 78–80.
5. Fredriksen, "Paul's Letter to the Romans," makes provocative overtures toward reconfiguring *pistis*, law keeping, and justification.

scholars agree, the final *pistis* here, God's *pistis*, does not refer to God's belief, faith, or trust in something. Rather it intends God's *faithfulness* or *fidelity* to his people. By what right, then, can we exclude this fidelity nuance the very next time we encounter *pistis* language in Romans, at verse 3:21 and following?

Consider the following passages, in which I have substituted *allegiance* in place of the more traditional *faith* in all of the places in which the *pistis* word family appears. The first is from Romans 3:21 and following:

> But now the righteousness of God has been manifested apart from the law, although the Law and the Prophets bear witness to it—the righteousness of God through the *allegiance* of Jesus the Christ[6] for all who *give allegiance*. For there is no distinction: for all have sinned and fall short of the glory of God, and are justified by his grace as a gift, through the redemption that is in the Christ Jesus, whom God put forward as a propitiation by his blood, through his *allegiance*.[7] (Rom. 3:21–25)

> Therefore, since we have been justified by *allegiance*, we have peace with God through our Lord Jesus the Christ. (Rom. 5:1)

Now moving on to Galatians:

> Yet we know that a person is not justified by works of the law but through the *allegiance* of Jesus the Christ,[8] so we also *have given allegiance* to the Christ Jesus, in order to be justified by the *allegiance* of the Christ[9] and not by works of the law, because by works of the law no one will be justified. (Gal. 2:16)

> It is no longer I who live, but the Christ who lives in me. And the life I now live in the flesh I live by the *allegiance* of the Son of God,[10] who loved me and gave himself for me. (Gal. 2:20)

> You are severed from the Christ, you who would be justified by the law; you have fallen away from grace. For through the Spirit, by *allegiance*, we ourselves eagerly wait for the hope of righteousness. For in the Christ Jesus neither circumcision nor uncircumcision avails for anything, but only *allegiance* working through love. (Gal. 5:4–6)

6. Or, "through *allegiance* to Jesus the Christ." See the subsequent discussion regarding the translational options.

7. Or, "to be received by *allegiance*."

8. Or, "through *allegiance* to Jesus the Christ."

9. Or, "by *allegiance* to the Christ."

10. Or, "by *allegiance* to the Son of God."

Now Philippians:

> Rather, I consider everything loss because of the surpassing greatness of know-
> ing the Christ, Jesus my Lord. On his account I have suffered the loss of all
> things and consider them as rubbish, in order that I may gain the Christ and
> be found in him, not having my own righteousness by the law, but that which
> comes through the *allegiance* of the Christ,[11] the righteousness of God based
> upon *allegiance*—that I may know him and the power of his resurrection, and
> the fellowship of his sufferings, being conformed to his death, that by any means
> possible I may attain the resurrection from the dead. (Phil. 3:8–11)

Or consider 1 Corinthians:

> For since, in the wisdom of God, the world did not know God through wisdom,
> God was pleased through the folly of the proclamation [of a crucified king] to
> save those who *give allegiance*. (1 Cor. 1:21)

> Now, brothers and sisters, I bring to your attention the gospel that I gospeled
> to you, which you received, on which you stand, and through which also you
> are being saved—that is, if you hold fast to the word that I gospeled to you,
> unless you *have given allegiance* in vain. (1 Cor. 15:1–2)

If we remember that the allegiance concept welds mental agreement,
professed fealty, and embodied loyalty, foregrounding allegiance makes excellent contextual sense in all of these crucial passages. Moreover, fidelity
or allegiance terminology would appear to be an acceptable translation of
pistis (and other words with the *pist-* root) in a great many other less-central
passages in Paul's Letters and the rest of the New Testament as well (e.g.,
Rom. 1:5, 8, 12; 1 Pet. 1:5–9; Rev. 2:13; 14:12). But how likely is it that Paul
had this allegiance dimension of *pistis* in mind in the salvation-oriented
passages given above?

I would argue that the probability that Paul specifically intends to foreground the allegiance aspect of *pistis* in passages such as these is moved from
possible to highly probable when we consider that, for Paul, Jesus above all
is the Christ or the Lord. "Jesus is Lord" is in fact where the gospel above all
reaches a climax. When Paul speaks of Jesus *Christ*—and note that he does
speak in this way every time Jesus is mentioned in all of the passages quoted
above—*Christ* is not a last name or a meaningless addition; it is an honorific
designation.[12] It means Jesus the Messiah, Jesus the long-anticipated but now-

---

11. Or, "through *allegiance* to the Christ."
12. On "Christ" as a meaningful honorific title, see Novenson, *Christ among the Messiahs*.

ruling Jewish-style universal *king*. I cannot overstate the importance of this. In other words, Paul everywhere presupposes that the most basic identity of Jesus is that of the enthroned divine-human king, the actively ruling Son of God. So contextually the most obvious and natural way to speak about the proper relationship between the king and his people is allegiance or loyalty.

My suggestion that *pistis* language is best translated in the above passages as "allegiance" quickly shoves us into deep scholarly waters. That it is possible that some of Paul's *pistis* language could intend, as I have argued, allegiance or loyalty or faithfulness rather than "faith" is well known to scholars who specialize in the study of Paul's Letters. For example, just to mention some very recent literature, N. T. Wright declares, "For Paul, *pistis* is the personal allegiance to the God who was now to be known as 'the God who raised Jesus from the dead'; personal confession that 'Jesus is Lord.'"[13] Michael Gorman helpfully describes faith for Paul as "believing allegiance" or "trusting faithfulness."[14] Meanwhile, John Barclay, in his *Paul and the Gift*, frequently speaks in ways that would suggest that he thinks Paul construes faith as allegiance: "What now counts for worth is only one's status in Christ, and the consistency of one's allegiance to him"; "[Paul's] allegiance is now exclusively to Christ, the source of his new life in faith."[15]

In particular, Richard Hays has contended that some of the passages in Paul that have traditionally been translated "by faith in Jesus Christ" would be better translated "by the faithfulness of Jesus Christ." (Hence my footnotes regarding the possible alternative translation "by the *allegiance* of the Christ" and so forth in several of the passages previously cited.) That is, for Hays, in some vital salvation passages Jesus is the subject who acts in an obedient manner, bringing about salvation through his obedient actions, rather than the object toward whom "faith" is directed. Many scholars have been convinced by Hays's arguments, while many others, especially James Dunn, have argued to the contrary.[16] I cannot enter into this technical discussion

13. Wright, *Paul Debate*, 14.

14. Gorman, *Becoming the Gospel*, 93 (cf. 69).

15. Barclay, *Paul and the Gift*, 397, 398 ("allegiance" appears 34 times in Barclay's book). For Barclay, however, at other times "faith" is primarily the (interior?) recognition of the reconstituting nature of the Christ gift: "Faith is not an alternative achievement nor a refined human spirituality, but a declaration of bankruptcy, a radical and shattering recognition that the only capital in God's economy is the gift of Christ crucified and risen" (384–85; cf. 390n5). Perhaps faith, then, is best understood as an allegiance to the Christ predicated on the recognition that nothing apart from this allegiance has saving value.

16. For Hays's original articulation and further refinement, as well as the "Once More" response of Dunn (reprinted in the second edition of the book for convenience's sake), see Hays, *Faith of Jesus Christ*.

here. But I do want to point out that the fact that Hays's argument for *pistis* as Jesus's obedient actions, his faithfulness, has proved convincing to many scholars is telling, for it shows that nearly all New Testament scholars accept the idea that *pistis* can in principle mean something very close to allegiance for Paul, even if Hays's specific Jesus-as-the-acting-subject application has not convinced everyone.[17]

With regard to the basic thesis offered in this book, it is not strictly necessary for us to adjudicate whether certain instantiations of *pistis* intend the Christ as the subject who has performed the faithfulness or whether they instead intend the Christ as the object toward which our fidelity is directed, because it is certain that in numerous places Paul intends the Christ as the object of *pistis*, even if he might occasionally be the subject.[18] For example, Jesus is the object toward which *pistis* is directed in texts such as Galatians 2:16b (in verbal form as "we have *given pistis* unto the Christ Jesus" [*hēmeis eis Christon Iēsoun episteusamen*]); Ephesians 1:15 ("the *pistis* in the Lord Jesus that accords with you"); Philippians 1:29 (in verbal form as "to *give pistis* unto him" [*to eis auton pisteuein*]); Colossians 2:5 ("your *pistis* unto the Christ"); Philemon 5 ("the *pistis* that you have toward the Lord Jesus"); and 1 Timothy 3:13 ("*pistis* that is in the Christ Jesus"; cf. 2 Tim. 1:13; 3:15).

So in short, undoubtedly in many passages the Christ Jesus is the object toward which *pistis* is directed for Paul, and it is contextually plausible that fidelity or allegiance is an acceptable meaning for *pistis*, so the basic thesis of the book can be established. Thus, for example, to bring out the proper nuance of Jesus as the object of *pistis*, Colossians 2:5b–6 should be translated as something like, "I rejoice while seeing your orderliness and your *allegiance* unto the Christ-king. Therefore as you have received the Christ-king, Jesus the Lord, walk in him." Yet at the same time, with regard to the theology intended by several important passages, whether the Christ is the subject embodying allegiance or the Christ is the object toward which allegiance is directed is not certain. Moreover, it is sometimes a critical interpretative decision, especially with respect to the complex question of how we are found to be "right" with God. Justification and allegiance will be discussed further in chapter 8.

17. For recent discussion, see Bird and Sprinkle, *Faith of Jesus Christ*.

18. In Rom. 1:17, Paul's *ek pisteōs eis pistin* probably shows that he intends to speak at various times both of Jesus's allegiance to God and human allegiance to the Christ with his *pistis Christou* language in Romans (see esp. chap. 2, n. 22 herein). In "Reconsidering the Righteousness of God" in chap. 8 it is argued that a subjective genitive ("the allegiance of Jesus the Christ") in Rom. 1:17 and 3:22 better explains participatory dimensions of "the righteousness of God."

Obedience of Faith and Law of the Christ

Construing *pistis* as allegiance also casts fresh light on several old puzzles in Paul's Letters. For instance, famously Paul twice speaks of his gospel as aimed to produce what has been traditionally termed "the obedience of faith":

> *The gospel* concerning his Son . . . through whom we have received grace and apostleship to bring about *the obedience of faith* in behalf of his name among all the nations. (Rom. 1:3, 5)

> Now to him who is able to strengthen you according to *my gospel* and the proclamation of Jesus the Christ, according to the revelation of the mystery kept secret for long ages but now disclosed and through the prophetic writings, having been made known according to the command of the eternal God in order to bring about *the obedience of faith* among all the nations. (Rom. 16:25–26)

Notice in both instances that the gospel is directed toward bringing about this "obedience of faith" (*hypakoēn pisteōs*), especially among the nations.

But what Paul might mean by this has been less than clear to scholarship, especially given that in some quarters *obedience* smacks of external performance (works righteousness) and hence is difficult to hold together in a gospel context with faith alone, if the latter is felt to mean trust in God's promise. If the great danger to the gospel is seeking our own righteousness through works because we are truly saved by trusting in Jesus's righteousness alone, then why would Paul speak of the purpose of the gospel as "the *obedience* of faith" since this could promote a works righteousness? In other words, if this were the chief danger, would it not have been better for Paul to say that he desires to bring about "faith alone" among all the nations rather than "the *obedience* of faith"?

The ordinary solution for those favoring traditional faith-alone constructions has been to fall back on the notion that the "obedience of faith" means the obedience that is produced by faith (even though this meaning is rare for a genitive construction in Greek), and that Paul, while abhorring the idea of confusing works and faith with respect to the gospel, nevertheless is anxious to see preestablished faith mobilized in obedient action, so he speaks in this way occasionally.[19] But it must be admitted that if this is truly Paul's intent, then he was somewhat sloppy in safeguarding his "only trust" aims.

---

19. What follows slightly modifies my earlier analysis in Bates, *Hermeneutics of the Apostolic Proclamation*, 94n111, in that a genitive of production for "the obedience of faith" is no longer accepted. For a fuller discussion, see Garlington, *"Obedience of Faith."*

There is a better solution. If we recognize that the climax of the gospel is Jesus's enthronement and that *pistis* is predominately allegiance, then Paul's point is lucid: the gospel is purposed toward bringing about *the practical obedience characteristic of allegiance to a king*—what I have termed *enacted allegiance*. The gospel and Paul's mission are aimed at bringing about *embodied allegiance* to Jesus the king among the nations. Paul's point is *not* that once we have a preestablished trust in Jesus's power to forgive our sins, then we are set free to do good works; rather it is that the gospel is that Jesus has been enthroned, so the only proper response is obedient allegiance to him as the king. It is true, however, that declaration of allegiance results in a forgiving release from the power of sin, so that it is possible to maintain allegiance by the Holy Spirit. The purpose of the gospel proclamation is to cultivate obedient allegiance to Jesus the king among the nations (cf. Rom. 15:18).

Also, *pistis* as allegiance helps us make sense of how "the law of the Christ," a concept that has remained ever enigmatic, might plausibly fit into Paul's theology. Once again, if the law is viewed as largely the problem, because it breeds temptation to seek to establish one's own righteousness through successful legal performance, then the words about "the law of the Christ" and "the perfect law, the law of liberty" (and the like) spoken by Paul and James become a real difficulty:

Bear one another's burdens, and so fulfill *the law of the Christ*. (Gal. 6:2; cf. Gal. 5:14; Rom. 13:9; Lev. 19:18)

To those without the law I became as one without the law (while not being without the law of God but under *the law of the Christ*) that I might win those without the law. (1 Cor. 9:21)

For *the law of the Spirit of life* has set you free in the Christ Jesus from the law of sin and death. (Rom. 8:2)

But the one who gazes into *the perfect law, the law of liberty*, and persists, not being a hearer who forgets but a doer who acts, this one will be blessed in his doing. (James 1:25; cf. 2:12)

Scholarship committed to a hard faith/law antithesis has generally had to fall back on problematic explanations of "the law of the Christ." It is suggested that it refers to the role of the law in a future messianic age, or merely aims back at the earthly Jesus's teachings (e.g., the golden rule), or is Paul's attempt to subvert his opponents' preferred language, or is a vague assertion to love others as Jesus taught and exemplified.[20] But if "faith in the Christ" is above all "allegiance to Jesus the king," then it immediately becomes obvious why early Christians would have spoken of the "law of the Christ" with esteem rather than with law-hating suspicion. Far from being at loggerheads, the rendering of *pistis* (and its accompanying release from the power of sin) and submission to the law of the Christ amount to nearly the same thing—to give *pistis* means to enact allegiance to the king by obeying his law. This is not an attempt to establish self-righteousness but a posture of servant-minded loyalty. The "law of the Christ" (and the like) is spoken of in a positive fashion because *pistis* is not fundamentally opposed to all law but involves enacted obedience to the wise rule that Jesus the king both embodies and institutes.[21]

Allegiance, Gospel, and Empire

Not only do considerations of language, context, and Jesus's kingship make overtones of allegiance probable in Paul's use of *pistis*; imperial rhetoric within the Greco-Roman world of Paul's day and age also enhances the plausibility of this interpretation. For the Christian gospel was not the only good news being promulgated. The Roman emperors were busy spreading their own version of the good news. The emperors, primarily through overseeing the deification of their fathers (whether natural or adoptive), were increasingly taking on divine claims and prerogatives for themselves. For example, Octavian (Caesar Augustus), the emperor who was reigning when Jesus was born, orchestrated to have the Senate decree his adoptive father, Julius Caesar, a god. When this happened it made Octavian "a son of a god" in the eyes of the Roman populace. And this is precisely what transpired, not just with Octavian, but with subsequent emperors as well. It is not difficult to see how Christian claims that Jesus was in fact not just a son of a god but the only Son of the one true God and the ultimate king would have been subversive (see Acts 17:7).

---

20. For a summary of these diverse scholarly views, see Martyn, *Galatians*, 548–49. Meanwhile, Martyn's own view is that the "law of Christ" means "the Law of Moses as it has been taken in hand by Christ himself" inasmuch as Christ has brought the law of Moses to its completion, restoring it in an act of new creation to its simple "love for the neighbor" singularity (557–58).

21. On Jesus as the embodiment and self-giving royal pattern of the law, see Jipp, *Christ Is King*, 60–76, here 75, who summarizes, "Christ functions as a 'living law' in that, as exemplified in his self-giving death and in his implementation of the Torah in his teachings, love for neighbor is personified within his very nature. Paul sets forth the example of Christ's love for neighbor as a pattern to be imitated by the churches."

We see this reflected in the use of *pistis* in Revelation, for instance, when Jesus commends the church at Pergamum, a city that hosted a temple to the divine Augustus, a city called the place "where Satan's throne is" (2:13). Jesus says to his church, "You did not deny your *pistis* to me" (*ouk ērnēsō tēn pistin mou*). That is, the church is commended for remaining allegiant to Jesus as the divine king of kings, even in the face of death.

Other terms that we today traditionally associate with Christianity were also popular as part of imperial propaganda. In the broader Greco-Roman world, the word *euangelion*, "gospel," could mean good news of military victory or of the emperor's birth or reign. The term *kyrios*, "lord," along with *sōtēr*, "savior," was a favored term used by the emperor. In fact if one had ceased to be a Christian and wanted to prove that to the Roman authorities, then one could offer a sacrifice in the presence of a statue of the emperor while saying "Caesar is Lord," which was understood in such contexts as incompatible with the sworn confession "Jesus is Lord." We have a detailed description of this process in the letter of Pliny to the emperor Trajan, written around AD 112.[22] Pliny certainly understood that allegiance to Jesus as a sovereign was more fundamental to Christianity than anything else, even if it is not readily recognized today.

Many other terms that the early Christians favored had a definite currency within imperial rhetoric—for example, *eirēnē* (peace), *basileia* (kingdom), *eleutheria* (freedom), *dikaiosynē* (righteousness), *ekklēsia* (assembly), *parousia* (coming or royal arrival).[23] As part of this broader cultural climate, the Greek word *pistis* and its rough Latin equivalent, *fides*, had sociopolitical overtones of loyalty to the emperor (or other patrons) as well as reciprocity in receiving benefits in exchange for demonstrated loyalty.[24]

This patron-client, imperial context clearly informs Luke's use of the *pistis* word group in his description of the conversion of the Philippian jailor. Luke is at pains to point out that Philippi is a *Roman* colony (Acts 16:12) and that both the magistrates and the jailor are initially in the thrall of the Roman imperial system (16:20–24). Thus when Paul and Silas respond to the jailor, saying, "*Pisteuson* upon the Lord Jesus, and you will be saved; you and your household" (16:31), we are justified in construing this as an exhortation for the jailor to transfer his ultimate allegiance from the emperor to the enthroned

22. See Pliny the Younger, *Ep.* 10.96. The text of Pliny's letter can conveniently be found in Stevenson, *New Eusebius*, 18–20.

23. For a quick primer on ways in which Paul's gospel interfaced with Greco-Roman imperial propaganda, see Gorman, *Apostle of the Crucified Lord*, 107–9; for an advanced treatment, see Winter, *Honours for the Caesars*.

24. See Morgan, *Roman Faith and Christian Faith*, 60–65, 77–95.

Jesus. Moreover, after hearing the proclaimed "word of the Lord" (the gospel), the jailor's allegiance, and that of his household, is immediately embodied. Disobeying the previously issued command of the magistrates to keep the prisoners secure (16:23), the jailor no longer guards them. Instead he promptly washes the wounds of Paul and Silas, he and his household are baptized, and they rejoice while eating together (16:32–34). After this, the magistrates are still clients of the emperor, as is indicated by their grave concern at having imprisoned and beaten Paul and Silas as *Roman* citizens (16:37–39), but the jailor has transferred his allegiance by bodily serving the ambassadors of the Lord Jesus (Paul and Silas) rather than the clients of the emperor (the magistrates).

So, since "Jesus is Lord" is at the heart of the gospel, not only does *pistis* (and cognates) probably shade toward the meaning of allegiance in relevant texts in the New Testament; this meaning also fits contextually into Paul's Letters and makes excellent sense within the larger Greco-Roman imperial world.

Faith and the Promise

Even granting the evidence in favor of *pistis* as allegiance rehearsed thus far, some may still object that this construal is difficult to square with Paul's treatment of Abraham's faith. For Paul in his discussion of Abraham seems to offer a description of *pistis* as trust or belief in God's promises in a fashion that might preclude understanding *pistis* as fundamentally concerned with allegiance to Jesus as Lord. Moreover, when Paul is seeking to illustrate what *pistis* means, the example of Abraham cannot be dismissed as merely marginal to the issue at hand. On the contrary, it is Paul's parade example, for he uses it extensively in Romans 4 and Galatians 3 precisely to describe how salvation is by *pistis* rather than by works of the law. Can *pistis* as allegiance and *pistis* as trust be reconciled?

Trusting the Promise-Making God

In describing Abraham's response to God's promise that Abraham would have offspring as numerous as the stars (Gen. 15:1–6), Paul states that Abraham did not weaken in his "faith" (*pistis*) even though he knew that his own physical body was all but *dead* and that the aged Sarah was also *dead* (with regard to the womb):

> He did not weaken in *pistis* when he considered his own body, which was as good as dead (since he was about a hundred years old), or when he considered the *deadness* of the mother, Sarah. No unbelief [*apistia*] made him waver concerning

the promise of God, but he grew strong in his *pistis* as he gave glory to God, fully convinced that God was able to do what he had promised. (Rom. 4:19–21)

Paul's use of *pistis* here shows that this word in and of itself does not map perfectly onto the English word *allegiance*; rather it can and does often refer to mental assent to a certain proposition and confidence in the reliability of God's promise. Here for Paul *pistis* does mean something like "trust." But I submit that our English term *allegiance* is a larger category capable of subsuming the notion of mental assent to the reliability of God's testimony (belief) or of God's promises (trust), while also foregrounding the idea that genuine mental assent goes hand in hand with an *allegiant* or *faithful* (*pistis*-full) living out of that assent. In other words, yes, Paul and others do say that we must believe or trust, but these metaphors are best adjusted and subsumed within the richer category of *allegiance*. Consistent trust in situations of duress over a lengthy period of time is *allegiance*.[25]

Paul goes on to state that it was Abraham's *pistis* (trust) in God's promise that resulted in a right standing before God, saying, "That is why his *pistis* was 'counted to him as righteousness'" (Rom. 4:22, citing Gen. 15:6). Then Paul bridges from Abraham to his audience, the members of the churches in Rome, and by extension also to the church today, affirming that God will deal with the church just as with Abraham:

But the words "it was counted to him" were not written for his sake alone, but for ours also. It will be counted to us who trust [*tois pisteuousin*] in him who raised from the dead Jesus our Lord, who was delivered up for our trespasses and raised for our justification. (Rom. 4:23–25)

That is, when we, the church, trust (*pisteuō*, from the same root as *pistis*) certain specific promises given by God, the result is that right standing before God is reckoned or credited. How can this notion of *pistis* as trust in God's promise and his life-from-the-dead power be more precisely situated in relation to the idea that we are saved by *pistis* alone in the sense of allegiance to Jesus as king?

A Specific Promise

Notice, first of all, that although Paul appeals to Abraham's example of trusting in God's promises as the premier example of exercising *pistis*, Paul

25. For a helpful analysis of "faith" with regard to Abraham, see D. Campbell, *Deliverance of God*, 384–86, who emphasizes that *pistis* is better described as fidelity or faithfulness (rather than merely belief or trust) when it perseveres over the course of time under circumstances of difficulty—as it clearly had in the case of Abraham.

cannot mean that trust in just any arbitrary promise of God results in eternal salvation, for that might bypass Jesus altogether. Paul is not saying that we are eternally saved simply when we trust the promises of God *in general*—as if we could enjoy eternal salvation by trusting God's promise to bring climactic judgment on Moab (Isa. 25:10) or God's promise that anyone seeking to refound Jericho will do so at the expense of losing his firstborn (Josh. 6:26; cf. 1 Kings 16:34). Why is this sort of "faith" in God's promises not eternally saving? Because it is directed toward the wrong object. We know that final salvation is through Jesus the Messiah alone. As Peter says about Jesus in his speech before the Jewish leadership, "There is salvation in no one else, for there is no other name under heaven given among humans by which we must be saved" (Acts 4:12).

Even in this specific example in Romans 4, Abraham's *pistis* is not trust in the promises of God in general, but rather it pertains to the arrival of a specific offspring in the midst of seeming death, a seed, Isaac, that will yield many offspring in anticipation of yet another singular seed that is the deeper referent—a seed who will emerge from a state of even more profound deathly barrenness (first from the virgin womb and then from death itself) to produce many offspring, Jesus as the Messiah.[26] As Paul puts it in Galatians, "Now the promises were made to Abraham and to his offspring. It does not say, 'And to offsprings,' referring to many, but referring to one, 'And to your offspring,' who is the Christ" (3:16). Although obviously Paul was well aware that Isaac was the immediate offspring of Abraham in fulfillment of the promise (see Rom. 9:7), Paul's conceptual move proves that he saw that the promise to Abraham was not exhausted with the arrival of Isaac, but that it anticipated Jesus the king as the final fulfillment.

If we pay careful attention to how Paul applies the case of Abraham to the church, it becomes even more apparent that he does not consider "righteousness" to be credited on the basis of *pistis* in God's promises in general. The content of the promise is very specific:

> But the words "it was counted to him" were not written for his sake alone, but for ours also. It will be counted to us who trust [*tois pisteuousin*] in him who raised from the dead Jesus *our Lord*, who was *delivered up for our trespasses* and *raised for our justification*. (Rom. 4:23–25)

Paul indicates that saving *pistis* is directed toward God not arbitrarily but toward God as the one who has orchestrated the gospel itself. In other words,

26. For further discussion, see Jipp, "Reading the Story."

when Paul defines the content of saving *pistis* here, what he offers is a brief summation of the gospel, the eight-part narrative about the career of Jesus the Messiah that we traced earlier. Yet here it is compressed even further. Paul mentions death for sins, God's action in raising Jesus from the dead, the lordship of Jesus, and the effectiveness of this good news for our obtaining right standing before God.

Dimensions of Allegiance

What follows in the rest of this section is particularly vital to the whole book. It is really a continuation of our discussion of Abraham from the previous section. If salvation is truly by allegiance alone, then undoubtedly it is worth pondering what allegiance entails. If we synthesize the biblical data, we discover that saving allegiance includes three basic dimensions: *mental affirmation* that the gospel is true, *professed fealty* to Jesus alone as the cosmic Lord, and *enacted loyalty* through obedience to Jesus as the king.

This is a deliberate alternative to classic definitions of "faith." For instance, Saint Augustine determined that faith (*fides*) has two primary components: (1) "the faith which is believed"—the content that must be intellectually affirmed; and (2) "the faith by which it is believed"—the interior commitment of "faith" that takes place in the heart/mind.[27] Meanwhile, during the Reformation a threefold definition of faith developed among Luther's followers: (1) *notitia*—the content to be intellectually apprehended; (2) *assensus*—intellectual agreement that the content is true; and (3) *fiducia*—trust or a disposition of reliance (rooted in the will/affections as variously defined).[28] This trifold definition of faith is still used by many Lutheran and Reformed theologians today.[29]

My claim is that *fiducia* (or "the faith by which it is believed") has been slightly misaimed for three reasons. First, the climax of the gospel has been misidentified within *notitia* as forgiveness rather than as acknowledgment of kingship that leads to forgiveness. Second, it imposes faulty dimensions of "interiority" (speculations about psychological states interior to the individual) on *pistis* with respect to the ancient evidence. And third, it does not foreground the lived reality of *embodied fidelity* sufficiently.

27. Augustine, *Trin.* 13.1.2–5. See Morgan, *Roman Faith and Christian Faith*, 11–12, 28–30, and esp. 224–30, 444–72, where she shows that Augustine's definition of "the faith by which it is believed" is anachronistic with regard to the NT time period.

28. Melanchthon's *Loci communes theologici* of 1521 gives the classic threefold definition of *fides* as *notitia*, *assensus*, and *fiducia*. It can be found in contemporary English translation: Melanchthon, *Commonplaces*.

29. E.g., Sproul, *Faith Alone*, 75–88.

So, restating the matter in slightly different terms to ensure maximal clarity: in texts that refer to ultimate salvation, *pistis* can (but does not in every context or instantiation) include *intellectual agreement* that the eight stages of the good news correspond to reality, *confession of loyalty* to Jesus in recognition of his universal reign, and an *embodied fidelity* as a citizen of his realm. Let me expand on each of these three facets.

Intellectual Agreement

Although believing certain facts about Jesus does not immediately result in salvation, believing certain facts is required as a minimal starting point. Put in slightly more technical terms, giving intellectual assent to certain facts about the Jesus story is a *necessary*, but not a *sufficient*, condition for salvation. Is there, then, a bare minimum of facts to which me must cognitively agree before we can be saved? Yes. It is the outline of the gospel that we have already discussed in detail in the previous chapter. That is, in order to be saved, it is necessary that one must mentally agree that the following are true statements.

The Gospel: An Outline

Jesus the king

1. preexisted with the Father,
2. took on human flesh, fulfilling God's promises to David,
3. died for sins in accordance with the Scriptures,
4. was buried,
5. was raised on the third day in accordance with the Scriptures,
6. appeared to many,
7. *is seated at the right hand of God as Lord*, and
8. will come again as judge.

If a person can affirm that these statements are all true (that is, that they point to real historical and cosmic events and entities), then he or she can be said to agree intellectually that the gospel of Jesus the Christ is true. That individual is not thereby saved, but has fulfilled an essential basic requirement for salvation. This of course prompts a further question: How *intellectually certain* must a person be about these truths for them to count?[30]

---

30. It also demands a myriad of special-case questions that are beyond our scope—e.g., What of those who have never heard the gospel? What of those who have experienced serious

Gospel as mental furniture. Does an individual need to have consciously thought through and self-appropriated each stage? No. A person only needs to have passively or tacitly accepted each portion as true or real inasmuch as he or she has come to understand the story of Jesus. Those seeking salvation need not to have consciously, so to speak, put a check in each box while moving down the list. But they do need to have intellectually affirmed the basic shape of the outline as part of the mental furniture from which they seek to live, even if a given person couldn't name and describe those pieces of furniture at any specific moment. In fact, I feel certain that many devout Christians throughout the ages have never consciously affirmed these eight stages and would have had great difficulty seeking to name or explain them all. Our salvation—praise be to God—is not dependent on our being outstanding teachers, scholars, evangelists, catechists, or even especially adept learners with respect to the gospel.

Certain enough to yield. What about levels of certainty or about nagging doubts? I, for instance, am one hundred percent certain that I am not a pencil, that my wife is not a coffee mug, and that as I draft this book at my desk right now, I am employed as a university professor. But matters of history are frequently more dicey, and we can rarely attain to perfect certainty about events in the past, especially in the far distant past. For example, I am 99.999 percent certain that citizens of the United States have walked on the moon, and 98 percent confident that the philosopher Seneca, the apostle Paul's contemporary, committed suicide, but I put the odds at only about 10 percent that the physical description of the apostle Paul found in the apocryphal late second-century document *The Acts of Paul* offers any genuine historical remembrance of what he actually looked like.[31]

Fortunately, we do not have to speculate about what level of intellectual certainty is required for salvation, because the flip side of the allegiance-alone coin spells out the boundary for us—*we must be intellectually certain enough that we are willing to give our allegiance (pistis) to Jesus as our true king.* That is, "believing" the gospel in a saving sense entails embracing the story about Jesus contained therein as intellectually true, but especially the "Jesus

---

emotional or physical abuse to such a degree that they cannot truly hear the gospel right now because their sociological or psychological condition will not allow them to hear it? What about those who are mentally incapable because of immaturity, birth defects, injury, or illness? These poignant questions cannot be answered here.

31. On Seneca's suicide, see Tacitus, *Ann.* 15.62–64. Paul is described by the character Onesiphorus: "And he saw Paul coming, a man small of stature, with a bald head and crooked legs, in a good state of body, with eyebrows meeting and nose somewhat hooked, full of friendliness; for now he appeared like a man, and now he had the face of an angel." *Acts of Paul* 3.2 (Schneemelcher, 2:213–70, here 239).

is Lord" portion as its concise summary, so that one swears fealty to Jesus and begins to submit to the reign of God that Jesus is effecting. If a person is intellectually confident enough in the truth of the gospel that she or he is willing to give allegiance to the Jesus who is described in that gospel as the universal *Lord*, then the intellectual-agreement requirement for salvation has been satisfied.

Intellectual agreement and Scripture. So, for example, when Paul talks about the content of trusting (using the verb *pisteuō*) that will result in "justification" for us, he is focusing on the mental-agreement dimension of *pistis*, while urging that one must trust in God's ability to raise the dead (as he did for Jesus and will do for us through union with "Jesus our Lord") for righteousness to be credited. For Abraham this meant that God would raise up a seed (offspring), Isaac, from Abraham's and Sarah's bodily deadness in anticipation of Jesus. For us it means that God has similarly raised up a seed, Jesus the Messiah, from the deadness of the grave, and that our deadness in sin can be changed to life through union with him. Paul gives a compressed version of the gospel as a summary of the content that must be affirmed (as in Rom. 4:23–25 cited above). So when Paul puts forward Abraham as the premier example of how we are found to have right standing with God by *pistis* rather than works, it is the mental-agreement-with-the-good-news portion of *pistis* that is being foregrounded, as that is wedded to trust in the midst of death.

Meanwhile, somewhat akin to what we find in Romans 4, in the Gospel of John the *pistis* word group frequently emphasizes cognitive affirmation—the determination that various pieces of testimony and evidence are true (e.g., John 1:7, 50; 2:22–23; and scores of other passages), so that one can thereby come to participate in eternal life through and in the Christ (see esp. John 20:31). In fact, much of the evangelistic logic of the Gospel of John can be found in one compressed statement in which John explains why Jesus performed his miraculous water-to-wine sign during the wedding at Cana: "This, the first of his signs, Jesus did at Cana in Galilee, and manifested his glory. And his disciples *gave pistis* unto him" (2:11). That is, the miraculous deeds that Jesus is described as performing (and other pieces of testimony) are signs; they are intended to point beyond themselves to a further reality. These signs pull back the veil, showing that despite his humble and ordinary appearance, Jesus as the incarnate Son already truly possesses divine glory, and that he will return to glory alongside the Father once he is "lifted up"—that is, lifted up on the cross and lifted up to his rightful position of heavenly glory alongside the Father (John 3:14–15; 8:28; 12:32–34; cf. 17:1–5). Through the phrase "lifted up," Jesus's crucifixion has intentionally been conflated by John with his exaltation to kingly rule, so that we can recognize the paradoxical glory-in-weakness. And when a glimpse of Jesus's glory is obtained, the one who has caught the glimmer is compelled to give *pistis*—that is, to affirm that the various strands of testimony about Jesus in John are true.

This is not to say, however, that simply because intellectual assent is fore-grounded for *pistis* in John, *pistis* in John is thereby devoid of a loyalty demand. For example, notice the way *pistis* and obedience can be paralleled: "Whoever *has pistis* in the Son has eternal life; whoever does not *obey* the Son shall not see life, but the wrath of God remains on him" (John 3:36).[32] It is clear here that the salvific *pistis* action is closely aligned with obedience so that it cannot be separated from it. So, then, a few verses earlier, when we read the most famous salvation statement in the Bible, "For God so loved the world that he gave his only Son, that whoever *gives pistis* unto him should not perish, but have eternal life" (John 3:16), we must bear in mind that although John frequently foregrounds mental affirmation, *giving pistis* unto Jesus is more than belief (mental assent), for in the final analysis *giving pistis* is bound up with obedience—enacted loyalty. In the Gospel of John, then, the Jesus to whom *pistis* is owed is the very Jesus whose career is defined by the eight-stage outline of the one true gospel—with it assumed that Jesus is the Son of God whose reign is now at hand.

Confession of Loyalty

So the first dimension of allegiance is intellectual agreement with the truthfulness of the foundational Jesus story, but it also requires more. The second necessary component is confession of loyalty to Jesus as king. As confirmation, consider that both of these dimensions of allegiance—mental agreement and confession of loyalty—are in fact present in Paul's clearest statement about what is essential for salvation. In Romans 10, after sketching the difference between a righteousness by means of the Mosaic law (which in the final analysis does not result in righteousness at all) and a righteousness by means of *pistis*, Paul speaks of the nearness of that righteousness. The "righteousness by *pistis*" is as close as the proclaimed "word of *pistis*" (that is, the proclaimed fidelity-demanding gospel message) when it is found in the heart and the mouth. Paul says, "If you *confess* with your mouth that Jesus

32. As evidence that the range of meaning for *pistis* in John can include fidelity, consider John's words about the crowds and Jesus: "Now when he was in Jerusalem at the Passover Feast, many *gave pistis* [*episteusan*] unto his name when they saw the signs that he was doing. But Jesus *did not pistis* [*ouk episteuen*] himself to them, because he knew all people" (2:23–24). The same verb, *pisteuō*, is used in both cases. But the second instantiation intends Jesus's recognition that the crowds would not show "good faith" toward him if he were to entrust himself fully to them—that is, they would not reciprocate by being faithful or loyal to him.

is *Lord* and you *give pistis* [believe] in your heart that God raised him from the dead, you will be saved" (Rom. 10:9). And Paul continues, explaining why this is so: "For with the heart a person *gives pistis* [believes] and is made right, and with the mouth a person confesses and is saved" (Rom. 10:10). Moreover, for Paul, Jesus's absolute lordship is anything but mere lip service: "For none of us lives to himself, and none of us dies to himself. For if we live, we live to the Lord, and if we die, we die to the Lord. So, whether we live or die, we are the Lord's" (Rom. 14:7–8). Jesus's lordship is regarded as absolute and all-encompassing (1 Cor. 8:6; Phil. 2:9–11; Col. 1:18).

Confession assumes intellectual affirmation. A saving confession depends on agreement that a certain state of affairs holds true about the universe. In Romans 10:9–10 Paul asserts that one must cognitively affirm ("believe" is preferable for the verb *pisteuō* here) that it is true that Jesus really was "raised from the dead."[33] If, as I have argued, Paul actually holds to the eight stages outlined earlier as the nonnegotiable gospel facts that must be believed for salvation, why does Paul here identify only one of those facts as essential? Yet something else must be essential, for Paul also demands the confession of Jesus as Lord, which entails belief in his enthronement. So Paul can't intend a statement of the minimum necessary belief. The resurrection is probably singled out because it was (and still is) the most controversial point of dispute among those who do not think that Jesus was who he claimed to be.

In other words, Jesus's resurrection from the dead is both the most controversial and the most central historical "fact" that must be upheld, so Paul points to it as a way of compactly referencing the network of additional gospel facts that an affirmation of the resurrection entails by association. We should remember that all communication, but especially teaching, involves offering both compressed summary and expansive description at suitable times. By pointing to Jesus's resurrection from the dead as what is necessary to hold mentally as real, Paul is merely condensing the gospel facts that he elsewhere expands, evoking the larger gospel narrative by association.

Public declaration. Additionally, notice that in the other portion of the verses under discussion, Romans 10:9–10, Paul states that for a person to be saved, he or she must "confess" with the mouth that "Jesus is Lord." It is important to recognize that Paul does *not* say "if you confess with your mouth that Jesus fulfills the Davidic promise" or "if you confess with your

33. As in Rom. 10:9, when *pisteuō* is followed by *hoti*, it is usually best translated "believe that" because mental agreement with a proposition is being foregrounded (e.g., Matt. 9:28; Mark 11:23–24; Luke 1:45; John 8:24; Rom. 6:8; 1 Thess. 4:14; James 2:19). Here the word "heart" (Greek: *kardia*) is a comprehensive term for all the dimensions of the mental life (intellectual, rational, emotional).

mouth that Jesus died for your sins." With regard to confessing, the focus lands squarely on one specific stage of the gospel—Jesus as *Lord*. Why? This is not mere happenstance.

Confession of Jesus as Lord is an expression of allegiance to him as the ruling king. Paul is pointing at our need to swear allegiance to Jesus as the Lord, the ruling sovereign, precisely because this lordship stage of Jesus's career expressly summarizes a key aspect of the gospel, describes Jesus's current role in earthly and heavenly affairs, and is the essential reality that must be affirmed to become part of God's family. Public acknowledgement of the acceptance of Jesus's rule is the premier culminating act of *pistis*. The verb that Paul selects to describe what is necessary, *homologeō*, refers in this sort of context to a public declaration, as is made clear by the "with your mouth." Paul does not envision raising your hand in church or silently praying a prayer in your heart as a sufficient "confession" (nor does Paul say that such an action couldn't initiate salvation, but he clearly intends something more substantive). Paul is talking about something public and verbal, like what might happen at an ancient baptism—although we must reserve discussion of this until chapter 8.

We might compare Paul's use of *homologeō* to the use of that same word in Luke's Gospel. Jesus says, "Whoever *acknowledges* me before men, the Son of Man will also *acknowledge* him before the angels of God" (Luke 12:8; cf. Matt. 10:32). Or again we might compare it to Paul's voluntary public declaration when on trial before Felix in Acts 24:14, when he "confesses" that he belongs to "the Way" (a term used to describe the earliest Christians collectively [cf. Acts 9:2]). What is essential for salvation? Public declaration that *Jesus is Lord* is at the bedrock, because this designates mental agreement with the gospel and the desire to live a life of personal fidelity to Jesus as the sovereign ruler of heaven and earth.

Embodied Fidelity

Now, circling back to our earlier discussion, I have asserted that saving allegiance includes three components. The first is *intellectual agreement* to the truthfulness of the eight stages that comprise the gospel. The second is the public *confession of loyalty* to Jesus as Lord. The third is *embodied fidelity* to Jesus as Lord. It is not enough merely to confess allegiance to Jesus in order to attain eternal salvation; the gospel is aimed at evoking "the obedience of *pistis*," practical allegiance (Rom. 1:5; 16:26; cf. 15:18–19). Paul tells Timothy to flee vices such as greed and to pursue virtues, summarizing: "Fight the good fight of *pistis*. *Take hold of the eternal life* to which you were called and about which you *made the good confession* in the presence of many witnesses" (1 Tim. 6:12). Timothy must actualize his confession of allegiance to Jesus by persisting victoriously in *pistis* through his enacted loyalty.

Moreover, in Matthew, Jesus himself indicates, in what is perhaps the most terrifying statement in the New Testament, that confessing that he is Lord is not on its own sufficient to secure eternal salvation. Allegiance includes obedient action:

> Not everyone who says to me, "Lord, Lord," will enter the kingdom of heaven, but the one who *does* the will of my Father who is in heaven. Many will say to me on that day, "Lord, Lord, did we not prophesy in your name, and cast out demons in your name, and do many powerful deeds in your name?" And then I will declare to them publicly, "I never knew you; depart from me, you *workers* of lawlessness." (Matt. 7:21–23)

The context in which this passage is situated pertains specifically to entering true life ("enter through the narrow gate!"—7:13), a warning against false prophets ("by their fruit you will recognize them!"—7:16), and the necessity of putting Jesus's words into practice ("everyone who hears these words of mine and *does* them will be like a wise man who built his house on the rock"—7:24). So the point in context is that even those who have confessed Jesus as Lord and who claim (on the basis of their own questionable testimony) to have performed good works in Jesus's name may not have truly *enacted* fidelity to Jesus as Lord. Notice Jesus calls them "*workers* of lawlessness," meaning their wicked practices are at issue. Professed allegiance is not sufficient; the allegiance must be realized by genuine, albeit not perfect, obedience. *Pistis* must be embodied. In fact, because salvation is a bodily journey, it cannot be any other way.[34]

This chapter has focused on *pistis* ("faith") as allegiance. We have briefly looked at ancient evidence for *pistis* as allegiance outside and inside Paul's Letters, discussed how Abraham's "trust" in the midst of deadness connects to allegiance, and analyzed various subcomponents that define saving

---

34. On the necessity of embodiment in the journey of salvation, see Green, *Conversion in Luke-Acts*. Green shows that contemporary ideas of non-bodily conversion are by and large a legacy of Cartesian dualism as it impacted emerging religious psychology—all of which has been decisively challenged by recent developments in neurobiology. Conversion is inescapably marked in the body (in brain remolding and in other somatic markers); moreover, Luke-Acts describes both conversion and salvation using the framing metaphor of a bodily journey (e.g., Luke 3:3–14; 9:51–62; Acts 9:3–18; see Green, *Conversion in Luke-Acts*, 53–163).

allegiance—intellectual assent to the gospel, professed loyalty to the Christ, and embodied fidelity. To explain how this third dimension, embodied fidelity or enacted loyalty, does not conflict with Paul's claim that we are saved by *pistis* but absolutely not by works (especially of law), we will need more space. I will take up this topic in the question-and-answer portion of the next chapter.

——— FOR FURTHER THOUGHT ———

1. Why might it be important theologically to think "Jesus the Christ" whenever you see "Jesus Christ"?

2. In phrases of the form "*pistis* of Jesus the Christ," what are the two major interpretative options for what this phrase means? Does the difference matter?

3. How has the "obedience of faith" typically been understood in most Protestant traditions? How might *pistis* as allegiance bring clarity to Paul's specific intention?

4. What are some possible understandings of how "the law of the Christ" fits into Paul's theology?

5. How does the Roman imperial context of the New Testament inform the meaning of *pistis* with respect to Jesus?

6. What is the difference in meaning between "belief," "trust," and "allegiance" in common parlance today?

7. With regard to the story of Abraham as recounted by Paul, we are saved not by "faith" in God's promises *in general* but by what? Briefly yet precisely sketch how Paul describes the matter in Romans 4.

8. This chapter has claimed that the threefold definition of *pistis* as consisting of *notitia*, *assensus*, and *fiducia* is inadequate with respect to the New Testament witness. Explain these terms and why they might be insufficient. Why might this matter for the church?

9. It has been proposed that saving *pistis* can be described as consisting of three components. Can you list and briefly explain (in your own words) the three essential components?

10. Why is mental agreement with the gospel as "true" insufficient for salvation on its own?

11. If God is forgiving, why is enacted allegiance required for final salvation?

5

QUESTIONS ABOUT
ALLEGIANCE ALONE

It is time for a question-and-answer session. But first, let's briefly recap. The first chapter sought to deconstruct deficient but popular understandings of faith. In the second it was argued that there is only one true gospel and that this one gospel is attested by Paul. In chapter 3 we discovered that Jesus and the Evangelists proclaim this same gospel in the Gospels, including Jesus's future rule as king of heaven and earth. In its essence, this gospel is not that "all have sinned and fallen short of God's glory," and so "we are saved by trusting in the sufficiency of Jesus's death for our sins." These statements contain important truths, but they truncate and distort the gospel, which instead *climaxes* and is directed most emphatically toward the enthronement of Jesus as the Christ. We are indeed saved by *pistis*, traditionally translated "faith," but when this word is applied to the question of salvation, it is best to speak of loyalty or allegiance, since saving "faith" is directed toward Jesus as the actively ruling king.

But with this claim, a multitude of related questions and possible objections readily spring to mind that have not yet been addressed: Doesn't allegiance require self-effort and in so doing preempt God's grace? How can allegiance be reconciled with Paul's teaching about works? What of the law? How can we be saved by allegiance if our allegiance is less than perfect? Many other questions need to be addressed as well.

In this chapter, working topically, I will begin to answer these questions. Although some satisfactory answers can be given at this stage of the book, exhaustive answers are out of the question—entire books have been written on the subtopics addressed here. Even complete answers still remain just beyond our reach, as what we mean by *salvation* will remain underdetermined until we can discuss the matter more fully in subsequent chapters.

In what follows, each section starts with a hypothetical question—although many of these questions are not fully hypothetical, as colleagues, friends, and students have often asked them as I have presented this material. My hope is that after pondering this chapter, the reader will have a better sense of why it is true to say that we are saved by allegiance alone, even if the reader still has unanswered questions regarding salvation, for this topic will be addressed more fully later.

Grace and Allegiance Alone?

Question: If salvation is by grace (a gift), then how can it depend on our allegiance to Jesus?

The Bible is absolutely clear that we cannot earn eternal salvation. No person on the basis of self-effort—by living a clean life or doing some heroic deed—can approach God and say, "If you are truly a just and fair God, then you *owe* me eternal life; I am a good person and I deserve it." If we think otherwise, it is because we have an unrealistic assessment of God's holiness, his righteous standard, and the depths of our own wickedness. Paul makes this abundantly clear in Romans 1:18–3:20, especially through his climactic assessment of the pervasive nature of the sin problem and the resulting implications:

> For we have already charged that *all*, both Jews and Greeks, are under the power of sin, as it is written: "*None is righteous, no, not one*; no one understands; no one seeks for God. *All have turned aside*; together they have become worthless; *no one does good, not even one*." (Rom. 3:9–12)

Since in the final analysis *all* are dominated by sin apart from the Christ, the implication is that right standing with God cannot follow from "works of the law"—that is, performance of the covenantal commandments given by God to Moses (or any other system of commandments). On the contrary, such commandments in the end only serve to heighten our awareness of the degree to which we have transgressed the holy standard that God has given (see Rom. 3:20; 7:7–14; 7:21–25). Humans are entirely undeserving of God's gift of salvation because they have been unfaithful to him. In consequence, salvation must come as a gift, by grace. Lest we miss the point, Paul underscores it by using two terms together, the adverb *dōrean* ("as a gift," "without payment") and the noun *charis* ("grace," "gift"), to stress emphatically the unmerited nature of the gift, saying that through the saving action of the Christ we are "justified by his grace [*charis*] as a gift [*dōrean*]" (Rom. 3:24).

Thus, it is certain that if we are to be saved, it must come from outside ourselves, as an undeserved gift from God (Eph. 2:5). God graciously takes the saving initiative in both corporate (Rom. 5:6; Titus 3:4–7) and personal salvation (Acts 13:48). A positive affirmation of the necessity of God's saving initiative with respect to the individual (e.g., "No one can come to me unless the Father who sent me draws him"—John 6:44) must be balanced with Scripture's affirmation that God has *in some sense* already taken that saving initiative for all because he desires that all be saved (e.g., "And I, when I am lifted up from the earth, will draw all people to myself"—John 12:32; cf. 1 Tim. 2:4). Various Christian traditions (e.g., Reformed, Arminian, Catholic) systematize this *in some sense* very differently, as it is disputed whether God's saving initiative truly extends to all individuals (or merely to the elect) and the degree to which it can be resisted. Regardless, it is agreed that God does not call or select either individuals or groups of people for salvation on the basis of *prior* allegiance or loyalty to him, but only on the basis of his own inscrutable desire to show mercy to the undeserving (Rom. 9:1–26; 11:5–6). These are bedrock truths that we must not lose sight of in our subsequent discussion.[1]

Yet not even traditional understandings of faith as belief or trust in Jesus's saving work claim that humans have no active role to play in salvation. On the contrary, most everyone would affirm that God requires us to perform at least one concrete action in response to God's grace, to respond "in faith," however we define it, to God's offer of salvation in Jesus. In fact, Jesus himself states as much in the Gospel of John. When the crowds ask Jesus, "What must we do, to be doing the works of God?" Jesus responds quite simply, "This is the work of God, that you *pisteuēte eis* the one whom he has sent" (John 6:28–29). Regardless of how we translate *pisteuēte eis*, whether "believe in" or "trust in," or as I am tempted to translate it, "give allegiance to," there is no doubt that *pistis*, to whatever degree it constitutes a "work," is required—and this is not felt to preclude grace under the traditional understandings of faith.[2]

The matter, I submit, is essentially no different if we understand *pistis* as allegiance to Jesus, the cosmic king. We are still saved by grace through *pistis*; salvation comes from outside ourselves as the Christ gift. Yet we must respond

1. For further discussion, see "Order of Salvation" in chap. 8.
2. For more on *pistis* language in John, see "Dimensions of Allegiance" in chap. 4.

to that gift by giving allegiance to Jesus as *Lord*. The offer of salvation is free, but it absolutely *does* come with strings attached. Obedient loyalty to the king is required as a condition of acceptance.

John Barclay shows that "grace" (*charis*) has been susceptible to six differentiable meanings for those who have interpreted Paul's Letters: (1) *superabundance*—the size of the gift; (2) *singularity*—the pure benevolence of the gift; (3) *priority*—giving at the ideal advance time; (4) *incongruity*—lack of merit in the recipient; (5) *efficacy*—the ability of the gift to achieve its intended purposes; (6) *noncircularity*—the absence of obligation to reciprocate by giving a gift in return. Paul himself does not necessarily "perfect," or take to its extreme limit, each one of these nuances of grace. In fact, he does not even include all of them in his own understanding of grace, as noncircularity in particular is alien to Paul. In other words, Barclay has convincingly demonstrated that it is a misunderstanding of grace (gift) in antiquity and in Paul's Letters to suggest that grace could not truly be grace if it requires obedience as an obligatory return. We are undeserving of God's gift of the Messiah—shockingly so!—in ancient contexts as well as contemporary. Yet the modern notion of the "pure gift" (a gift that requires no reciprocation) seeks to perfect grace along the wrong axis and does not align with the ancient evidence pertaining to grace.[3]

Contemporary Christian notions of grace also frequently fail to take into account the *effective* nature of grace. That is, the aim of God's gift of the Christ is to set us free from our slavery to sin, the law, and evil powers and to transform us so that we become new creatures, righteous in the Messiah (Rom. 5:20–21; 2 Cor. 5:17–21; Gal. 1:1–6; 6:15; Titus 2:11–14). In the Christ, we are ruled by grace, "*grace reigns* through righteousness unto eternal life" (Rom. 5:21; cf. Rom. 5:17; 1 Cor. 15:10). It is inappropriate, then, to suggest that God's gift of the Messiah, if the gift is accepted and subsequently held, would be ineffective in bringing about God's transformative aims. So we should not set grace at odds with the required behavioral changes (good deeds) associated with allegiant union to Jesus the king.

3. Barclay, *Paul and the Gift*. On the implausibility of "pure gift" (i.e., a noncircular gift) for Paul and for his social world as well as for the way in which grace is "perfected" (extended to its farthest limit) in six different ways, see 24–78. Barclay further demonstrates that God's saving grace is always unmerited for Paul, but that Paul consistently requires embodied obedience in response to that grace for it to result in final salvation (439–42, 493–519, 566–69). For further discussion regarding how God's grace obligated a return gift from the recipient (including charitable giving) in early Judaism and nascent Christianity, sometimes with the return gift linked not simply with reward but with personal forgiveness of sin, see Sir. 3:30; Tob. 12:9; Luke 11:41; 1 Pet. 4:8; 2 *Clem.* 16.4; Anderson, *Charity*; Downs, *Alms*, esp. 18–25, 125–29, 175–201.

In short, we cannot say in an unqualified fashion that final salvation is by grace and by faith apart from embodied obedience, for this misunderstands the nature of both *charis* ("grace") and *pistis* ("faith") in antiquity and in Paul's Letters. We must recognize the bankruptcy of our current selves, especially our self-centered indulgences and ambitions. Through participation in the Christ's death and resurrection, we must die to our old selves with the Messiah and become new selves, and in so doing follow the road of obedient service that our Lord commands by enacting allegiance. For Paul "faith" recognizes we are utterly dead and totally undeserving of God's grace, but the grasping of God's life-from-the-dead grace demands a trajectory of loyal obedience.

Irresistible Grace and Free Will?

Question: But doesn't the Bible teach that God chooses us even before we can choose him, so grace is not only prior to our "faith" but also irresistible?

Grace in the sense of God's prior activity precedes "faith," for God first had to bring about the good news before it could be proclaimed and before allegiance to Jesus as Lord could be confessed (Rom. 10:9–14). Moreover, God is the creator, and every good gift comes from God (James 1:17), so we must affirm God as the ultimate source of "faith" and all else.

Regarding the "prior" and "irresistible" nature of God's grace as it pertains to salvation, however, much more could be said. The Letter to the Ephesians, for example, combines these ideas in a powerful way when it says that God "chose us in him before the foundation of the world" and that "in love he predestined us for adoption" through Jesus the Christ (1:4–5). In my judgment these verses, and others like them, do prove that God orchestrates all human affairs, seeing both the beginning and the end of matters pertaining to human salvation. Note, however, that the focus is on God's choosing of *the church* for salvation in advance, not God's choice of individual humans for salvation (let alone for damnation) except inasmuch as they are part of the church.[4] In other words, Paul is affirming that his audience (the Ephesians) are part

---

4. In the classroom, I find that many contemporary English-language readers of the Bible individualize and personalize the text prematurely, taking the "we" and "us" in the text immediately as "I" and "me" and considering "you" to be a direct personal address. In Eph. 1:3–14, that Paul is speaking primarily of God's election of the collective church is made clear by the "we" and the "us." Moreover, in English "you" can refer either to an individual or to more than one person, but Greek marks the difference—and in this passage the "you" is plural. For further discussion of individuals and corporate groups in the order of salvation, see "Justification as Union, Not Order" in chap. 8.

of the one church, and hence that they have been chosen by God before the creation of the world for salvation.

Although philosophical consistency suggests that it is almost certainly the case that God—who transcends ordinary categories of space and time—knows in advance the eternal destiny of each individual person, this is not Paul's point here or elsewhere (contra Calvin and others).[5] Even Paul's example vis-à-vis Pharaoh in Romans 9:16–23 does not speak directly about Pharaoh's eternal fate, but only shows that God may harden individuals in order to assist others and to bring greater glory to God's own self. God retains the prerogative to reshape that vessel of wrath into something new even as he uses it as an instrument of his mercy. Misshapen potter's clay was not generally thrown away or destroyed in antiquity but rather put back on the wheel and crafted afresh (for evidence, see Jer. 18:4–6 as the background to Rom. 9:16–23). Even in this particular case, as the Bible presents the matter, God's hardening is in full cooperation with Pharaoh's free will, as the God-ordained consequences of Pharaoh's own choices move him to a state of ever-greater (but from *his* vantage point still potentially revocable) hard-heartedness.[6]

Ephesians 1:3–14 does show that God chose the church for salvation in the Son even before creation. God also can choose individuals for distinct purposes before they are born. For example, Jacob is chosen for special privilege over Esau, even though God ultimately finds a way to bless them both (for Esau's blessing, see Gen. 27:39–40 and Gen. 36). Accordingly, if some Christians[7] prefer to theorize that God irresistibly chooses individuals, not just the collective church, this does not mean that those individuals would

5. Barclay, *Paul and the Gift*, 569, puts it summarily: "The priority of the gift is everywhere presupposed, but Paul rarely draws out predestinarian conclusions, as in the *Hodayot* [of the Dead Sea Scrolls] or in the theologies of Augustine and Calvin." That is, Paul himself is not nearly as interested in perfecting *the volitional priority* of God's personal electing grace (God's choosing specific individuals before their birth for final salvation) as some of Paul's interpreters have been. While God's all-encompassing knowledge of the past, present, and future is everywhere presupposed (e.g., Rom. 11:33–36; 1 Cor. 2:7; Eph. 3:9), and Paul frequently speaks of specific events that God has arranged in advance (Rom. 8:28–30; 1 Cor. 15:51–55; Gal. 3:8; Eph. 1:3–14; 2:10; 1 Thess. 4:16; 2 Tim. 1:9), Paul's emphasis is consistently on God's choosing of the Christ and the corporate people of God in the Christ, not on individual predestination unto eternal life or damnation.

6. Regarding free will in the midst of divine action, although most of the time Exodus states that God will harden or has hardened Pharaoh's heart (e.g., 4:21; 7:3; 10:1) to save others, sometimes it states that Pharaoh hardened his own heart (e.g., 8:15, 32). Eventually Pharaoh's heart turns and he releases the Israelites before his heart is hardened once again for pursuit. Similarly, the temporary, revocable hardening of "Israel" in Rom. 9–11 is for the salvation of the gentiles (Rom. 11:25). Compare how God hands the wicked over to the consequences of their freely chosen but ever-accelerating disobedience in Rom. 1:24, 26, and 28, while remembering that Paul affirms that such disobedience can be transformed into obedience in the Christ (Rom. 12:1–2).

7. The biblical evidence for such a view is slender. See "God Chooses the Son" in chap. 8.

actually *experience* that grace as irresistible in a way that would violate their free will as these individuals move linearly through time. For we, unlike God in God's own eternal self-existence, are not beyond time so that we can see our own end or the end of others; rather we are inescapably time-enmeshed creatures, compelled to make choices (experienced as truly free) at specific moments that will somehow move us toward our eternal destination.[8]

So, even if those who speculatively affirm a primordial choice by God to graciously favor some specific individuals with salvation and to deny it to others happen to be right, nevertheless *pistis* as an enduringly experienced free choice is still necessary for salvation. The real question, then, is not whether salvation by allegiance alone denies grace—in my judgment it does not deny grace properly understood (see the previous section) any more or less than traditional understandings of "faith" inasmuch as the activity of *pistis* is the only thing demanded regardless. Rather the true question is how *pistis* interfaces with works and the law of Moses.

Works and Allegiance Alone?

Question: If we are saved by allegiance alone, and allegiance involves concrete acts of obedience to Jesus the king, then does this not violate the principle that we are saved by faith, not by works?

The way that I have framed the question above is a common way of phrasing such a question, but it is a bit loaded, for it assumes rather than demonstrates as probable that Paul believed that works are both the opposite of faith and immaterial (if not dangerous!) to eternal salvation. That is, it presumes that Paul and the earliest Christians did not believe that "works" in any way contribute to our salvation. But this is incorrect.

Works as the Basis for Eternal Judgment

Regarding the role of works in salvation, although many systematic treatments attempt to skate around this issue in a variety of ingenious ways, Paul himself states that we will be judged on the basis of our deeds:

> But because of your hard and impenitent heart you are storing up wrath for yourself on the day of wrath when God's righteous judgment will be revealed.

8. This classical theological position—God as beyond time—has been challenged within modern theologies that stress God's openness to the future, process, and God's being as bound up with eschatological completion. By and large I do not find these challenges persuasive.

God will render to each one according to his works: to those who by steadfastness in well-*doing* seek for glory and honor and incorruptibility—*eternal
life*; but for those who are self-seeking and do not *obey* the truth, but obey
unrighteousness—wrath and fury. (Rom. 2:5–8)

Paul affirms that God, on the day of judgment, will "render to each one according to his works," or even more precisely, that God "will *pay back*" at the
judgment in relation to works. And given that Paul describes this as "the day
of wrath" in conjunction with judgment and the granting of "eternal life,"
there is no real doubt we are talking about the *final* judgment here. Moreover,
after the passage I just cited, Paul goes on to say that it is not the hearers of
the law but the "*doers* of the law" who will be justified (Rom. 2:13), and that
what is rendered on this day of judgment will extend even to sins committed
in secret (Rom. 2:16). Paul is firm even if some modern commentators are not:
we will be judged, at least in part, for eternal life *on the basis of* our works.

Some scholars, however, do not accept this view. For example, John Piper
and Thomas Schreiner (among others) suggest that Paul's preposition *kata*
("according to") in Romans 2:6 is extremely important, signaling that we will
be judged for eternal life not *on the basis of* our works but only *in accordance
with* our works.[9] This interpretation, however, problematically suggests that
the conceptual spheres of these phrases can be tidily separated. But this is true
neither in English nor in Greek. For example, the sentence "In accordance with
the rise in temperature, I changed from pants into shorts" does not ordinarily
exclude "on the basis of the rise in temperature" as part of the reason for the
change in clothing. The same holds for *kata* in Greek. Moreover, in contexts
comparable to Romans 2:6 elsewhere in the Bible, *kata* gives the norm or the
standard for judgment in a way that moves beyond mere congruency to basis.[10]
Even more vital is the context of Romans 2:6, where Paul moves immediately
from the statement that we will be judged *kata* works to a description of concrete doing in 2:7–8 in such a way that the description of the doing appears
to define fundamentally (not just correlatively) what Paul means by judgment
kata works. All of this makes it unlikely that Paul was deliberately separating
congruence from basis. Judgment for eternal life in accordance with our works
but not on the basis of our works cannot be maintained.

Some of those who are particularly eager to rescue the idea of "faith alone,
not works" seek, in squeamish alarm, to propose two judgments (or separate

9. Piper, *Future of Justification*, 103–11, esp. 109–10; Schreiner, "Justification," 71–98, here
78 and 97.
10. See Ps. 61:13 LXX [Ps. 62:11]; Prov. 24:12; Matt. 16:27; John 7:24; 8:15; 2 Tim. 4:14;
1 Pet. 1:17; Rev. 2:23 (cf. BDAG, s.v. *kata* def. B.5.β).

stages within the one judgment)—one on the basis of deeds that is for the purpose of determining rewards only, and another on the basis of "faith alone" that determines eternal destiny.[11] But this ignores what Romans 2:5–8 plainly indicates, that on the basis of *works* the *eternal verdict* is rendered; specifically, eternal life is given to "those who by steadfastness in well-*doing* seek for glory and honor and incorruptibility." Meanwhile, wrath and fury are poured out on those who "are self-seeking and do not *obey* the truth, but obey unrighteousness." *Concrete actions and their results* (works) are the basis of the judgment—doing or not doing certain things and the specific results obtained (albeit the list of approved and disapproved actions and deeds remains somewhat general).

Given the obvious machinations of attempting to rescue the faith-alone system in suggesting two judgments, it is currently more popular to see only one final judgment here, but to see salvation as granted on the basis of faith alone, with it understood that this faith necessarily *caused* sufficient good works, so that Paul can speak in this way. In other words, a typical solution is to suggest that faith, the act of decisive trust or belief, comes first, and then good works naturally flow as a secondary effect, like a river from a spring. As Thomas Schreiner puts it, "Works are the necessary evidence and fruit of a right relation with God. They demonstrate, although imperfectly, that one is truly trusting in Jesus Christ."[12] Yet there are problems with this works-are-not-the-basis and works-are-the-necessary-evidence approach of Schreiner, Piper, and others.[13] There is a simpler solution.

Might it not be better to affirm that when Paul speaks of salvation by *pistis* in Jesus the Christ, not by works, that he speaks of allegiance to Jesus as the sovereign king? That is to say, we really are eternally judged, just as Paul indicates, in part on the basis of our works, but these works are part of *pistis* as embodied allegiance or enacted loyalty. *Pistis* is not the polar opposite of works; rather *pistis* as ongoing allegiance is the fundamental framework into which works must fit as part of our salvation.

11. E.g., see Wilkin, "Christians Will Be Judged," 25–50.
12. Schreiner, "Justification," 71–98, here 97.
13. Piper, *Future of Justification*, 103–16, esp. 110, gives a representative statement: "I think the best way to bring together the various threads of Paul's teaching on justification by faith apart from works (Rom. 3:28; 4:4–6; 11:6; Eph. 2:8) is to treat the necessity of obedience not as any part of the basis of our justification, but strictly as the evidence and confirmation of our faith in Christ whose blood and righteousness is the sole basis for our justification." In addition to the implausibility of a separation between congruence and basis with regard to Rom. 2:6 (as just discussed), see my treatment of faith (*pistis*) and grace (*charis*) as inclusive of embodied obedience in chaps. 4 and 5, respectively, as well as the further exploration of justification in chap. 8.

The relationship between *pistis* and works is not one of cause to effect but rather of overlapping nested categories. The larger category or set (*pistis* as allegiance) can include a portion of the smaller category or subset (works as embodied allegiance) as the Holy Spirit empowers us for right living. To show that this is true, it needs to be demonstrated further that Paul does not oppose works in general in favor of *pistis*, but rather that works are integral to final salvation. As we shall see later, what Paul does adamantly oppose is works as a system of salvation predicated on successful performance of rules, rather than works as the embodiment of *pistis* (fidelity) to Jesus the king.

More on Salvation by Works

If one were to encounter Romans 2:5–8 and think that it is the sole text in which Paul announces that we will be eternally judged on the basis of our works, then one might perhaps be excused for dismissing it as an obscure text that is best ignored. However, we cannot do this. For in a closely related passage Paul again affirms that we will be judged after death according to *what was accomplished* while in the body, and on that basis we will be rewarded or punished:

> For we must all appear before the judgment seat of the Christ, that each one may receive what is due *for that which he has done through the body*, whether good or evil. (2 Cor. 5:10)

Other texts in both Paul's Letters and the rest of the New Testament also indicate that our works will be taken into account on the day of judgment. Consider the vision of the final assize in the book of Revelation:

> And I saw the dead, the great and the small, standing before the throne. Books were opened. Then another book was opened, which is the book of life. And the dead were judged by what was written in the books *in accordance with their works* [*kata ta erga autōn*]. The sea gave up the dead who were in it, Death and Hades gave up the dead who were in them, and they were judged, each one of them, *in accordance with their works* [*kata ta erga autōn*]. And Death and Hades were cast into the lake of fire. This is the second death, the lake of fire. And if [the name of] anyone was not found written in the book of life, he or she was cast into the lake of fire. (Rev. 20:12–15)

Now within this vision, regardless of how we parse out the exact details of what these various books might contain, it is clear that the final verdict is rendered by examining together *both* the books in which "works" are recorded *and* the Lamb's book of life. To introduce two separate judgments (e.g., one for rewards and one for eternal life) is merely to introduce an unnecessary complexity because, so it is felt, salvation *must be* by "faith, not works." But the conflict is illusory, for Paul himself, that great champion of *pistis* not works, elsewhere stresses that certain deeds, if they persist without any repentance or modification, will result in our exclusion from the kingdom of God and our destruction:

> For you may be sure of this, that everyone who is sexually immoral or impure, or who is greedy—that is, an idolater—has no inheritance in the kingdom of the Christ and God. (Eph. 5:5)

And again:

> Now the works of the flesh are evident: sexual immorality, impurity, sensuality, idolatry, sorcery, enmity, strife, jealousy, rages, rivalries, dissensions, divisions, envies, bouts of drunkenness, orgies, and the like. I warn you, as I warned you before, that those who do such things will not inherit the kingdom of God. (Gal. 5:19–21)

Failure to "inherit the kingdom of God" certainly sounds like exclusion from eternal life. That eternal life (not merely rewards) is indeed at stake with regard to these matters of performed obedience is made clear as Paul continues in Galatians: "For the one who sows to his own flesh will from the flesh reap *destruction* [*phthoran*], but the one who sows to the Spirit will from the Spirit reap *eternal life*" (6:8).[14]

The contrast shows that eternal life is indeed the issue with regard to inheriting or not inheriting the kingdom. And it must be remembered that Paul is addressing the Christian community—not just those outside the church—in all of these texts that state that our actual (not just intended) obedience is a nonnegotiable essential with regard to our final salvation. As the author of Hebrews states, Jesus is "the source of eternal salvation for all who *obey* him" (5:9). Furthermore, other texts in the New Testament only reinforce the notion that those who continue to practice wickedness rather than obeying the Christ will have no share in God's eternal kingdom (e.g., 1 Cor. 6:9–11; 2 Thess. 1:5–10; Rev. 22:15).

---

14. The word *phthoran* pertains to decay, corruption, perishability, and destruction, so when placed as an opposing parallel to eternal life, as in this passage, it is best to translate it not as "corruption" (e.g., NRSV, ESV) but as "destruction" (e.g., NIV).

Allegiance Alone and the Law? (Part 1)

Question: If Paul and other New Testament authors indicate that our eternal verdict will be rendered on the basis of works (at least in part), then how does our salvation relate to obedience to God's law or other rules?

It is hoped that the reader has been convinced that Paul and the other New Testament authors regarded our actual obedience to Jesus the king—that is, the deeds that we perform in enacting *pistis*—as essential to our final salvation. Why then is Paul so strident in his polemic against works? I think we can now provide an answer.

Inasmuch as it pertains to salvation, in short, Paul does not oppose all works—in fact he demands good works as embodied loyalty. But Paul is absolutely against something more specific: "works *of law.*" That is, Paul opposed the idea that anyone can perform the works of the law (as given by God to Moses)—and by extension any other rule-based system—in order to establish or confirm righteousness before God. To show why this is so, it is helpful to gain at least a rudimentary acquaintance with recent scholarly conversations that have helped us nuance these matters more accurately, and then we will move to the examination of some specific texts.

The New Perspective on Paul

Lively and often heated discussion about salvation (especially *justification*, roughly, "right standing before God") has occupied the center of the study of Paul's Letters among professional scholars for approximately the past thirty-five years. This is not the appropriate place to retell the whole story of what has been termed the New Perspective on Paul, especially because many others have told it well already and the interested reader can easily follow up.[15] For our purposes, the main point is that in response to groundbreaking work by Krister Stendahl, E. P. Sanders, James Dunn, N. T. Wright, and many others, a broad spectrum of New Testament scholars have come to question ways of reading Paul's Letters, especially Romans and Galatians, that had become traditional since the Protestant Reformation in the sixteenth century. The issue at hand, for our purposes, is not so much whether this reassessment is correct but the manner in which it helps us ask different questions of the text than we might otherwise have been prepared to ask.

So, then, what is the gist of this recent scholarly discussion about salvation in Paul's Letters? In brief, it is claimed that two of Paul's most important

---

15. Westerholm, *Perspectives Old and New on Paul*; Zetterholm, *Approaches to Paul.*

letters, Romans and Galatians, had been systematized by Reformers such as Martin Luther, John Calvin, and especially their spiritual descendants as if Paul was trying to teach his ancient congregations how a person comes to be saved—namely, "by faith, not by works." In arriving at this conclusion, however, the Protestant Reformers, so this scholarly story goes, had in fact *falsely projected their caricatured conceptions of medieval Catholic teaching*—that is, that Catholic teaching demands "works" as a condition for salvation—*onto ancient Judaism*. So allegedly (but there is at least *some* truth in the matter) the Protestant Reformers had determined that the ancient Jews were much like the medieval Catholic church in demanding a works-based system in which salvation could only be earned by accruing sufficient merit by performing certain deeds. Specifically, the Reformers judged that the ancient Jews quite uniformly believed salvation could only come by remaining obedient to the Mosaic commands (as interpreted), so that salvation might be earned through performing the commands sufficiently well, so that the good deeds might outweigh the bad at the final judgment.

The Protestant Reformers believed that Paul was the great champion of the gospel and liberty for the earliest church over against Paul's Judaizing opponents. In the face of opposition from Jewish Christians and their allies, Paul above all others was the one who preserved the "good news" that we are saved as a free gift by faith alone, not by works. Moreover, Paul was not just a champion for the church during ancient times; for the Reformers he was also a champion for their own day and age. For them, Paul's Letters could be wielded to show that the medieval Catholic salvation-by-works system was a corruption of the one true gospel. The Reformers especially objected to the notion that the "works" required by the sacrament of penance could contribute to the forgiveness of mortal sins committed post-baptism or that the works demanded by the indulgence system could guarantee reduced time in purgatory (see chap. 8 for more discussion). According to the Reformers, the genuine good news—the gospel—was, still is, and always shall be that we are saved by faith alone and grace alone apart from any such works that we might accomplish!

Regardless of whether this scholarly reassessment has correctly described the real position of the Reformers, medieval Catholicism, or ancient Judaism (and professional opinions on these matters vary considerably), it is beyond dispute that this reassessment has had the salutary effect of forcing all serious interpreters of Paul and the New Testament to step out of habitual ways of reading these texts and to seek to become reacclimated. And as we move outside the box to reframe, common sense (as well as inspection of the texts in question) suggests that it is unlikely that Paul's main goal would be to outline a program for his ancient Christian readers regarding how to enter into salvation, since Paul indisputably regards his readers as already having decisively entered. Moreover, E. P. Sanders and others have shown that most ancient Jews believed that they were born into covenant membership as *an ethnic privilege* (chosen by God by *race* as much as by grace), and hence that they were moving toward final salvation so long as they did not flagrantly disregard the commands.[16]

Thus, when we read about "justification" in Paul, which has traditionally been regarded as denoting the first step of salvation, the moment at which we enter into "right" relationship with God through Jesus, we ought to begin with at least a modicum of suspicion that Paul's language about justification might be more flexible than has been encouraged by the traditional Reformation-inspired systems.[17] The upshot of all this is that when in Galatians, for example, Paul stridently opposes certain individuals who are perverting the gospel (1:6–10) or who are not acting in line with the truth of the gospel (2:11–14), because they are pushing the necessity of maintaining Jewish customs connected to the Mosaic law (see Gal. 4:10, 21; 5:1–4; 6:12–13), Paul is probably not as concerned with perversions regarding how an individual might *enter into* right relationship with God as he is with false ideas about *what can truly demarcate* the people of God as the genuinely "declared to be in the right" people of God—although the issues overlap and cannot be entirely separated.[18] That is, the nub of the question with which Paul is wrestling is this: Do the people of God have right standing with God through performing a legal code, or is it by allegiance (*pistis*) to the Christ as the Holy Spirit works in the community to actualize the power of God for salvation?

Works of Law as Rule Performance

As we have already discovered, Paul does not think works are immaterial to salvation. Paul says that works will form the basis of eternal judgment (at least

---

16. Sanders, *Paul and Palestinian Judaism*.

17. See Wright, *What Saint Paul Really Said*, 113–33, here 119: "Justification . . . is not a matter of how someone enters the community of the true people of God, but of how you tell who belongs to that community." For discussion of justification in the so-called order of salvation, see "Order of Salvation" in chap. 8.

18. To clarify, I am not saying that Paul (as it pertains to salvation) was only concerned with the law as a false socioreligious boundary marker and that he was therefore not concerned with actual legal performance. For most Jews in Jesus's day, eternal salvation was both an ethnic gift and contingent on adequate (albeit not perfect) covenant maintenance through obedience to God's commandments (as variously understood). Yet I am signaling that Paul's *pistis*-versus-works-of-law polemic is more about false ways of demarcating the basis of the people of God's righteousness than about how an individual might first come to be "declared right" (although Paul would also certainly affirm that circumcision and works of law are inadequate entry points).

partially) and that lived obedience is essential for salvation. Non-embodied *pistis* is not *pistis* at all, but rather a dead thing, as James so forcefully reminds us (2:17, 26). Paul does not oppose works in general (good works are both desirable and inevitable); what he opposes are works as part of a race-based, performance-demanding, rule-oriented system of salvation that fails to recognize the worthlessness of such criteria in the wake of the Christ event. As Paul himself puts it:

> For as many as are by means of the works of law, they are under a curse; for it is written, "Cursed is everyone who does not persist in *all* the things written in the Book of the Law, in order to do them." (Gal. 3:10, citing Deut. 27:26)

Here Paul shows why works of the law are insufficient for right standing with God. The one who does not successfully perform *all* the commandments written in the Book of the Law (that is, the law of Moses as found in the first five books of the Bible) finds that the curses that are attached to the covenant as sanctions for disobedience inevitably come crashing down on the one attempting to perform the works. That Paul has in mind covenant curses such as those mentioned in Leviticus 26 and Deuteronomy 27–28 is clear, for he has drawn his Old Testament quotations from these contexts. Paul continues:

> Now it is evident that no one is justified before God by the law, because "The righteous one will live by *pistis*." Now the law is not by *pistis*, rather "The one who *does* these things shall live by them." (Gal. 3:11–12, citing Hab. 2:4 and Lev. 18:5)

Having just mentioned "works of the law" (Gal. 3:10), Paul now makes the contrast between *pistis* and works of the law (performing the commands) more precise. He indicates that the works-of-the-law approach is fundamentally different in orientation than the *pistis* path ("the law is not by *pistis*"). Moreover, the *pistis* path succeeds whereas the works-of-the-law approach fails specifically because successful *performance* of *all* the commands is demanded by the law if *life* is going to result—but as we have just discovered in 3:10, the law itself testifies that the commandments cannot be successfully performed, and the covenant curse is the inevitable result.[19]

19. If most Jews in this time period did not think it necessary to keep the *entire* law of Moses in order to attain to final salvation (as has been established by E. P. Sanders and others), why might Paul think this to be true (Gal. 3:10; 5:3; cf. James 2:10)? One possible solution is that Paul believes that Jesus opened up a new era of salvation history. Jesus the Christ's climactic fulfillment of the law, in which he brought the law to its terminal goal (Rom. 10:4) and forged a new covenant (1 Cor. 11:25; 2 Cor. 3:6), has left provisions in the law for forgiveness devoid

We see here that Paul construes "by works of law" and "by *pistis*" as different paths to right standing, one that succeeds "by *pistis*" and one that fails. We also see that Paul's complaint against works is rooted in specific limitations of the Mosaic system and, we might surmise because Paul himself suggests it, limitations in *any rule-based system*. Paul argues that even before the law of Moses was given, trespasses still had a death-dealing effect (e.g., see Rom. 5:12–14 and 7:9–10). So the problem is not specific to the Mosaic law but extends to all rule-based systems because they inappropriately rely on successful performance of enumerated commands.

The problem need not be that the individual in question is inappropriately trying to "earn" salvation by trying to establish his or her own righteousness (nor is this possibility excluded), but it could merely stem from a failure to see that grace, the gift of the Christ event, has shown that *all forms of worth that could determine a person's righteousness are empty*. This would explain why, for instance, Paul's concern in Galatians is not just circumcision but *both* circumcision (performing a command) and uncircumcision (not performing a command); the Galatians must see that *both* are a matter of total *indifference* (Gal. 5:6). All that matters is re-creation "in the Messiah" through allegiance.[20]

Moreover, even if some of Paul's compatriots were not convinced that perfect performance of *all* the commands was necessary for salvation, Paul himself seems to have felt that Scripture points to the necessity of obedience to all the commands ("cursed is the one who does not continue to do *everything* written in the Book of the Law" [Gal. 3:10, citing Deut. 27:26]). Such obedience is impossible. Likewise, for Paul the person who makes circumcision necessary becomes responsible for obedience to "the *whole* law" (Gal. 5:3). Because a person cannot obey the entire law, the result is that the covenant curses come upon the one attempting the rule-based performance.

Yet there is good news in the midst of the gloomy prospect of the covenant curses. For the curses have indeed fallen, but Jesus has taken these curses upon himself: "The Messiah redeemed us from the curse of the law by becoming a curse for us!" (Gal. 3:13). And in so doing, Jesus the Christ has delivered the blessing of Abraham that God promised the gentiles,[21] which Paul understands to be the gift of the Holy Spirit, received through *pistis* (Gal. 3:14). Paul is opposed to "works of law" inasmuch as they demand performance of the

---

of power (e.g., the Day of Atonement in Lev. 16). So now anyone who would approach God through the law must attain to the impossible standard of perfect obedience. See Das, *Paul, the Law, and the Covenant*, 145–70.

20. See Barclay, *Paul and the Gift*, esp. 391–94, 404–6.

21. God had promised Abraham, "In you all the families of the earth will be blessed" (Gen. 12:3), a point that Paul has already emphasized in Galatians (3:8).

commands in an attempt to establish or otherwise demonstrate righteousness but are unsuccessful in securing it.

Another text also gets at one of Paul's basic objections to works of the law. Paul invokes the metaphor of a race. In this race, the gentiles have obtained the prize of righteousness, but Israel, tragically, has fallen short. How has this come about?

> What shall we say, then? That gentiles who did not pursue righteousness have attained it—that is, a righteousness that is by *pistis*; but that Israel who pursued *a law* that would lead to righteousness *did not succeed in reaching that law*. Why? Because they did not pursue it by *pistis, but as if it were based on works*. They have stumbled over the stumbling stone. . . . For, being ignorant of the righteousness that comes from God, *and seeking to establish their own*, they did not submit to God's righteousness. For the Christ is the end of the law for righteousness to everyone who *gives allegiance* [*panti tō pisteuonti*]. (Rom. 9:30–32; 10:3–4)

Here we find out something further. Paul is opposed to "works of law" not merely because they are unsuccessful at meeting the performance requirement (and so leading to righteousness and life) but also because such works could, for Israel, smack of an attempt to establish *their own righteousness* rather than acquiescing to the true demarcation for God's righteousness—*pistis*, rendered allegiance to Jesus as the Christ, the messianic stone that God has placed as a gift in Zion.

Does Paul indicate that some of his compatriots were self-righteously seeking to "earn" their own salvation by accumulating sufficient good deeds? This possibility is not excluded, but it is better to suggest that the weight of Paul's critique lies subtly elsewhere. As John Barclay puts it, Paul's compatriots were mistakenly insisting that "God's righteousness should recognize as its fitting object, the righteousness defined in their own Torah-based terms"[22]—and in so doing they were failing to recognize that the Torah had in fact reached its *telos* (goal or fulfilling end) in the Christ event. That is, Paul regarded his compatriots as falsely believing that God gives his gift of righteousness only to those who prove themselves worthy—and that God's "worth" system was enshrined in the performance-demanding Torah. The importance of this subtle difference is that Paul is not critiquing the *general* human attempt to "earn" salvation by doing good deeds or self-righteousness as much as he is hinting that *all merit-based systems fail to grasp the totally unmerited nature of the Christ gift*—a gift that can be accessed only by *pistis* to the king.

22. Barclay, *Paul and the Gift*, 540.

Allegiance Alone and the Law? (Part 2)

Question: If the law of Moses represents a genuine, God-given standard but at the same time does not result in righteousness, is it the case that the good works necessary for salvation and the good works that the law demands are different?

To frame this question in slightly different terms, when Paul and other New Testament authors affirm that our works will be taken into account in rendering a verdict regarding our eternal destination, are these good works different than the works demanded by the law of Moses?

Salvation and Obeying the Law of Moses

The answer, like much else, is a complicated yes and no. It is no inasmuch as we will not be assessed on the basis of our performance of specific rituals or moral commands in the Mosaic law apart from how these inhere in loyal obedience (*pistis*) to Jesus as Lord. God will not judge us on the basis of whether we ate meat with the blood still inside it, as is forbidden by Leviticus 19:26, apart from whether such a command is required for us by allegiance to Jesus. (And for some this regulation perhaps is demanded because of their particular circumstances or life mission, but for most of us it is not.) God will not judge us on the basis of whether we have broken the commandment "You shall not steal," except inasmuch as such a command is demanded for us by allegiance to Jesus. (And for all of us, this command is binding for allegiance to Jesus—although one might be able to think of a Robin Hood scenario where concern for the weak might permit it in the face of corrupt hording.)

So while the answer is no because it is the allegiance to the king himself that counts rather than performance of the Mosaic law, it is also yes since allegiance (*pistis*) to Jesus as king demands obedience to the deepest intentions of the law of Moses (see Matt. 5:17–48) even though this law has now reached its climactic goal (Rom. 10:4). At the final judgment, we will not be evaluated on the basis of whether we kept a list of rules such as the Ten Commandments, except inasmuch as genuine fidelity to Jesus the king demanded it. We are not saved by heaping up good works on our eternal balance sheet. We are saved by *pistis* rendered unto Jesus as *Lord*, and this involves a qualitative rather than quantitative enacted faithfulness to Jesus in real-life situations. I will speak to the issue of infidelity or disloyalty to Jesus the king subsequently.

Law, Excitable Flesh, and Spirit

How are we, devoid of an absolute rule-based standard such as the law of Moses, supposed to be able to make determinations about what constitutes obedience to Jesus the king? We are to obey the Lord Jesus's commands through the discerning and empowering aid of the Holy Spirit—and in so doing we will fulfill the good works that all along the law was designed by God to aim toward. The result is that the true intention of all the commandments are fulfilled, especially the love command. As Paul himself puts it:

> For the commandments, "You shall not commit adultery, You shall not murder, You shall not steal, You shall not covet," and any other commandment, are recapitulated in this word: "You shall love your neighbor as yourself." Love renders no evil to a neighbor; therefore love is the fulfillment of the law. (Rom. 13:9–10)

So we fulfill the true aim of the specific commandments pertaining to the other when we love the neighbor as the self, and this comes about when we walk in the Holy Spirit (see Gal. 5:13–18).

But why is the aid of the Holy Spirit necessary? Why can't we please God simply by remaining obedient to the Ten Commandments or God's other moral instructions? Because of the powerlessness of our flesh, God had to do something for us. He had to send his Son. And furthermore, we needed the gift of the Spirit. Paul puts it this way:

> For God has done what the law, weakened by the flesh, could not do. Having sent his own Son in the likeness of sinful flesh and for sin, he condemned sin in the flesh, in order that the righteous requirement of the law might be fulfilled in us, those who walk not according to the flesh but according to the Spirit. (Rom. 8:3–4)

The law of Moses was powerless to effect sufficient good works on its own steam, for even though the law is God's holy and righteous standard, it actually made the sin problem worse! How so?

Imagine that you are a small child and that your mother has just made a wonderful batch of chocolate chip cookies. She has placed them on a low shelf to cool. On a crisp morning, you prance into the kitchen and are suddenly overwhelmed by the homey and rich smell. With bright and hopeful eyes, you ask your mom for a cookie, but she curtly says, "No, not until after lunch," and promptly leaves the kitchen, returning to coffee and a magazine in the living room. Hungry and disappointed, you are all alone with the cookies.

Now, prior to your mom's "No," the cookies were already highly desirable. But as soon as the commandment, the "No," entered in, the desire suddenly heightened, because now they were *forbidden* cookies. Your mother's law, her commandment, had come alongside your flesh-based desire and made the problem worse (cf. Rom. 7:7–8). You wanted a cookie before, but now you *desperately* want a cookie!

This heightening of desire is the fundamental way that a rule-based system operates on humankind—and this even prior to the coming of the Mosaic commandments, as is illustrated by the story of Adam, Eve, and the forbidden fruit. This is one of the reasons Paul is absolutely certain that a rule-based system devoid of Messiah-allegiance cannot result in righteousness. It does not alleviate the sin problem; it exacerbates it by exciting the flesh (cf. Rom. 7:14–23). But God through the Christ has set us free from the death-dealing effects of the law by doing what the law could not do: "For God has done what the law, weakened by the flesh, could not do" (Rom. 8:3). God has sent his Son "in the likeness of sinful flesh," and in so doing he "condemned sin in the flesh" (Rom. 8:3; cf. Jesus's taking on the curse of the law in Gal. 3:13). God did this so that "the righteous requirement of the law might be fulfilled in us" when we walk "in accordance with the Spirit" rather than "in accordance with the flesh" (Rom. 8:4).

Several other texts similarly indicate that the good works God requires for our salvation are performed as part of our allegiance to Jesus as actualized by the agency of the Holy Spirit. This is an additional reason why salvation by allegiance alone does not preclude grace. The good works that are required for salvation are embodied via a gift by the Holy Spirit as the Holy Spirit operates with and through us. Yet these good works embodied in conjunction with the enabling Spirit are not optional extras—our salvation depends on their real, albeit imperfect, actualization: "For if you live according to the flesh you will die, but if by the Spirit you put to death the *deeds* [*praxeis*] of the body, you will live. For as many as are led by the Spirit of God, these are sons of God" (Rom. 8:13–14).

So the Mosaic law, even though it is God-ordained, nonetheless was subject to the limitations of all such rule-based systems. Law makes the sin problem worse by exciting the flesh. Thus it cannot result in the kind of righteousness that God desires. As Paul puts it elsewhere, "For the letter kills, but the Spirit makes alive" (2 Cor. 3:6). That is, the letter of the law associated with the Mosaic covenant kills, but the Holy Spirit supplies life. Why? Because the Spirit sets us free from the performance demands of the Old Covenant (2 Cor. 3:17), allowing us to be transformed into the image of Jesus the Christ (2 Cor. 3:18). The good works that the law was really directed toward all along are indeed fulfilled for those who walk in accordance with the Spirit:

> But I say, walk by the Spirit, and you will not consummate the desires of the flesh. For the desires of the flesh are contrary to the Spirit, and the desires of the Spirit are contrary to the flesh, for these are opposed to each other, so that you do not do the things you want. But if you are led by the Spirit, you are not under the law. Now the works of the flesh are evident: sexual immorality, impurity, sensuality . . . (Gal. 5:16–19)

In other words, allegiance to the Christ entails life in the Spirit (which is precisely what it means to be part of the church) rather than life under the law—and this allegiance is manifest as a concrete way of life that puts to death the flesh's wicked practices. It also means that the fruit of the Spirit will be embodied, but not necessarily in a simple cause-and-effect relationship between initial "faith" (as "belief" or "trust") and subsequent "good deeds." Rather the Spirit's actions in the midst of the community that *continues* to profess "Jesus is Lord" is the cause, and the effect is spiritual gifts that manifest "good deeds" performed as ongoing allegiance (see 1 Cor. 12:1–3). In other words, initial declared allegiance (*pistis*) to Jesus the king causes a union with the king and his body, and the maintenance of this union is an embodiment of allegiance, a lived obedience that includes good deeds within its purview. So there is not a simple cause-and-effect relationship between "faith" and "works"; rather *pistis* is quite simply not *pistis* at all if it is not embodied and embedded in the allegiant community.

So, in sum, for Paul, salvation requires the performance of concrete works (deeds) in loyal submission to Jesus as the king (i.e., salvation by *pistis* necessarily entails enacted allegiance), but Paul stridently opposes the idea that good works can contribute to our salvation when performed as part of a system of rule keeping apart from the more fundamental allegiance to King Jesus. In other words, the real "faith" versus "works" divide in Paul is more accurately framed as a divide between *works performed as allegiance to Jesus the king* versus *works performed apart from new creation in the Christ*. And the latter usually but not always takes the form of a system that seeks to establish righteousness through performing prescribed regulations.

Paul views the by-*pistis* path (the allegiance path) as fundamentally different than the by-works-of-law path, even though both avenues equally demand good works for final salvation. One path succeeds through Holy Spirit–infused union with Jesus the Messiah; the other fails. Good deeds are required for salvation even though (apart from allegiance to Jesus the king) they are not on their own in the least bit meritorious. Nor can the good deeds necessary for salvation be enumerated or definitively prescribed as part of a salvation system without running afoul of Paul's teaching here. *Pistis* alone counts—loyalty to Jesus that is pragmatically expressed in obedient and willing service to him as the king.

Struggling with Sin?

Question: Since we are all disloyal to Jesus—we have sinned in the past, sin in the present, and will sin in the future—how can our salvation depend on our allegiance alone?

First, it must be remembered that when Christians, using the traditional terminology, speak of salvation by *faith* alone, they are not asserting that nothing else is involved from the divine side. Obviously, they are not suggesting that we are saved by faith alone, so therefore God didn't have to act in sending his Son to die for our sins. What is being claimed is that faith, enabled by grace, is the only contribution that *we make* to our salvation. I am making precisely the same claim, that we are saved by *pistis* alone, but that many contemporary understandings of "faith" dangerously and illegitimately shade out the loyalty-demanding portion of *pistis*. I am also suggesting that all too frequently the object toward which *pistis* is directed in contemporary Christianity (and also in much Reformation-era Christianity) is blurry, inasmuch as it centers on Jesus as a sin offering rather than as the fidelity-demanding king.

Imperfect Allegiance

So if allegiance (*pistis*) to Jesus as Lord is the only contribution that we can make to our salvation, then what of our ongoing sin problems? Are these not fundamentally acts of disloyalty? Yes, they are. We truly are saved by allegiance alone, but *perfect* allegiance is neither demanded for salvation in this earthly life nor is it possible any more than is perfect faith (or zero doubt) as traditionally understood. (What is demanded is transformative union with Jesus—see chap. 8.) Although sin has been decisively defeated and no longer controls us (Rom. 6:11–14), both our own experiences of failure and Scripture make it clear that we cannot live entirely sin-free lives on this side of glory, even with the aid of the Holy Spirit. As John puts it in his First Letter, "If we say we have no sin, we deceive ourselves, and the truth is not in us" (1:8; cf. 1:10). And then he continues, giving us a much more encouraging report: "If we confess our sins, he is faithful and righteous to forgive us our sins and to cleanse us from all unrighteousness" (1:9).

If perfect allegiance is neither demanded nor possible, then *how much* allegiance is sufficient? What if I give considerable allegiance most every day, but somehow every fourth Tuesday I find myself grossly disobeying the Lord Jesus? Personally, I have found myself in this predicament, wrestling with certain repeated sins that seem to have a stranglehold on me—and I know for certain that I am not alone in my repeated failings. I am convinced that through my confession of Jesus as the Lord and my overarching desire to actualize that confession through lived obedience, God (through the Spirit) and I are working in tandem in such a fashion that I never find myself entirely giving up the fight against sin. We are saved when our confessed and imperfectly maintained allegiance unites us to Jesus the king, for he has already been declared righteous, and we share that righteous standing (see chap. 8 for further discussion). Allegiance must be a settled conviction and basic disposition. Yet what if a person is not just struggling with sin but has fundamentally turned his or her back on Jesus in word or deed?

Treason against Jesus

In considering sin as disloyalty to the Lord Jesus, a closely related question arises: What about blatant treason? Is there any hope for those who have not merely temporarily lapsed or acted selfishly (i.e., in their own interests) more than in the interests of King Jesus, but have fundamentally denied him? Yes, there is hope, as the example of Peter, who denied Jesus three times but who was reinstated, makes certain. Meanwhile, another traitor, Judas, despite his remorse, committed suicide and was never reconciled (Matt. 27:3–5; Acts 1:16–19, 25). So treason is at least sometimes reversible through renewed allegiance; yet reversal, even for those who were at one time followers of Jesus, is not an inevitable outcome.

In fact, Jesus states that for those who blaspheme not just against Jesus himself but against the Holy Spirit, the sin is eternal and there is no possibility of forgiveness (Matt. 12:31; Mark 3:29; Luke 12:10). The contexts in the Synoptic Gospels in which we find this saying do, however, suggest that this irreversibility is not due to God's lack of willingness to forgive should repentance occur but rather to the inability of the blasphemer to take the initiative in repenting.[23] It seems best, then, to suggest that the lack of a possibility for

---

23. In Matthew and Mark, Jesus's opponents accuse him of driving out evil spirits by the power of the prince of demons (see Matt. 12:22–32 and Mark 3:22–30). They are so muddled by their hatred of Jesus that they are identifying the good work of the Spirit as the work of

forgiveness arises from the human side rather than from the divine: God would forgive the one who has blasphemed the Spirit if that person could right the ship enough to see good as good and evil as evil—and in so doing begin to choose the good in returning to God.

How Much Allegiance Is Required?

Question: If our salvation depends solely on allegiance to Jesus as Lord, how can I be sure that I have been loyal enough?

When I find myself wondering whether my allegiance is enough, I am forced to remind myself that this is to ask the wrong question. Indeed, those who are concerned enough to ask it are probably those who are in the least danger of a lack of allegiance—although they may be drawing nigh to a risky legalism. To seek to quantify or develop a set of hard and fast rules by which one could measure sufficient loyalty is antithetical to the gospel—indeed, it is precisely this rule-based approach that causes Paul so much consternation in his polemic against works of law. Enacted loyalty is required as the Holy Spirit empowers us, and this enacted loyalty means a settled intention and truly changed bodily behavior. But a personalized description of how much loyalty is necessary for me or for you is not only impossible; it is wrongheaded.

Allegiance cannot be quantified or enumerated. How would you feel if you were getting married and your spouse wanted a list of rules issued in advance describing how far he or she could go sexually in a relationship with another before it would be considered cheating? Or what, if you were a soldier during wartime, would your general think if you wanted a list defining how much military aid you could give to the opponent before it would be considered treason? The desire for an enumerated list is often indicative of one of two things: either a failure to know and trust the goodness of Jesus the king or a what-can-I-get-away-with orientation.

It is better to ask *what sort* of allegiance than *how much*, because allegiance depends on what Jesus the king commands each of us individually to do and whether he determines now and at the final judgment that you and I have given *pistis*. If we give *pistis* to Jesus as Lord by declaring allegiance, determining to

---

evil, and vice versa. Meanwhile, in Luke the context is public confession of loyalty to Jesus in the presence of hostile authorities (see Luke 12:8–12; cf. 11:14–23). When hostile authorities speak against Jesus himself, they might possibly still be forgiven, but if they declare that the good Spirit-empowered Christian work is in fact evil, they are beyond the pale. In brief, if a person becomes so depraved that she or he can no longer identify evil or good correctly, then the eternal spiritual risk for that person cannot possibly be overstated, so Jesus issues this warning.

enact loyalty, and showing through bodily doing that our determination was not just lip service, then we can rest assured that his death on our behalf is utterly and completely efficacious—all of our sins are forgiven in the Messiah (even our selfish acts of temporary disloyalty). And the Holy Spirit invariably comes alongside us to assist us in faithful living.

But can we get a rough answer to the question of *what sort* of embodied loyalty is necessary? That is, can we get an approximate idea of what actualized loyalty to the Lord Jesus should look like, perhaps enough to gain assurance or sound a necessary alarm? Scripture does give us a broad description by way of an inverse picture, describing what sorts of activities enacted loyalty *forbids*—"sexual immorality, impurity, sensuality, idolatry, sorcery, enmity, strife, jealousy, rages, rivalries, dissensions, divisions, envies, bouts of drunkenness, orgies, and the like" (Gal. 5:19–21)—and we can only conclude, while still leaving space for God's desire to show stunning mercy to all (Rom. 11:32; 1 Tim. 2:4), that persisting unchecked in these activities without change leads to condemnation.

The First Letter of John also gives helpful guidelines that we can use to measure whether we are truly enacting loyalty in such a fashion that the eternal kind of life is ours as a present and future possession—although we must resist turning any such guidelines into a legalistic prescription. Consider especially the specific actions mentioned:

And by this we know that we have come to know him [Jesus the Christ], if we keep his commandments. (2:3)

The one who claims to be in the light yet who hates his brother is still in the darkness. (2:9)

If anyone loves the world, the love of the Father is not in him. Because all that is in the world—the desires of the flesh and the desires of the eyes and the arrogance associated with material possessions—is not from the Father but is from the world. (2:15–16)

No one who denies the Son has the Father. The one who confesses the Son also has the Father. (2:23)

If you know that he [Jesus the Christ] is righteous, you know that everyone who practices righteousness has been born of him. (2:29)

No one who abides in him [Jesus the Christ] keeps on sinning; no one who keeps on sinning has either seen him or known him. (3:6)

> No one born of God keeps on sinning, because God's seed remains in him. He is unable to keep on sinning because he has been born of God. (3:9)

> We know that we have moved from death into life, because we love the brothers and sisters. The one who does not love remains in death. (3:14)

> By this you know the Spirit of God: every spirit [of prophecy] that confesses that Jesus the Christ has come in the flesh is from God; every spirit that does not confess Jesus is not from God. (4:2–3)

In weighing these various statements, we should notice how many of them pertain to concrete deeds: keeping Jesus's commandments, ceasing from persistent sinning, practicing righteousness, turning away from hatred and worldliness, and loving the brothers and sisters. It seems that John left his ultimate test for last:

> The one who *gives pistis unto* [*ho pisteuōn eis*] the Son of God has the testimony in himself. . . . And this is the testimony: God has given us eternal life and this life is in his Son. The one who has the Son has life; the one who does not have the Son of God does not have life. (1 John 5:10–12)

Giving *pistis* unto the Son of God is what results in eternal life. John makes it evident that this test is definitive when he states his overall purpose in writing:

> I write these things to you *who give pistis unto* [*tois pisteuousin eis*] the name of the Son of God, in order that you may know that you have eternal life. (1 John 5:13)

So John explicitly avows that his primary purpose is to grant confidence to those who have given *pistis* to the Son of God. We can have confidence in knowing that our embodied loyalty is indicative of eternal life when we see a reflection of our own actions mirrored in the guidelines. Non-enacted *pistis* is not *pistis* at all but a dead thing. Although there may be important subjective ways to test whether we have assurance of our salvation (e.g., inner peace that we are God's children, as that peace is facilitated by the Spirit [Rom. 8:16]), nevertheless the objective guidelines given by John are helpful to us in weighing whether our *pistis* is genuine.

This chapter has sought to clarify the salvation-by-allegiance-alone proposal. Grace is a multifaceted concept, but construing *pistis* as allegiance does not violate Paul's understanding of grace. Quite the opposite: for Paul, acceptance of the Christ gift demands embodied allegiance (obedience) as an obligatory return. Meanwhile, Scripture is clear that we will be judged, at least in part, on the basis of our works. "Faith" and works are not unrelievedly opposed to one another, but rather Paul's *pistis*-not-works polemic seeks to undercut any rule-based system—and the law of Moses is Paul's premier example—that enshrines an alternative system of worth and preempts allegiance to the king. Rule-based systems ally with sin by exciting the flesh, making the sin problem worse, not better. But living in allegiance to Jesus means walking in step with the Holy Spirit as the Spirit is present in the midst of the people of God. Through the Spirit a person practices allegiance—that is, she or he embodies the good works toward which the law was aimed. Initial declared allegiance (*pistis*) to Jesus the king forges a union with the king and his body (the church), and this union is upheld subsequently through embodied allegiance, an enacted loyalty that is inclusive of good deeds. Our allegiance to Jesus the king is not perfect, but our imperfect but maintained allegiance is sufficient to sustain a union with Jesus the king, so that we are forgiven "in him" as we are joined to his death and resurrection. Allegiance cannot be quantified, but Scripture does give us general measures to help us weigh whether our imperfect allegiance is genuine.

FOR FURTHER THOUGHT

1. What is the difference between a gift and a legal obligation? What are a couple ways in which a gift might cause a nonlegal obligation?

2. Can the grace of the Christ gift be *prior* without it involving the eternal predestination of individuals? How could grace be prior yet still demand actual obedience (including good works) for salvation?

3. What does it mean for a gift to achieve its intended purpose? What is the purpose of the Christ gift?

4. Can you describe a time when someone lavished grace on you? Can you think of a situation into which you can bring God's grace to someone else?

5. How does our time-bound status affect our spirituality? Do you struggle more with the past, the present, or the future? Why?

6. The New Testament attests that we will be judged for eternal life at least in part on the basis of our works. It may be that preestablished *pistis* can be described as *the sole cause* of subsequently produced saving works,

but a more complex model has been suggested here. What's another way to think about the relationship between *pistis* and saving deeds?

7. When Paul speaks about justification by *pistis*, why might it matter if this language pertains more to getting in or to demarcating what it means to be in?

8. In what sense does salvation *not depend* on our obedience to the law? In what sense does our salvation *absolutely depend* on our obedience to the law? Explain how this seeming paradox can be resolved.

9. Can you explain why, specifically, obedience to the Mosaic law as an aim in and of itself could not result in final salvation?

10. In considering the necessity of embodied allegiance (enacted loyalty) for salvation, do you think in the past you have been underconcerned or overconcerned with the necessity of obeying Jesus for eternal life? How has that impacted your past journey with God? What kind of concern should you maintain in the future?

11. Do you agree that it is wrongheaded to ask *how much* allegiance to Jesus is required for salvation? Why or why not?

12. What rules of thumb appear in Scripture to help us gauge whether our allegiance is genuine? Why do you think these rules are framed mostly in negative terms (describing what sort of behavior indicates a lack of genuine allegiance) rather than in positive terms?

6

RESURRECTION INTO NEW CREATION

It is surprising that my first sermon was not my last. In the middle of a sleepy summer, when attendance was low, I was invited by a beleaguered pastor to fill the pulpit for a small, elderly Presbyterian congregation in my hometown in rural Northern California. I am certain the pastor deserved a vacation. But I fear whatever rejuvenation he received while away may have been promptly depleted upon his return. I knew the pastor well. In fact, I had dated his daughter some seven years prior during high school and early college. That relationship had been quite serious, and he was fond of me, so undoubtedly he deemed me sufficiently competent and sober-minded for the task at hand.

Little did he know that for the past several years my seminary professors had been dumping theological gunpowder into my brain, tamping it down firmly with a Greek New Testament and Hebrew Bible, and then, heedless of the possible consequences, packing in more. With only a few ministerial outlets into which I could safely discharge the compressed fuel, I had become a walking kingdom-of-God powder keg. And the fuse was lit when I stepped into the pulpit that quiet Sunday. After the opening prayer, I exploded. I hope the pastor, upon return from his vacation, was able to safely extract the theological shrapnel from the kindly but unfortunate little old ladies who happened to be sitting in the first rows.

Figuring I might have one and only one chance to reach this audience, I had prayerfully (but perhaps not prayerfully enough!) determined that I needed to awaken them to full kingdom-of-God life by hitting them with the most jolting and paradigm-shifting material at my disposal. I no longer remember my sermon's official title, but the unofficial title could have been "Forget about Heaven!—It's All about Living in the Kingdom of Heaven Today and Eventually in the New Creation!" With all the frothy enthusiasm of my seminary training bubbling out, I explained in eager detail that the Christian tradition's emphasis on heaven as the final reward for salvation was misguided, for the final vision of the Christian story does not involve us floating off to heaven, but heaven coming down to earth. There was a general look of bewildered confusion on the faces of the congregants. This was a strange teaching. Undoubtedly a few knowing looks regarding fresh seminarians were surreptitiously exchanged.

The congregation was kind enough to invite me back for a second Sunday. And although the sermon was delivered with equal lather, it seemed to go tolerably well. But at the conclusion of the sermon, when I broke protocol by including a Q and A and then forgot to prepare the benediction, quickly fumbling out Colossians 3:1–10—which, amid some very encouraging words about putting on the Christ, also exhorts the audience to avoid "sexual immorality, impurity, passion, evil desire, and covetousness"—I think they determined that although I was undoubtedly entertaining, my style and teaching might be disorderly. Through the experience I did learn an important lesson that should have been obvious from the get-go: when speaking in a pastoral capacity to a new audience, one must first build trust by giving the familiar. Subsequently, if one determines that the audience needs to hear new truths, those truths must be introduced gently, humbly, and gradually. Fortunately, I have had opportunities to fill the pulpit more successfully since that time.

I tell this story to illustrate that there are deeply held convictions about heaven as the final reward among Christians—convictions that are not easily modified. Despite a near consensus among academics that the Bible does not teach that heaven as traditionally understood is the final goal of redeemed humanity, traditional convictions about heaven remain very stable in the church because, as a legacy of Western civilization, they are perpetually reinforced by the media and popular culture. For example, for the last several years the book *Heaven Is for Real*, which recounts the to-heaven-and-back experience of four-year-old Colton Burpo, has been a hot topic among many Christians, with the conversation overflowing into the non-Christian community. In fact, although released several years ago, as I draft this book right now, the book is currently still a top-ten best seller in Christian Living on the website of the world's largest book retailer. Moreover, it has recently been released as a major motion picture. I am not making a judgment about the validity of Colton's reported experiences. I am merely signaling that these kinds of stories remain popular, and as they become part of the cultural fabric, they tend to reinforce the overriding conviction that heaven is the ultimate goal for redeemed humanity.[1]

Accordingly, I am more convinced than ever that the sermon that I preached that sleepy Sunday more than a decade ago contained the germ of ideas that the church still needs to hear. The reader, however, can heave a sigh of relief. For in what follows I will not attempt to redeliver my enthusiastic but unwise homily. Instead I will do something more important—synthesize some major themes in the story of salvation. For if final salvation is not primarily about the individual soul going to heaven, but about embodied *transformation* as the individual participates alongside others in the holistic restoration of the entire cosmos, then the logic of the allegiance-alone proposal takes on greater coherence. Allegiance to Jesus the king is the basis of citizenship in the new Jerusalem. Moreover allegiance entails an invitation to rule alongside him and is the foundation for transformation into his image.

Since the story of salvation is heavily traversed ground, special attention will be given to features of the story that are often neglected. In fact, I am going to begin the story in an unusual place—at the end, the grand finale, the appearance of the new heaven and the new earth.

The New Heaven and the New Earth

For those who enjoy being carried along by a gripping story until the plot tension resolves in a magnificent climax, I must apologize. Spoiler alert! I am about to tell you how the most marvelous story that the world has ever known concludes—well, at least I'll tell you a portion of the conclusion, for much remains a mystery. But I do not want to apologize overly much for playing spoiler, because God felt that it was imperative for his church to know something of the beautiful final glory toward which God is moving history.[2] We can be confident that God wants us to know something of the grand finale, because the enthroned Lord Jesus sent a vision of the end to the prophet John.

1. For a thoughtful discussion of heaven and the present-yet-future kingdom of God, see McKnight, *Heaven Promise*.
2. For a comprehensive discussion of the doctrine of last things, consider Middleton, *A New Heaven and a New Earth*.

Things Old and New

Jesus's very last recorded scriptural words for the church, then, are found not at the end of the Gospels but in Revelation.[3] Notice how Jesus's final words point at *vetera et nova*, things old and things new:

> Behold, I am coming soon, bringing my recompense with me, to repay each one for what he has done. I am the Alpha and the Omega, the first and the last, the beginning and the end.
>
> Blessed are those who wash their robes, so that they may have the right to the tree of life and that they may enter the city by the gates. Outside are the dogs and sorcerers and the sexually immoral and murderers and idolaters, and everyone who loves and practices falsehood.
>
> I, Jesus, have sent my angel to testify to you about these things for the churches. I am the root and the descendant of David, the bright morning star. (Rev. 22:12–16 ESV)

So, at the end of the salvation story, we do not find humans in heaven; rather we discover they are city-dwellers, still on earth.

In addition to Jesus, who self-attests that he is "the Alpha and the Omega" (the first and last letters of the Greek alphabet) and "the beginning and the end," in what way do we see the old and the new combined in this passage? In the beginning of the biblical story we have humans, Adam and Eve, inside a secluded garden containing not just one but two specific trees: the tree of life and the tree of the knowledge of good and evil (Gen. 2:9). After eating from the tree of the knowledge of good and evil—which involved a rejection of God's prerogative to define what is good and evil for humanity—they are placed outside the garden. A cherubim with a flaming sword prevents their access to the other tree, the tree of life (Gen. 3:24). Now in Revelation we find that the original *garden* has become a magnificent *city*, so the progress of life and culture has somehow been taken up into God's redemptive work.

So the movement from garden to city is a new development. Yet not all is new, for a vestige from the garden remains—*the tree of life*. Some of the people described in this final vision in Revelation are practitioners of evil, like Adam and Eve in their disobedience, and they remain *outside* with no access to the tree. Others have washed their robes. And given the overall trajectory of the Christian story toward resurrection, we have every reason to believe this vision,

---

3. Amid so much toxic speculation (and, frankly, bad popular-level teaching) on the book of Revelation, students looking for a healthy entry point should consider Bauckham, *Theology of the Book of Revelation*; Koester, *Revelation and the End of All Things*; Gorman, *Reading Revelation Responsibly*; Beale and Campbell, *Revelation*.

no matter how symbolic, intends real people with real physical bodies. They can go through the gates *inside* to the tree of life. After they are removed from the garden, there is nothing that Adam and Eve can successfully do to return to the tree, but those in the new Jerusalem who have chosen to wash their robes can freely access the tree. So the human ability to move from outside to inside, to approach the tree of life, is a new feature of the story as well. The story of salvation, then, is in the final analysis the story of how resurrected humans can enter into the new Jerusalem and eat from the tree of life because they have washed their robes, but how some nevertheless remain in disobedience outside the city. Moreover, it is not a story about how we can get back to the primitive paradise of Eden, but the story of how God can enfold the progress from garden to city into his redemptive plan. But where is this city?

After the climactic scenes of the return of the Messiah as a rider on a white horse, the binding and banishment of Satan and his minions, and the final judgment in Revelation 19–20, John sees not a vision of heaven but something more startling: "Then I saw a new heaven and a new earth, for the first heaven and the first earth departed, and there was no longer any sea" (Rev. 21:1; cf. Isa. 66:22). I want to say a couple things about this vision of a new heaven and a new earth.

Describing the New Heaven and Earth

How can we describe the new heaven and new earth that John sees? First, in the preceding chapter, Revelation 20, when judgment was rendered by the Christ from the great white throne, John saw "the earth and the heaven" flee from the presence of the judge (Rev. 20:11). That is, John saw the old heaven and the old earth disappear. Other biblical authors describe this event using related imagery. For example, the author of Hebrews says that although the earth and heavens are the work of the Son, nevertheless "they will wear out like a garment," they will be rolled up, and "like a robe they will be *changed*" (1:11–12). And we discover as the Letter of Hebrews continues that the change envisioned in relationship to this heavenly Jerusalem that will emerge is not a total discard of the old earth and heaven but a shaking of the present created order, and only the elements of eternal value will persist (11:22–29). God is a consuming fire able to melt the present order and remove the dross, so that what results is so radically pure and new that it is appropriate to call it "a new creation," even though it includes elements from the old creation. Essentially the same imagery is found in Peter's Second Letter, where it states that in association with the day of the Lord, "the heavens will be set on fire and dissolved, and the elements will melt while burning," so that what eventually comes forth can be called "new heavens and a new earth," a place where righteousness dwells (2 Pet. 3:12–13). So even though John states in Revelation that the first heaven and earth have "passed away," the new heaven and new earth is best understood not as a brand-new creation from nothing but as containing elements of the old creation that have been purified and radically recrafted so as to be taken up into the new.

Second, there is a puzzling feature of this new heaven and new earth, for John notes in relation to it that "the sea is no more." From the distant lens of our contemporary world—where the sea is often associated with warm sandy beaches, dancing ocean spray, and relaxing vacations—this may seem both odd and disappointing. What? No ocean in the resurrection age? As with much in Revelation, we know that this image and others like it function as powerful symbols, so it is difficult to know when we are to press such symbols in service of a literal, historical future occurrence or when God intends the symbol to evoke a different sort of truth. For example, when the Christ returns as a historical event, should we expect him to appear on an actual white horse, with a sword literally extending from his mouth (Rev. 19:11–15)? It doesn't seem likely. As Saint Augustine helpfully reminds us, the Scriptures "are in the habit of making something like children's toys out of the things that occur in creation, by which to entice our sickly gaze and get us step by step to seek as best we can the things that are above and forsake the things that are below."[4] With the sword extending from Jesus's mouth, it is more plausible that we are dealing with a metaphor designed to point us to a higher reality—and probably also with regard to the absence of the sea. Toward what higher reality, then, are we pointed by the missing ocean in this vision?

Once again, the end of the biblical story points us back to the beginning. When Genesis opens, we find the created order is a vast watery chaos—"the deep"—a limitless primordial ocean: "The earth was formless and void, and darkness was over the face of the deep" (Gen. 1:2). As creation progresses, this watery mess is bounded, tamed, and controlled by God's creative word. For example, God speaks "the expanse" into existence and uses it to make a division within the deep between the waters in the heavens and the waters below the heavens (Gen. 1:6–8). God then commands the waters below the heavens to be gathered into one place, so that dry land appears. Later we discover that the land itself serves to bottleneck a freshwater supply that likewise holds a threat if it were to be unleashed. For without these separators functioning properly to control the water, the dry land would be overwhelmed. The undifferentiated life-destroying brine of "the deep" could appear once

---

4. Augustine, *Trin.* 1.1 [§2] (Hill).

more. Creation could be undone—which is precisely what happens when "all flesh" (excluding Noah and those with him) is destroyed in the flood: "All the fountains of the great deep burst forth, and the windows of the heavens were opened" (Gen. 7:11). Thus, the roar of the ocean serves as a reminder to the people of God. In creation, God told the haughty ocean waves, "This far shall you come, and no farther, and here shall your proud waves be stayed" (Job 38:11; cf. Ps. 65:7; 89:9). The ocean is a mighty destructive force, a wild threat to life associated with terrifying beasts (Ps. 74:12–17), especially evil pagan empires that harm the people of God (Dan. 7:2–3; Rev. 13:1). But in the past God has subdued the ocean, including the beasts, so that although the waves threaten, God is sovereign (Jer. 5:22; Ps. 93).

John's vision in Revelation describing an oceanless new heaven and new earth thus anticipates but goes beyond the vision of the Old Testament. In the Old Testament, God promises in his covenant with Noah that he will never destroy all flesh again by unbounding the reservoir of waters (Gen. 9:11). Moreover, God will one day slay the great writhing dragon of the sea (Isa. 27:1–2). A river flowing from the temple will make the Dead Sea fresh (Ezek. 47:1–12). Yet John's vision brings this line of thought a step further. At the end of God's story the sea will not even exist! John's vision indicates that the danger posed by the untamed waters (and the beasts associated with the waters) in times past and present *will no longer even be possible* in the new heavens and the new earth. The perilous sea will not just remain tame but will have been entirely removed. John's vision of an oceanless new order, then, is best read as announcing the utter and absolute removal of all external threats to life for humankind.

Divine Presence Interrupted and Regained

In the final words of Jesus in the Bible, we find that humanity has advanced from the primitive garden to a marvelous city. But we haven't yet explored the nature of the city. John's vision of the new heavens and the new earth centers upon the splendor of the bride, the new Jerusalem: "And I saw the holy city, new Jerusalem, coming down out of heaven from God, prepared as a bride adorned for her husband" (Rev. 21:2 ESV). As the new Jerusalem descends, John hears a booming voice coming from the heavenly throne:

> Behold, the dwelling place of God is with humankind. He will dwell with them, and they will be his people, and God himself will be with them as their God. And he will wipe every tear from their eyes, and death shall exist no longer.

Neither mourning, nor crying, nor pain will exist any longer. For the former things departed. (Rev. 21:3–4)

And so we discover the defining characteristic of the eternal city, the new Jerusalem: it is comparable in purity and joy to a bride. It is a place where those who have been burdened by grief are perfectly consoled. Above all else it is *the abode of God with humanity*.

We are invited to consider the coming together of God with God's people as akin to a wedding banquet and the subsequent consummation of the marriage. That is, the coming together will be so celebratory, satisfying, and ultimately intimate that the metaphor of a wedding is the best language that God can give us to describe the union, even though it is clear that the union is not itself sexual. Jerry Walls, in *Heaven, Hell, and Purgatory*, speaks of how heaven will fulfill our deepest yearnings, and how sexual desire and consummation in this earthly life is merely "a foretaste of even greater delights in the world to come."[5] As the scenes of the great biblical drama roll past our mind's eye, we recognize that this declaration—"Behold, the dwelling place of God is with humanity"—is a fitting climax to the story God has been directing all along. In the new Jerusalem the companionship that God and humans enjoyed prior to the fall is restored. Yet the story of the recovery of direct fellowship is more complex than we might guess, for it is the climax of Old and New Testament teachings about fellowship with God.

Divine-Human Companionship Disrupted

Before Adam and Eve eat from the tree, God is described as walking with them in the cool of the day. Prior to the fall, this divine-human companionship was the norm. Yet once the camaraderie is disrupted by the desire of humanity to define good and evil for itself (rather than accepting God's superintending moral role), Scripture ceases to describe this direct, unimpeded fellowship between God and humanity. After the fall, God still yearns to dwell with his people, but humans are not at a suitable level of holiness so as to be directly in God's presence.[6]

The Tabernacle

Through Moses at Mount Sinai, God gives his people instructions to make a tabernacle (or tent), which will facilitate human-divine fellowship through

---

5. Walls, *Heaven, Hell, and Purgatory*, 28.
6. For a biblical theology focused on God's desire to be present with humans, see Beale and Kim, *God Dwells among Us*.

a mediated system. No mortal will be able to enter into God's presence apart from successfully traversing the graded levels of purity and holiness that the tabernacle facilitates and enshrines. To draw near unto God's presence, one must be properly purified. In fact, although an ordinary priest could offer sacrifices on behalf of a worshiper at the altar in the outer courtyard of the tabernacle, and could at special times enter the inner sanctuary (where the showbread, menorah, and incense altar were stationed), only the high priest could enter the most holy place. And the high priest could do this but once a year on the Day of Atonement, at which time he would approach the ark of the covenant where God was enthroned between the cherubim, and bring the blood of a sacrificial offering (see Lev. 16), covering over the sins for the year.

The Temple

Much later the tabernacle, a mobile tent-like structure, would provide the conceptual pattern for God's fixed palace—the temple built by Solomon. Although it was believed that God dwelt in the holy of holies of the temple in a special fashion, nevertheless God's presence was understood to transcend such earthly limitations. Solomon's dedicatory prayer, offered when the temple was completed, makes this clear: "Look, the heavens, even the highest heaven cannot contain you; how much less this house that I have built!" (1 Kings 8:27). This first temple was destroyed by the Babylonians, only to be rebuilt in the sixth century BC. It was in the process of being enlarged during the time of Jesus. Yet God had grander plans, for his desire was to dwell not in a temple but *directly* with humans once more.

The Incarnation

The taking on of human flesh by Jesus the Son, who preexisted with God the Father, is the shocking yet fitting master stroke in the divine plan for restoring divine-human fellowship. God walking in our very midst, his glory nevertheless disguised, mediated, and tempered by human flesh. In his Gospel, John famously describes Jesus's incarnation, but English translations struggle to capture how the incarnation advances God's plan to dwell with his people: "And the Word became flesh and dwelt among us" (John 1:14). That is, the Word (Greek: *Logos*) that was present with God the Father in the beginning (1:1), and through whom God the Father made the universe (1:3)—the very Word who can indeed appropriately be called "God" in his own right (1:1, 18)—is declared by John to have "dwelt among us." In the Greek of this verse it is clear that John is drawing upon the Old Testament image of the *tabernacle*, the *skēnē*, the tent. For John says, "The Word [*Logos*] became flesh and tabernacled [*eskēnōsen*] in our midst." So Jesus is compared to the tabernacle, a very much this-earthly building that nevertheless housed God's presence—a divine-human intermingling.

Jesus's human flesh was just like the Old Testament tabernacle—which was constructed of typical building materials such as wood, dyed yarns, cloth, skins, precious stones, and gold—in that both appeared from the outside as nothing more than an ordinary (albeit ornate in the case of the tabernacle) structure that nevertheless concealed God's presence and glory. Since no physical description of Jesus is ever given in Scripture, it is safe to assume that when one looked at his body, stature, hair, eyes, and skin, one saw nothing uniquely special that would suggest divinity (cf. Isa. 53:2). An observer could only begin to equate Jesus with the divine presence when she or he contemplated the signs that Jesus was performing, his mighty deeds such as turning the water to wine, the healings, and his raising of Lazarus from the dead. In seeing the signs, one could see the glory, and in seeing the glory one could begin to exercise believing loyalty toward Jesus (see John 2:11). As John, in speaking of this tabernacling of Jesus in our midst, says, "We have seen his *glory*, glory as of the only Son from the Father, full of grace and truth" (1:14).

John extends this tabernacle comparison by inviting us to consider Jesus to be *beth-El*, Hebrew for "house of God." In Genesis 28:10–19 the patriarch Jacob had fallen asleep in a certain location, using a rock as a pillow. While he slept, he saw angels ascending and descending upon stairs or a ladder, and he determined that he was at an important intersection between heaven and earth. So he named the place *beth-El*. Thus, when we find Jesus describing himself to Nathaniel, "You will see heaven opened, and the angels of God ascending and descending on the Son of Man" (John 1:51), the point should not be lost upon us: Jesus has come as the true tabernacle, the ultimate house of God.

Preliminary Access Regained

The incarnation may indeed be the most surprising moment in the story of the restoration of companionship between God and humans, but Jesus's crucifixion is another significant moment in this story. Describing this event, the New Testament writers use imagery from the temple to describe the significance of Jesus's death. The Gospel writers tell us that upon Jesus's death the curtain in the temple that separated the most holy place from the outer chamber "was torn in two, from top to bottom" (Mark 15:38; cf. Matt. 27:51; Luke 23:45). The author of Hebrews explains the theological significance of this rending of the curtain, and it becomes clear that the meaning of this event pertains to the restoration of fellowship between God and humanity.

Before the curtain was torn in two, the high priest could enter the most holy place but once per year, for the way was "not yet opened" (Heb. 9:8). Yet in his death Jesus the Christ as the great high priest offered his own blood, passed through the outer holy chamber, through the curtain, and went into the heavenly most holy place, of which the earthly most holy place is but a shadowy copy. He "entered once for all" (Heb. 9:12) and in so doing blazed the trail into the most holy place, so that other humans can also enjoy direct access to the divine presence:

> Therefore, brothers, since we have boldness for accessing the holy places by the blood of Jesus, by the new and living way that he opened for us through the curtain (that is, through his flesh) and since we have a great priest over the house of God, let us approach with a true heart by the full bearing of *pistis*, with our hearts sprinkled clean from an evil conscience and our bodies washed with clean water. (Heb. 10:19–22)

So humanity is able to draw intimately near to God once again—go into God's very presence—through the perfect mediation of Jesus the Christ's offering. Yet this restoration of fellowship, like much else in Christian theology, has an *already* but *not yet* dimension during the present church age. In the here and now we have the privilege of spiritual access to God the Father, but the immediacy of gazing upon God (via his image) face to face must await the resurrection age.

Complete Restoration

After Adam and Eve's disobedience, God took the initiative in seeking them out, bringing his presence near to them. God also initiated fellowship with Abraham, with Moses and Israel through the tabernacle, with Israel and the gentile nations through the temple, and with all humanity through the incarnation. Should we be surprised, then, if we find that the biblical story ends with God climactically drawing near to his people once more, as God brings the heavenly Jerusalem down, so that God and humanity can dwell together? Fellowship between God and humanity has been so completely restored that, as John reports, there is no longer need for a temple at all in the new Jerusalem: "And I did not see a temple in it, for the Lord God the Almighty is its temple, and the lamb" (Rev. 21:22).

In the story of God's relationship with humanity, the answer is always grace—God approaching us. In the final analysis, we don't go to heaven; *God brings his heavenly abode down to earth*, having re-created the universe so that there is a new (that is, radically renewed) heaven and earth. We do not go to God, but *he comes to us*.

Living in the New Jerusalem

We have just explored the manner in which the biblical narrative anticipates one goal of final salvation: God and humans will dwell together on the earth once again. Humans will have unmediated access to God. They will enjoy the river of the water of life that flows from the throne of God and of the Lamb (Rev. 22:1). They will have access to the tree of life once again—it will bear twelve kinds of fruit, and its leaves will bring healing to the nations (Rev. 22:2). But this is not the end of the story of God and humanity; it is more like the first chapters in the second volume of an ongoing saga. Can we learn anything about what life and culture will be like as humans dwell with God once again in this new heaven and new earth? As John is carried away in the Spirit to a tremendously lofty mountain, he sees "the holy city, Jerusalem, descending out of heaven from God" (Rev. 21:10).

The description of the new Jerusalem gives us insight into what it will be like to be a citizen of that dynamic city. The city is described as having "the glory of God," a thick wall (approximately 216 feet thick!), and twelve gates inscribed with the names of the twelve tribes of the sons of Israel. Moreover, the wall has twelve foundations containing the names of the twelve apostles.

In seeking to interpret this imagery, we must tread carefully, bearing in mind the symbolic nature of the vision as it is doubtful that a literal, physical city with the precise features should be anticipated as a future reality.[7] What is clear from the vision itself is that the wall, along with the gates, is that which divides the holy inhabitants of the city from the disobedient sinners who must remain outside the city (Rev. 22:14–15). Thus, the wall signifies that the true people of God are encompassed by the apostolic foundation, implying that its citizens are those who have given allegiance to Jesus as king on the basis of the apostolic testimony. Jesus appointed twelve apostles to show symbolically that he was reconstituting Israel around himself—and in so doing he redefined what it means to be a member of the family of God. To be a citizen of the

---

7. Regarding why the description of the new Jerusalem should be considered symbolic rather than literal in all its details, see Beale, *Book of Revelation*, 1063–67. Beale aptly summarizes, "To construe [Revelation] 21:9ff as a vision of a future literal city is to miss its fundamental symbolic nature," but at the same time "this means not that there will be no literal new cosmos but that the point of the vision is the focus on the exalted saints as the central feature of the new order" (1064–65).

new Jerusalem means to have welcomed the apostolic testimony about Jesus (the eight stages of the gospel discussed earlier) so as to have entered into the community that is guided by the Spirit and the apostolic witness. Meanwhile, although the gates serve the same function as the wall (separating God, the Lamb, and the saints from the sinners who dwell outside the new Jerusalem), they have two other important functions.

Home at Last

First, the gates allow the redeemed to access the city. The imagery suggests that the new Jerusalem, having descended from heaven, is gradually populated as its citizens arrive at the city as the goal of their pilgrimage. The city is a beacon of light toward which the pilgrims can walk, for the glory of God provides the light, and the Lamb of God is the lamp (Rev. 21:23; cf. Isa. 60:19). Those pilgrims who stream most readily to the new Jerusalem undoubtedly are those who all along have found this world to be a place that is hostile, alien, and unwelcoming—at best a place of exile and temporary refuge. These pilgrims, like Abraham, never settled, because they were "looking forward to the city that has foundations, whose architect and builder is God" (Heb. 11:10). Such people long ago realized that their true citizenship was in heaven (Phil. 3:20), and they have been eagerly awaiting the consummate establishment of the kingdom of God "on earth as in heaven" (Matt. 6:10). Their allegiance is to Jesus the king, and when his throne is established in the new Jerusalem, they find they are for the first time in their true home as they worship in his presence (Rev. 21:5; 22:1–3).

The Gathering and Advance of Culture

Second, the gates permit the collection and advance of culture in the new Jerusalem. "The nations will walk by its light, and the kings of the earth will bear their glory into it, and its gates will never be shut by day, for night will not exist there" (Rev. 21:24–25). This image of the new Jerusalem hearkens back to the reign of King Solomon, when foreign dignitaries such as the Queen of Sheba came bearing gifts to Jerusalem, coming to learn of God's manifold wisdom (1 Kings 10:1–13). This image of the pilgrimage of the nations is expanded by Isaiah, who envisions the nations flowing into the exalted Jerusalem in the last days in order to learn the ways and laws of God (e.g., 2:1–4). In speaking of the future glory of Jerusalem, Isaiah declares, "Nations will come to your light, and kings to the brightness of your shining" (60:3). When the nations stream into the renewed Jerusalem, they bear their best: "The abundance of the sea will be turned to you, the wealth of the nations will come to you" (Isa. 60:5). The items gathered are listed as bronze, silver, gold, iron, frankincense, camels, rams, and precious building materials. In short, the gates of the new Jerusalem are forever open to those things of God's good, renewed creation that deserve to be celebrated and welcomed.

But at the same time, the gates do not permit culture to advance in the new Jerusalem in unwholesome ways. As John sees in his vision: "Nothing unclean will ever enter into it" (Rev. 21:27). Since the new Jerusalem is repeatedly described as full of God's "glory" rather than human self-glory (Rev. 21:11, 22), John sees a city whose inhabitants undertake cultural progress in precisely the opposite way as did the builders of the tower of Babel.

The constructors of the tower are said to have acquired a technology of oven-baked bricks and mortar, but they did not offer this cultural achievement to God's glory. In fact, quite the opposite. By a manipulative and self-serving technical mastery of the created order, they sought to pierce the heavens in order to "make a name" for themselves (Gen. 11:4). Yet God scattered these hubristic builders. Citizens of the new Jerusalem are instead like Abraham, who did not seek to make a great name for himself at all, realizing that a great name is something that the promise-fulfilling God *bestows as a gift* on his servants. God promised Abraham, "I will . . . make your name great" (Gen. 12:2), and bless all the families of the earth through Abraham (Gen. 12:3). The seed of Abraham, who ultimately is Jesus the Messiah, has allowed the blessings to the nations to flow forth through the Holy Spirit. In response, the nations, healed of their desire to make a name for themselves, can offer their cultural achievements to God in the new Jerusalem. And as these cultural gifts enter, the new Jerusalem is not a static city but a city growing in beauty and magnificence. This vision has important implications for the fundamental value and dignity of work as we bear God's image.

Seeing the Face of the Glorified Lamb

Finally, life in the heavenly Jerusalem will above all else be characterized by worship. The heavenly Jerusalem, now established on earth, contains at its center "the throne of God and of the Lamb" (Rev. 22:1). The followers of Jesus as citizens of the new Jerusalem will bow before the throne and gaze upon God's glory: "His servants will worship him" (Rev. 22:3). Unlike in the past, when it was deemed dangerous for the people of God to enter into the very presence of God, now it is clear that such obstacles have been utterly removed, as we are told that humans have access to "the throne of God and of the Lamb" (Rev. 22:3). Moreover, "they will see his face, and his name will be on their foreheads" (Rev. 22:4). Yet the marvel of viewing face to face the glorified

Lamb on God's throne[8]—the climax of final salvation for the individual (and ultimately for the community of the saints)—can only be fully appreciated in conjunction with the Bible's theology of image, the subject of the next chapter.

How, then, can we best describe the biblical vision of the final horizon of salvation? Contrary to widespread cultural assumptions in the Western world and much popular Christian teaching, the final goal of salvation in the Christian story is not the individual soul reaching heaven. On the contrary, heaven is discussed very little in the Bible and is best regarded as a temporary abode with God in anticipation of the more glorious next act in the divine drama. God will radically recraft the present cosmic order, refining everything. The transformation will be so dramatic that when he sees the vision, John is compelled to exclaim, "I saw a new heaven and a new earth, for the first heaven and the first earth departed" (Rev. 21:1)!

Humans will not return to the primitive garden of Eden. God will bring down a city, the new Jerusalem, showing that God accepts and values the best elements of culture and development. Work will no longer be burdensome toil. As we rule alongside the Messiah, our work will be a service-oriented stewardship of creation that causes culture to continue its progress. Life will flourish. The gates and the walls of the city show that good and evil will be decisively separated; nothing impure and no evildoer will ever enter the city. God will take up residence in the midst of the new Jerusalem. After the bodily resurrection, God's people, those who yield allegiance to Jesus, those whose robes have been cleansed by the blood of the Lamb, will enter it. We will eat fruit from the tree of life.

——— FOR FURTHER THOUGHT ———

1. What images or ideas did you most strongly associate with heaven when you were growing up? What images does our contemporary culture tend to perpetuate?

8. It is uncertain whether the face of Jesus or God (the Father) is intended with the "They will see his face, and his name will be on their foreheads" (Rev. 22:4; cf. 14:1). However, the face of Jesus rather than of God (the Father) is more likely for three reasons: (1) the Lamb was the last mentioned, so he is the most natural referent for "his face" in Rev. 22:4; (2) in Rev. 19:12 Jesus has many crowns on his head and "a name written that no one knows but himself," so it is slightly more probable that "his name will be on their foreheads" refers to Jesus (cf. Rev. 6:16); and (3) in the OT God is described as having a face, but since "God is spirit" (John 4:24) and all language about God involves metaphor, it is unclear that God's visage can be seen physically even in the new Jerusalem apart from Jesus, as the full image of God, making it visible (although see Matt. 18:10).

2. The final vision in the book of Revelation circles back to the garden of Eden. What's the same, what has changed, and why is this significant?

3. The ocean is not the most pervasive symbol of primordial evil in our contemporary culture. If God was to give a new vision to John today and wanted to evoke a similar idea, what symbol do you think God might use? Why?

4. How is the incarnation both a fulfillment of earlier patterns and an anticipation of future things with respect to divine-human fellowship?

5. How, practically speaking, might it change our ethical choices when we remember that the final goal for redeemed humanity is not the soul floating upward toward heaven but God bringing the heavenly Jerusalem down to earth? (E.g., consider environmental ethics, bioethics, and interpersonal ethics.)

6. Given the purpose of the wall and gates in the new Jerusalem, do you think the church today should seek to erect similar "walls" and "gates" with respect to how it engages culture and the world? Practically speaking, what form might such "walls" and "gates" take?

7. What does "home" mean to you? Why is the new Jerusalem finally home for God's people in a way that nothing else has been?

8. What in contemporary culture do you feel will be refined so that it survives into the new creation? What dimensions of culture are pure dross that will be removed?

9. What can you personally contribute to culture today that will be fit to endure into the new Jerusalem in the future?

7

RESTORING THE IDOL OF GOD

When I had freshly completed my undergraduate degree—a bachelor of science in physics—after some scrambling, I managed to land a junior-level electrical engineering position. Our firm mainly engineered electrical systems for hospitals, college campuses, prisons, and so forth. Filled to the brim with potent ideas, I tackled spreadsheet calculations, wrestled with blueprint drawings of electrical systems, memorized strange facts about allowable amperages, and wrote specifications for transformers. Yet, in the midst of this hubbub, a growing sense of dread began to wash over me. Here I was, twenty-two years old, making an excellent salary and contributing to society in a meaningful way, but toward what ultimate end? I had a burning love for God in my heart and a desire to see God's kingdom grow. But how, I wondered, apart from those occasional conversations around the coffee pot that might tilt in a theological direction—and I lived for those conversations!—was my work of any *eternal* significance?

The dread grew into an aching emptiness, an irresistible yearning to make my life count for something beyond getting a nice house, raising some kids, and enjoying frequent excursions to ski slopes. As I sat at my desk laboring to meet project deadlines, I saw my life billow out in front of me as a gray nothingness. My work, as I saw it through my immature and deficient theological lenses, was meaningless. I became convinced that I needed to change career paths, otherwise I would waste my life or go insane (or probably both). I did change career paths, going to seminary for several years, returning to engineering for a season, and then finally completing a PhD in theology.

Throughout my life journey I have learned things that would have helped stave off the insanity had I stayed in engineering. As was discussed in the previous chapter, since the final goal of salvation is not the destruction of the created order, but its radical refinement, we can expect that the pure, true, and excellent elements of our labor will somehow be caught up into the new heavens and the new earth. In other words, the quality of our engineering (and other seemingly mundane tasks) matters not just for the here and now but for eternity. Although we do not know precisely how, there are elements of dignity and good in most of our earthly labors that will be swept up into God's marvelous new heavens and new earth. First, however, they will be refined, so that nothing impure enters through the gates into the new Jerusalem (Rev. 21:25–27). As the apostle Paul puts it with regard to the labor of building up the church—and I think his point can be extended to all our labors—"the fire will test what sort of work each has done" (1 Cor. 3:13). The cut corners and the compromises, the hay and straw, will be burned up, but the refined precious material will endure.

The bodily resurrection from the dead suggests an analogy. Our present bodies are like kernels of wheat, but our resurrected bodies will be like the full plant (1 Cor. 15:35–37). Our present bodies have a modest glory (in my case very modest) befitting our perishable earthly condition, but they will take on an immortal heavenly splendor (1 Cor. 15:40–43). Our present bodies are "soulish" (*psychikon*—some translations render this "natural"), but resurrected bodies will be "spiritual" (*pneumatikon*) (1 Cor. 15:44), even though still physical in accordance with Jesus's raised body.

If such is the case with our physical bodies, why would we think it any more or less so with our work? Our labor and its fruits in their present form are perishable and cannot enter into the new Jerusalem as they stand. Yet, in speaking of our bodies, Paul says, "Look! I tell you a mystery. We will not all sleep, but we will all be changed, in a moment, in the twinkling of an eye" (1 Cor. 15:51–52). The trumpet shall sound, and the dead will be raised imperishable. God will change us so that the mortal is swallowed up by immortality. Similarly, our transformed labors will contribute to the life and culture of the renewed creation.

Can we describe this transformation and renewal further? As a complement to the previous chapter, this chapter will outline a biblical theology of image bearing, especially as this connects to final salvation.[1] Not only is salvation resurrection unto new creation; it also entails holistic personal transformation so that we are like Jesus the king, who is the image of the invisible God. This

1. For a biblical theology of image and salvation, see Kilner, *Dignity and Destiny*; Lints, *Identity and Idolatry*.

transformation, strangely, ensues through a specific kind of "idol" worship and ends in our restoration as fully functional "idols" of God. For Jesus as the suffering-but-now-glorified king is the true idol of God, and our final salvation involves conformity to his image.

Created in the Idol (Image) of God

In our postmodern cultural milieu of ubiquitous but superficial social-connectedness, many, but especially young men and women, struggle with depression, feelings of estrangement, and purposelessness. For all of us, yet particularly for those who feel smothered by a blanket of individual despair and futility, the biblical doctrine that all humans are made in the image of God is truly good news. It gives assurance that each of us has a fundamental dignity and self-worth, since we have been made in God's image.

And in our fractured, alienating culture, it is vital that those concerned with God's truths continue to emphasize this encouraging image-of-God message. I do wonder, however, if the contemporary tendency, at least at the level of popular Christian teaching and preaching, to center "image of God" theology on the human essence (ontology) rather than on the human purpose (teleology) might give the doctrine short shrift. There is much more to be gained from the doctrine of divine image bearing than an appreciation of our own self-dignity; it is in fact determinative for our final salvation.

Although God surely wants humans to have an appropriate sense of self-worth—to be neither over- nor underinflated, and to be aware of our uniquely privileged station among all God's creatures—I think that God is even more concerned that we *act* as the image of God. Actually, it is best to say that the knowing and the acting are interrelated and mutually informing. This becomes apparent when we notice that when God speaks of our creation in God's own image, the focus quickly moves from the reality of image bearing to the purpose of image bearing:

> Then God said, "Let us make man in our image [*tselem*], after our likeness [*demuth*]. And let them *rule*. . . . So God created man in his own image, in the image of God he created him; male and female he created them. Then God blessed them. And he said to them, "*Be fruitful* and *multiply* and *fill the earth* and *subdue it* and *rule* over the fish of the sea and over the birds of heaven and over every living thing that moves about upon the earth." (Gen. 1:26–28)

There are several things to draw from this passage. First, notice that twice in this short passage (in 1:26 and then again in 1:28) the assertion that God made humans in God's own image is immediately followed by the human commission to *rule* over the other creatures. So the text urges the conclusion that humans are created in God's image so that they can undertake the fundamental task of ruling for God.

The purpose of bearing the image is so that the created order can receive proper governance, so that humans can bring the wise rule of God in a tangible fashion to creation. This is why Adam (and eventually Eve) is placed in the garden to "work/serve" it (from *'abad*, which relates especially to the word for servant or slave) and to "keep" it (from *shamar*, which pertains to superintendence: watching, guarding, and protecting). The prolifically wild fruitfulness of the created order needs to be actively marshaled; it needs to be directed, tamed, and tended so that humans, animals, plants, and the nonliving portions of creation can mutually benefit. This, among other reasons, is also why humans are instructed to be fruitful and to multiply: if the created order is ever to reach its maximum life-sustaining potential, it is necessary that many humans come into being and take up their God-given task of active service and governance.

As we ponder together the meaning of the "image of God" metaphor, I also wonder what new layers of meaning might surface if the cheery phrase "You are made in the image of God" were to be replaced by a translation that is more startling, "You are made as the *idol* of God." For the word "image" (*tselem*) that we find describing humans in Genesis 1:26–27 is frequently equivalent to "idol."[2] Reframing the discourse in this way might open up fresh vistas on the relationship between idols, temples, worship of idols, transformation, and how the fundamental human mandate to act as God's kingly representative to the created order connects to final salvation.

The Purpose of Idols/Images

If humans are made in the idol/image of God, it is surely worthwhile to ponder what further significance this might hold.[3] Christian theologians have made many different suggestions as to what makes humans unique from the animals in bearing the image of God. These suggestions have usually focused on specific mental or spiritual qualities that might be thought to

---

2. On *tselem* ("image") as roughly synonymous with "idol," see Num. 33:52; 2 Kings 11:18; 2 Chron. 23:17; Ezek. 7:20; 16:17; Amos 5:26.

3. Regarding what "image of God" does and does not involve, see Kilner, *Dignity and Destiny*, 85–133. Kilner ultimately determines that the "image of God" metaphor primarily intends connection to God and reflection of God.

give humanity a distinctive stamp. Could the "image of God" be the human ability to speak? To reason? To sign? To imagine? The capacity to create? The presence of the soul? Or is it possible that this "distinctive stamp" premise has been too hastily accepted in the history of Christian theology? Instructive for us are studies of how the "gods" were understood to relate to their respective idols and temples in the ancient Near Eastern environment in which Israel was situated.

When and how did an image or idol come to be regarded as a god or goddess in antiquity? In the ancient Near East, when an idol was crafted or carved, the idol was not believed thereby to have instantly become worthy of full veneration. The god or goddess in question was usually felt to have initiated the manufacturing process in the first place, so the idol was worthy of instant respect, but the idol still needed to be *imbued with the divine presence* through a ceremony. The premier place for an idol to reside was in a temple, and so after manufacture, the next step would ordinarily involve the ritualized induction of the idol into the temple.

In ancient Mesopotamia, the so-called mouth-washing ritual was the most prominent feature of the induction ceremony, the purpose of which was to enable the god or goddess (via the image) to eat, drink, and smell the incense offered to it. After the mouth-washing ritual, the image was then brought into the inner chamber of the temple, where it was stationed to receive daily offerings and other forms of worship. From the extant descriptions of idol-induction ceremonies, John Walton concludes that the ancient Babylonians believed that through induction "the material image was animated by the divine essence."[4] Ancient Egyptian ideas were similar, with the deity's *ba* (i.e., a portion of the deity's "spirit" or "soul") animating the image, allowing the idol, as a nexus between the divine and earthly spheres, to serve as a revelation of the deity's character and nature.

Nearer the time of Jesus, Minucius Felix, a late second- or early third-century Christian apologist, gives an insightful mockery of pagan idol worship that gives a handy compressed description of the process by which an idol came to be considered fully divine in his day and age: "When does the god come into being? The image is cast, hammered, or sculpted; it is not yet a god. It is soldered, put together, and erected; it is still not a god. It is adorned, consecrated, prayed to—and now, finally, it is a god once man has willed it so and dedicated it" (*Oct.* 22.5).[5]

---

4. Throughout this section, I rely especially on Walton, *Ancient Near Eastern Thought*, 113–34, here 115.

5. As cited by Gupta, "'They Are Not Gods!,'" 704.

The animation of the image by the god or goddess's presence, however, did not mean that the idol *merely represented* the deity but rather that the deity was *genuinely immanent* in the idol. For example, today when you hold a piece of paper containing the signature of another person, you usually don't feel that the person is truly present in and by virtue of the physical signature; rather you probably feel that the signature somehow vaguely "represents" the person's authorization. A legally binding signature represents personal legal consent. The representation idea with respect to idols went much further.

The nations surrounding Israel felt their idols did not just represent but actually were a localized manifestation of the god or goddess. They believed that the idol gave the worshiper genuine access to the presence of the god or goddess, because the image made the deity's presence real, actual, and tangible. This does not mean, however, that the idol and the deity were thereby deemed identical or coterminous; rather, the god or goddess was "the reality that was embodied in the image" but at the same time was transcendent beyond the specific embodiment in that discrete idol in such a fashion that the deity could be fully and equally present in other idols.[6]

From the above, we can conclude that what it meant to be in the image/idol of a god in the ancient Near East was not about having a singularly unique capacity, such as reason or a soul that might separate humans from the animals; rather the image served as a holistic manifestation of the divine presence to those who might encounter the deity in and through the image. Yet the deity remained transcendent beyond the image. Not just in the ancient Near Eastern world of the Old Testament but also during the time of Jesus, many pagans living in the Mediterranean region believed that their idols were a nexus of the mundane and the divine, a complex portal where heaven and earth kissed. As Nijay Gupta has recently concluded on the basis of his study of Greco-Roman cult statues, from the pagan vantage point idols (1) were not merely human creations but also divine; (2) were living; (3) were able to see, hear, and speak; (4) could sometimes move; and (5) were capable of "saving" their worshipers from illness, danger, or trouble.[7] To meet the image was to encounter the god or goddess who was imbued and manifested in the image and who acted through it.

Thus, applying these insights to humans as created in the image/idol of the God of Israel, when other creatures encounter humans, they are in the presence of God via God's idol. God has imbued his human-idols with his active presence. God breathes his breath/spirit (*ruach*) into the nostrils of the

---

6. Walton, *Ancient Near Eastern Thought*, 115–16.
7. Gupta, "'They Are Not Gods!,'" 712–18.

clay figure Adam, and he becomes a living *nepesh* ("person" or, traditionally, "soul") (Gen. 2:7). The idol of God, Adamic humanity, that has been placed in the garden-temple of Eden has in this manner been pervaded by the divine breath/spirit.[8] Hereafter, anyone who encounters Adam and Eve or their descendants (Genesis specifically stresses that the "image" is transferred through human reproduction—see Gen. 5:3) will be *dynamically* experiencing the God of Israel, for they will be in the spirit-presence of a genuine idol of God. While God remains transcendent above creation and is not coterminous with the human-idol, nevertheless humans as the idols of God serve as localized manifestations of the divine presence—junctures where God is present in a real and tangible way to all who encounter "the image" that has been imbued with the divine spirit or breath.

Why Were Images Forbidden by God?

To the best of our knowledge, ancient Israel was unique among its fellow ancient Near Eastern civilizations in forbidding idols. God's command to the Israelites not to craft or worship idols is ubiquitous in the Old Testament, but the classic statement is the second of the Ten Commandments, "You shall not make for yourself an idol [*pesel*], or any likeness [*temunah*] of anything that is in heaven above, or that is in the earth below, or that is in the water below the earth. You shall not bow down to them or serve them" (Exod. 20:4–5).

But when we seek a rationale for why God gave this unique no-idols command, we have less guidance. The reason given in the Ten Commandments is that God is a jealous God, faithful to punish sin through several generations, but even more prone to steadfast love toward those who would keep his commandments (Exod. 20:5–6). So the overriding reason is that God, as the only true God, is the only one who appropriately merits worship and service, and hence God is justifiably jealous when he does not receive his fitting due.

If this, however, were the only reason given for why God disallows idol worship, we might be tempted to conclude that God is petty. If humans fail to worship God or otherwise sin, shouldn't God be big enough to get over the slight? After all, even if I truly deserve a promotion at work, while recognizing the injustice, I shouldn't get jealous when I am passed over, but should accept

8. On ancient Near Eastern garden-temple complexes as applied especially to Eden, see Beale, *Temple and the Church's Mission*, 29–92, esp. 66–80; Walton, *Ancient Near Eastern Thought*, 122–25.

the circumstances as a trial, seeking redress or new employment if appropriate but retaining a spirit of equanimity. And if we humans should accept this sort of slight nobly, how much more God?

Job, in his suffering, seems to buy into this line of reasoning. As Job puts it when hurling his accusations back into God's face, "If I sin, what do I do to you? . . . Why have I become a burden to you?" (7:20). Even if Job has sinned in some serious way, which he maintains that he has not in fact done, Job wonders why God doesn't just get over it. "Why do you not carry away my transgression and cause my sin to pass away?" (7:21). And if God alone were affected when God is slighted, then we might conclude that Job has a valid point. But the truth is we are affected too. Thus, we shouldn't be surprised to discover that God's jealous desire to receive all the worship and glory is not for God's benefit alone, but also very much for ours.

Forbidden Images and Defaced Image-Bearers

How does unauthorized idol worship harm humanity? It results in a defacing, so that humans do not appropriately bear the glorious image of God to creation. That is, when a person is truly acting as the image of God, he or she serves as a genuine contact point between God and creation, mediating God's presence to creation (including other humans and all other creatures). But when a person worships false idols, the capacity to serve in this way is undermined. The glory of God that the image is to radiate has become distorted. So other humans, animals, plants, and the rest of the earth fail to experience God's sovereignty through that human as God would desire it to be exercised, and the creation falls into corruption. As Paul puts it, "The creation waits eagerly for the revelation of the sons of God" (Rom. 8:19). And why? Because it is awaiting the fullness of the *glory* of the children of God as they reign alongside the Son (Rom. 8:17; cf. Col. 3:4; 2 Tim. 2:12; Rev. 20:6). In fact, it is in association with the "freedom of the *glory* of the children of God" that creation is finally "released from its bondage to decay" (Rom. 8:21). In short, if I fail to act as the full image of God, then my neighbors, family, pets, livestock, and the places on the earth over which I have royal stewardship will be bereft of God's life-giving, wise, ordered rule.

The image of God that forms me is not lost as I become mired in sin, but the manner in which God is imaged through me is altered and mangled. We need look no further than the stories of murder, sexual degradation, violence, and hubris in Genesis 4–11 or Romans 1 (or we need but to turn on the news) to see what happens to other humans and to creation when humans fail to act as true idols, true image-bearers. How in practical terms does this defacing of the image of God happen in connection with idolatry?

False Reality and the Distorted Image

First, above all, the defacing of the image in conjunction with idolatry derives from a basic misconstrual of reality. The idols of the nations are false; they are not really imbued with the presence of a god or goddess. Unlike Adam and Eve who are given the spirit, as Jeremiah puts it, the idols "have no *ruach* ['breath' or 'spirit'] in them" (10:14). They are fraudulent, a lie, a deception, vain—that is, they have no status as "real" beyond the raw materials from which they have been crafted.[9] In speaking to the idols and the gods they purport to represent, Isaiah says, "Look, you are nothing, and your work is less than nothing" (41:24). In contrast, the God of Israel can assert about himself, "I am the first and I am the last; except for me there is no god" (Isa. 44:6). That is, God is the only genuine god, so when humans worship idols, they participate in a faulty assessment of reality. And just as a person who has been hoodwinked by a crooked used-car salesperson is harmed in practical ways when he finds his expensive car will not even reliably transport him to work, so also those deceived by idols will find their lives breaking down rather than joyfully flourishing. As the book of Jonah puts it, "Those who revere vain idols abandon their covenant love" (2:8).

Idolatry, Rationalization, and Moral Decay

Second, idols lead humans into practical harm because there is a tendency for the idol-maker to "trust in his own creation" (Hab. 2:18). Idols themselves are in truth speechless, but those who provide speech for them "utter nonsense," and those that seek divination from them "see lies," for "they tell false dreams and give empty comfort" (Zech. 10:2). In other words, there is a strong human proclivity to cause idols to "say" what we want them to say, and to hear from them what we want to hear. Thus, idols are used to legitimate and rationalize the self-serving interests of those who prophesy and interpret through them. The result is that, rather than being led by God and by the truth, the people are led astray so that they "wander like sheep" (Zech. 10:2).

---

9. Note, however, that even though the most primal truth is that an idol has no real existence beyond the material used to craft it ("we know that 'an idol is no real thing in the world,' and that 'there is no God but one'" [1 Cor. 8:4]), nonetheless idol worship can be co-opted by the demonic, so that idol worship can involve participation with evil spirits (see 1 Cor. 10:20).

As Paul explains in Romans, idolatry begins a process of accelerated moral degradation that culminates in a lack of God's glory among humans. Even though we know something of God's "eternal power and divinity" by observing the created order (Rom. 1:20), nevertheless we ignore the truths about God that we discover there when these conflict with our self-serving interests, and we make idols that will allow us to pursue our own misguided desires in place of the one true God: "Claiming to be wise, they became fools, and exchanged the glory of the incorruptible God for the likeness of the image of corruptible man, and of birds and of animals and of reptiles" (1:22–23). The result of this turn to images is that humans lack the necessary encounter with God's glory, for they have exchanged it for something nonglorious and utterly lifeless. So false-god worshipers are transformed by their idolatry until they cease to bear God's glory adequately. Because of the ubiquity of idolatry (in one form or another), the final outcome is that apart from the Christ *all* humans are radically bereft of God's glory: "For all have sinned and *lack the glory of God*" (3:23).

After making idols, we use them to rationalize our desire to satisfy our bodily cravings, especially our sexual appetite. God allows us to experience the consequences of our folly: "Therefore God handed them over in the lusts of their hearts to impurity, for the dishonoring of their bodies among themselves" (Rom. 1:24). The moral collapse gathers speed as humans are allowed to experience the consequences of their idolatry—a bankrupt mind that leads to "every kind of unrighteousness" (1:29), which Paul describes in painful detail by listing the sins that result (1:29–30).

Human Transformation and Image Worship

Third, idolatry is damaging to humanity because humans become like what they worship.[10] When we worship idols, we come to take on their qualities. As the psalmist says about idols:

> They have mouths, but do not speak;
>> eyes, but do not see.
> They have ears, but do not hear;
>> noses, but do not smell.
> They have hands, but do not feel;
>> feet, but do not walk;
>> and they do not make a sound in their throat.
> *Those who make them become like them;*
>> *so do all who trust in them.* (Ps. 115:5–8 ESV)

10. For a rich analysis of this biblical motif, see Beale, *We Become What We Worship*.

That is, the psalmist indicates that worship of an idol results in conformity to the idol, as the worshiper becomes increasingly like the idol—unable to see, hear, smell, or feel toward the truth.

Idol worship, in both its ancient and modern forms, involves a movement away from the domain of the real and thus a concomitant inability to engage the real accurately. In speaking of the false worship of the Israelites, the author of 2 Kings says, "They went after empty idols [*hebel*] and became empty" (17:15). The prophet Jeremiah echoes this sentiment, saying that in departing from true worship of Yahweh, the people of Judah "went after emptiness, and became empty" (2:5). So idolatry's trajectory away from the real leads the worshiper finally into a vacuum, a total disconnect from reality—the idol worshiper has become like the insensate idol. As such, she or he is in the end totally unable to use the senses to connect to the domain of the real—God's truth, beauty, goodness, and oneness as these can be accessed through encounter with God's creation, which God has given as a gift. Human encounter with God's glory has been exchanged for an encounter with false images so that humans lack the glory of God.

The good news, on the other hand, is that when we participate in worship of the one true God, the result is that we become increasingly sensate and insightful—we see, hear, smell, and touch the God-crafted reality of the created order, and we correctly recognize that it points to truths about God's very self. And in so doing we are set free to be fully human once again; that is, we are increasingly conformed to the image of the Son, the truly human one, the one who fully images God.

Bearing the Original Image

We often think of God and humanity as opposites. Humans are error-prone, God is infallible; humans are sinful, God is sinless; humans are mortal, God is immortal; humans are weak, God is all-powerful. This, however, is to reflect upon humans as we find them, not upon humans in light of God's ultimate intentions for them. All humans are made in the image of God. Yet the ability of fallen humanity to act as the idol of God (i.e., to represent God dynamically by exercising stewardship over creation) has been hampered by the fall. In the incarnation, Jesus comes to us as the genuinely human one, the fulfillment of God's intentions for what it means to be most completely human. The stunning mystery of what it means to be a flourishing human is this: to be fully human doesn't mean to be the opposite of God; it means to fully image God, to reflect and represent God flawlessly in God's entirety, glory, and splendor.

Jesus as the Complete Image of God

We find a description of the way in which Jesus as the beloved Son (cf. Col. 1:13) serves as the full image of God in the justly famous Christ hymn of Colossians:

> He is the image of the invisible God, the firstborn of all creation. Because by him all things were created in heaven and on earth, things visible and invisible, whether thrones or dominions or rulers or authorities—all things were created through him and for him. And he is before all things, and all things hold together in him. And he is the head of the body, the church. He is the beginning, the firstborn from among the dead, in order that he might be preeminent in all things. Because in him all the fullness of God was pleased to dwell, and through him to reconcile to himself all things, whether on earth or in heaven, making peace through the blood of his cross. (Col. 1:15–20)

In pondering the meaning of the hymn, we might wonder how it is that the Son can be called *the image* of God (cf. 2 Cor. 4:4), which implies something *visible*, when God is expressly described in it as *invisible*. This puzzle is actually an important clue to the meaning of the hymn. When the author of the hymn (the hymn was probably not composed by Paul; rather, he simply opted to include it in his letter) describes the Son as "the image of the invisible God," it is likely that the author is drawing on Jewish-Hellenistic traditions about the way in which things like "image" (*eikōn*), "wisdom" (*sōphia*), and "speech" (*logos*) were used by God to connect to the created order.

That is, because God is transcendent (above and separate from creation), various instrumentalities, such as speech, wisdom, and image, allow God to be active and immanent in creation. So, for instance, when God spoke various features of the universe into existence, saying, "Let there be light" (Gen. 1:3) and so forth, the *Logos* (word, speech, reason, rationality) was with God as God's agent in creation. As the Gospel of John states, "In the beginning was the *Logos*. . . . All things were made *through* him" (1:1–3). Meanwhile, the Jewish-Hellenistic philosopher Philo, drawing on Plato's ideas, could speak of "*logos*" and "image" as heavenly forms that brokered between God and the earthly realities that participate in the forms.[11] The book of Proverbs does not speak of the *logos* as present with God in creation but does give Wisdom the opportunity to self-attest regarding its role in creation: "The LORD possessed me at the beginning of his work" (8:22). Wisdom claims an intimate

---

11. For Plato on "image," see *Timaeus* 92c. For Philo on the relationship between the creation of humans in the image of God, platonic forms, and God's reason, see esp. *Opif.* 25, 31, 69. On the *logos* as image of God, see Philo, *Fug.* 101; *Spec.* 1.81.

role in laboring alongside God in crafting the cosmos: "I was beside him, like a master worker" (8:30).

Therefore when in Colossians 1:15 the Son is called "the image of the invisible God," we should recognize that this assertion is first of all a statement about the way in which the Son makes God, who is otherwise transcendent, immanent in creation. This corresponds well with what we have already learned about the purpose of idols or images in the ancient Near Eastern world more broadly considered: crafted idols were believed to make the heavenly deity local, concrete, and truly present on earth. Secondarily, however, in criticism of the Greco-Roman tradition but in continuity with the Jewish, here it is tacitly affirmed that only one thing can serve as the "idol" or "image" of God, and that thing is emphatically *not* a handcrafted idol made from wood, stone, or gold. Rather, only *a person*, a spirit-endowed living human, can adequately "image" God, bring God's wise rule to creation. The one who fulfills this image-bearing role is God's beloved Son, Jesus, who was a real human with a genuine physical body (Col. 1:22) and who has now been exalted as king to God's right hand (Col. 3:1). Indeed, as Joshua Jipp has forcefully argued, the kingly metaphor best explains how Jesus is the image of God for Paul.[12] If this is the case, then it becomes even more obvious that Jesus as the ideal king is a representative figure—the very image of God—so that our allegiance to him and his self-emptying ways will also involve a transformation into his image.

So Jesus in the flesh is the truly human one, the apex of God's design for humanity as made in God's image. And notice this point, for it is important: in discussing the manner in which Jesus is the image of God, Paul states, "In him all the fullness of God was pleased to dwell" (Col. 1:19). That is, although Jesus is not the only human to bear God's image, he is the only one who imaged God in a *complete* manner. If we consider the meaning of an idol/image within Paul's cultural world, then we find that in all likelihood Paul is hereby asserting that Jesus is the only "idol of God" that was *fully* imbued with the divine presence. Other human-idols reflect God, but they do not represent God in God's entirety. For all humans, apart from Jesus, the image and God's divine presence do not fully align, so that the divine presence is not perfectly mediated by the image—it is eclipsed or occluded. But with Jesus there is flawless alignment and pervasive presence. In case we missed it the first time, Paul makes much the same point further on in his letter when he warns the Colossians not to be taken in by the pseudo-wisdom of merely human philosophies and traditions. Jesus as the Christ is superior, because "in him the whole fullness of deity dwells bodily" (2:9). In other words, Jesus

---

12. On Jesus as the kingly image of God, see Jipp, *Christ Is King*, 100–127.

the king is the only image of God that fully houses the divine presence, so mere human wisdom could at best approach, but could never excel, that found in him. Jesus as the Christ-king is the fulfillment of the human mandate to bear the image of God.

Jesus as the Original Image of God

Not only is Jesus the full image; he is also the *original* image. Because chronologically Adam appeared first, then later Jesus, we might be tempted to think that Adam is the original image of God and Jesus the later copy that restores the image that had become distorted in the meantime. But Jesus is not merely the *recovery* of God's intentions for Adam and Eve. Jesus surpasses mere restoration in the way that a house in all its splendor (once it is fully constructed) surpasses its architectural blueprint. A blueprint is a real thing with intrinsic value both at its first issuance and after construction is complete (as a compact guide to the house's structure and systems). But once the house arrives, the blueprint has been surpassed by the deeper, fuller reality that it anticipated. In a like manner, Adam truly bore the image of God, but did so in a limited fashion. As the image of God, he was a type. He established a visible pattern that Jesus as the complete image surpasses—and this because, oddly, Jesus rather than Adam is the prototype, the original image of God. As Paul puts it, "Adam was a *type* of the one to come" (Rom. 5:14). The one to come, Jesus, was the fuller reality that Adam, the type, anticipated; Adam was a type of Jesus, a blueprint that anticipated the house, a visible imitation that anticipated the fullness that has now arrived in Jesus the king. Yet strangely the messianic prototype, the Christ-house, was present even prior to the Adam blueprint.

With Adam, Eve, and all Adam-shaped humanity prior to Jesus the Messiah, God was truly leaving a visible impress of his own presence. God was marking the created order with his decisive stamp, his imprint, his image. But as with many other visible pictures in the Bible, God intended Adam as image-bearer as an anticipation of a deeper, richer, fuller image-bearer who preceded him in a hidden fashion and would appear publicly in the future. Think here of Adam as an inky pattern left on a piece of paper from the strike of a wet stamp. God placed the inky pattern, Adam, in creation as an anticipation of the eventual appearance in history of the original stamp itself, Jesus the Christ, God's beloved Son. All humans participate in the ink-like pattern of Adam as that image of God through Adam is passed along.

But Jesus is the original image of God, and his appearance as a human in history provides defaced humans the opportunity to be renewed through contact with the heavenly original stamp rather than the earthly ink-like replica:

The first man was of the dust of the earth, the second man from heaven. As was the earthly man, so are those who are of the earth; and as is the man from heaven, so also are those who are of heaven. (1 Cor. 15:47–48)

So the first man, Adam, was an earthly prototype, and all his descendants are in his image in accordance with the Adamic pattern that he passes along to his offspring (see Gen. 5:3). But Jesus is the heavenly prototype for the earthly; he is the full image of God. If we remain in Adam alone, we are like garbled, waning ink marks on a piece of paper in our divine image bearing, but through our viewing of the original stamp, Jesus the Messiah, we can be restored. Our restoration is not just to the level of Adam prior to the fall, the vibrant first impression; rather the restoration is so all-surpassing that it is better to call it a new creation. We are made to conform not to the Adamic first impression but to Jesus as the primal stamp. In other words, the distorted way in which we bear the image of God is transformed by Jesus, who is the authentic image of God. How does this transformation take place? Intriguingly, we are most fundamentally changed by *gazing* upon Jesus.

Renewal through the Original Image

For the Christian, whatever else our final salvation might or might not entail, we can be certain that it will involve conformity to the image of the Christ, the very one who fully bears the image of God.[13] For Paul says, "Just as we have borne the image of the man of dust, we will also bear the image of the man of heaven" (1 Cor. 15:49). In another passage Paul goes even further, speaking about our conformity to the image of the Son as part of God's predetermined plan for the church. Jesus as the firstborn Son paved the way for many siblings to join the family as they come to share the Son's likeness or image:

For those God foreknew he also predestined to be conformed to the image [*eikōn*] of his Son, that he might be the firstborn among many brothers. Now, those he predestined, he also called; those he called, he also justified; those he justified, he also glorified. (Rom. 8:29–30)

It is the destiny of the saints that they will be conformed to the image of God's Son. For all those who are genuinely part of God's family, holiness and conformity to the image of the king are so inevitable that Paul can speak

13. On the renewal of our image through the image of the Christ, see Kilner, *Dignity and Destiny*, 233–310.

of these events in such a way as to suggest that they are a past, present, and future reality—those whom God has called he has justified and glorified.[14]

This conformity to the image of the Christ (and therefore to the image of God) comes about by looking fixedly upon Jesus. Although initially this might surprise us, when we weigh the theology of idolatry that we have already explored together, our surprise should abate. We become like that which we worship. Those who worship idols take on the attributes of those idols. If you worship something that cannot truly see, hear, touch, smell, or taste, then your own sensate abilities will likewise diminish in their ability to reliably lead you to the real truth: "Those who make them become like them; so do all who trust in them" (Ps. 115:8). But if Jesus is worshiped as the original God-ordained "idol of God," then the result will be conformity to King Jesus.

Several New Testament passages illustrate this point more fully. Paul describes this transformative viewing of the glorified Jesus: "And all of us who with unveiled faces are beholding as in a mirror the glory of the Lord are being transformed into the same image from glory into glory" (2 Cor. 3:18). Paul goes on to explain that this transformation is facilitated "by the Lord—that is, by the Spirit" (2 Cor. 3:18)—that is, in all probability, the Lord Jesus as functionally operative through the Holy Spirit.[15] We currently see the glory of the Lord Jesus, albeit indirectly (as if through a mirror). So this results in a slow transformation for us into the image of the Lord Jesus through the agency of the Spirit. This transformative viewing of Jesus as the authentic idol of God is so critical to our human transformation along the road to final salvation that the evil one urgently desires to prevent it: "The god of this world has blinded the minds of the *apistoi*, to keep them from seeing the light of the gospel of the glory of the Christ, who is the image of God" (2 Cor. 4:4). The *apistoi*, those who have not yielded allegiance to Jesus, are unable to participate in the transformative viewing that will result in conformity to the image of God in Jesus the Christ. Those who have given allegiance, however, fix their eyes on Jesus (Heb. 12:2) and on the things of God and the kingdom work that will endure into the ages (Matt. 6:22–23; 2 Cor. 4:18), knowing that

14. Those seeking to systematize the Bible's teachings about personal salvation must bear in mind that Rom. 8:29–30 speaks of God's activities on behalf of the collective people of God. This *group* is collectively predestined according to God's plan, justified, and glorified. But Rom. 8:29–30 does not delineate how individuals relate to the boundaries of this group, so this passage does not forthrightly say that any individual is inevitably predestined, justified, and glorified. For further discussion, see "Justification as Union, Not Order" in chap. 8.

15. For a defense of this interpretative option, see Bates, *Hermeneutics of the Apostolic Proclamation*, 160–81, esp. 178n186; for a full scholarly discussion, see Thrall, *Second Epistle to the Corinthians*, 1:273–97.

when we turn our minds to Jesus, he renews them as part of the transformative process that he is working in us (Rom. 12:1–2).

Bearing the Full Image

Now that we have explored together the theology of humans in the idol of
God, we can circle back to the beatific vision, as the saints gaze upon the face
of the Lamb directly in the new Jerusalem. As God's servants worship him, they
now have unobstructed access and can stare directly at the glorified Lamb, who
shares God's throne, and at his visage: "They will see his face, and his name
will be on their foreheads" (Rev. 22:4). This opportunity for direct viewing
represents a fundamental shift in the story of God's interaction with his people.

In the Old Testament several individuals are described as having seen God
"face to face," yet we notice that something always dampened, occluded,
reflected, or mediated the directness. This obscuring was necessary, for humans were unable to endure the full weight of a direct viewing of God's glory.
Even Moses, who famously is remembered as the greatest of all the prophets
because Yahweh "knew him face to face" (Deut. 34:10) and who is described
as speaking with God "face to face, as a man speaks with his friend" (Exod.
33:11), still did not view God's face directly. Rather the pillar of cloud would
descend into the tent of meetings and Moses would encounter God via the
pillar (the glory of which caused his face to shine). In fact, when Moses asked
to see God's glory, God explicitly told him, "You cannot see my face, for no
one may see me and live" (Exod. 33:20), and placed him in the cleft of the
rock as God caused his glory to pass by.

It is similar for others in the Old Testament. After wrestling and prevail-
ing over the mysterious being that accosts Jacob when he is alone, Jacob
declares, "I have seen God face to face, yet my life has been rescued" (Gen.
32:30). Yet this being is both described and encountered as "a man" (Gen.
32:24–25—Hebrew: 'ish), even if this man says afterward that Jacob has in
fact "striven with God" (Gen. 32:28—Hebrew: 'elohim). Meanwhile, as part of
the ratification ceremony in the giving of the law, it is said that Moses, Aaron,
Nadab, Abihu, and the seventy elders of Israel "saw God" and "beheld God,"
but only the area under God's feet is described, and it is said that the viewing
was as if through a clear piece of sapphire—again a mediated viewing. Once
again, God is described as speaking "face to face" with the people at Mount
Sinai, but we discover that this "face to face" encounter was "from the midst
of the fire" (Deut. 5:4; cf. Num. 14:14), signaling that God's presence was
indirect. We might infer that humans were not at a suitable level of holiness
to endure the full weight of God's glory.

In Revelation 22:4, as humans gaze upon the Lamb on the throne, we recognize that humans are now in a fit state to look upon God face to face. Jesus the glorified Lamb fully images God to those who view him—and as they gaze upon him, the final transformation ensues. *The viewing of the glorified Lord Jesus will result in our final transformation into his image, so that we also fully image God in the way that Jesus does.* The imperfect will disappear! Perfection will arrive (1 Cor. 13:9)! Right now we do truly view, know, and experience something of the transformative glory of God through Jesus, but only imperfectly as if through a cloudy reflection. The apostle Paul describes it this way: "For now we see in a mirror dimly, but then face to face; now I know in part; then I shall know fully, even as I have been fully known" (1 Cor. 13:12). That is to say, although currently we are "being renewed in knowledge in accordance with the image of [our] creator" (Col. 3:10), once the obscurity is totally removed, our encounter with Jesus, the glorified one, will result in a totally transformed understanding of God and God's ways—a conformity to the image of God in Jesus the Messiah (cf. Rom. 12:1–2). Our knowledge of God and God's ways, Paul indicates, will be akin to how God already entirely knows us and our ways. With his characteristic profound simplicity, the apostle John makes much the same point as does Paul. His words are a fitting climax to the theology of salvation through image viewing: "Beloved, right now we are God's children, and what we will be has not yet appeared; yet we know that when *he appears* we will be *like him*, because we will *see him just as he is*" (1 John 3:2).

God placed humans in Eden as idols imbued with his own spirit so that other humans and all creation could dynamically experience the sovereignty of God through the image of God borne by each human. Yet immediately the Adamic image of God became defaced and distorted through sin so that creation failed to receive its proper stewardship. Jesus the Messiah is the authentic, full image of God, the faultless representation. Jesus, who died for our sins, fully bears the image of God, and subsequently our own image can be renewed as we join the allegiant community in gazing upon him. So the end goal of salvation is that through allegiance we become fully human—that is, that we flawlessly mirror God because we have been fully conformed to the image of Jesus the Christ.

Salvation is resurrection into the new creation, yet it also involves our transformation into a glorious new image. Despite the Bible's fierce polemic against false idols, God's strange final saving intention is that we become *true idols*, dynamic created beings perfectly imbued with the presence of

God, radiating divine glory to other humans and to the rest of creation. Yet in working through these themes, we have not exhausted the topic of salvation. Fascinating and intensely debated aspects of salvation still need to be probed, especially justification.

——— FOR FURTHER THOUGHT ———

1. What aspects of your current life's work are toilsome drudgery? What would it mean for these same tasks to be a delight in the new creation?
2. Realizing that the final transformation can only be accomplished by God's re-creation, nonetheless, can you think of one or two ways in which the present realities of the kingdom of God can infuse your toil with delight now?
3. Why is it important to move beyond the mere fact of being "in the image of God" to the question of purpose? For what explicit purpose did God create humans in God's own idol/image?
4. Describe how, in antiquity, a hunk of wood might eventually come to be regarded as a god if brought through the proper process. Why is this important for a full understanding of a Christian theology of final salvation?
5. Why is the worship of idols forbidden in the Old Testament?
6. How does the viewing of false idols/images relate to human moral behavior? Why?
7. How is our final salvation connected to proper image bearing and image viewing?
8. Describe the content of some of the images that you view most often (e.g., perhaps on television or online). What impact do you think this has on your salvation?
9. Why is it important to recognize that Jesus rather than Adam is the original image of God?
10. In what way is our final salvation *more than* a restoration of our defaced, Adam-based image of God?
11. Given the overall theology of image explored in this chapter, how might viewing an icon, a picture of a holy person or a saint, possibly be of assistance in a journey of Christian salvation?

8

JUSTIFICATION
AND ALLEGIANCE ALONE

The previous two chapters examined the Christian vision for final salvation. Final salvation is not about the individual soul going to heaven after death; it is about resurrection into new creation. Our whole person—body, soul, and spirit—will be raised to new life by God, and we will do what humans were designed all along to do: we will act as "idols of God" who are fully imbued with the divine presence. That is, we will be perfect representations of God, as finally we are fully conformed to Jesus's image—the original, authentic image of God. The kingdom of God that was inaugurated with Jesus's first coming, especially with his enthronement at the right hand of God, will be brought to a fullness as that reign is actualized through us. The lost glory having been more than restored, Christians will rule over creation alongside Jesus the king as citizens of the new Jerusalem, the city that God will bring down to the earth. Allegiance to Jesus the king ultimately means that we reign with the king.

Yet this depiction of our final salvation only begins to answer our questions about salvation. Others remain, especially about how an individual comes to experience the benefits of this final salvation. That is, granted that the triune God—Father, Son, and Spirit—has acted in history to effect salvation, how is that salvation applied in individual cases? It is one thing to say "Jesus died on the cross to save us" and quite another thing to explain how the death of a single man nearly two thousand years ago can actually effect salvation for a person today. In seeking to explain, the Bible uses a number of metaphors to speak about our salvation—redemption, adoption, washing, clothing, regeneration, and more.

One particularly important, complex, and controversial metaphor is God's "justifying" activity and how it might relate to our "righteousness." These terms are both part of the *dikaio-* word family in Greek. As such, they are predominately forensic in nature, referring to legal uprightness or innocence. But their purview is not restricted to the individual, for justification's scope is ultimately as wide as creation (see Rom. 5:11–21; 8:19–21).

Paul especially favors this language, but his use is puzzling because he can speak of justification as a past, present, and future occurrence for the people of God (cf. Rom. 2:13; 3:24; 5:1; 1 Cor. 6:11; Gal. 2:16). How can a seemingly one-time event, this declaration of innocence, truly be past, present, and future for Christians? Moreover, upon my declaration of "faith," aren't my sins transferred or otherwise reckoned ("imputed") to Jesus and carried away on the cross, while his righteousness is given to me—glorious exchange!—so that God sees only Jesus's righteousness rather than my own sin when he looks upon me? It would seem that a personal, irreversible transaction has *already* occurred. If this model is correct, then Jesus has taken my sin upon himself, and I have been clothed in his righteousness. How, then, is there any room for *continued* allegiance in justification? Justification is clearly a complex matter.

Indeed, a principle cause of the Protestant Reformation was disagreement over how a person can come to be described as "right" or "just" before God. Protestants tend to favor a model of "imputed" righteousness, as above, and Catholics "imparted" or "infused." What's the difference? Why might it matter? And are there other ways of thinking about God's justifying activity that might prove fruitful? This chapter will seek to further the "salvation by allegiance alone" thesis by focusing on what Scripture teaches about righteousness and justification. As with the other topics broached in this book, the goal is not to exhaust justification (as if that were even possible!) but to consider new horizons in light of the main contours of the biblical teaching.

The Primacy of Union

So much has been written about justification by biblical scholars and theologians that there can be a danger of losing the forest amid the trees. In seeking to clarify how justification fits with the allegiance-alone proposal, my primary intention is to locate it properly within a larger scheme of personal salvation. This will also help clarify how to best conceptualize justification, assisting us as we assess imputation, impartation, and other possible models. As a starting place, I take it as axiomatic that we cannot treat justification as an abstract, isolated transaction carried out between God and the individual by virtue of the Christ's sacrifice, for *an individual's justification is entirely bound up with the union of the church to Jesus the king*.[1]

In rendering this judgment I am by no means alone. Although subsequently in the *Institutes* John Calvin is perhaps not as clear on the precise relationship between justification and union as one might wish, he nevertheless does clearly affirm the primacy of union in salvation.[2] Meanwhile, the great twentieth-century biblical scholar, medical doctor, and humanitarian Albert Schweitzer was so convinced of the centrality of union that he famously called the doctrine of righteousness by faith a "subsidiary crater" within the main crater or larger category of redemption through "being-in-Christ" (although I wouldn't follow Schweitzer's delineation of union in Paul in predominately mystical terms).[3] A tremendous number of contemporary biblical scholars and theologians are eagerly (and correctly!) pointing at the primacy of union or participation for soteriology.[4]

But if union with Jesus the king is key to understanding personal salvation, then it is worth asking what this union entails. The New Testament speaks of this union via a diverse array of metaphors and terms. These include language of location ("there is therefore now no condemnation for those who are *in* the Christ Jesus" [Rom. 8:1]), mutual indwelling ("you are *in me*, and *I in you*" [John 14:20]), and oneness of spirit/Spirit ("he who is joined to the Lord becomes one *pneuma* with him" [1 Cor. 6:17]), as well as diverse images drawn from agriculture, construction, the temple, marriage, and clothing. Moreover, I would follow Constantine Campbell in asserting that *union* in Paul (and arguably in the remainder of the New Testament too) should be qualified as involving nuances of *participation, identification*, and *incorporation*.[5] Not only is union a robust theological category firmly evidenced in the New Testament; it is able to organize and explain how activities, metaphors, and theological categories that might otherwise seem independent (e.g., justification,

1. Personal human salvation is also bound up with God's refining salvation of the created order in general, as discussed in chaps. 6 and 7.

2. See esp. Calvin's opening remarks on salvation in *Institutes* 3.1.1–2 (Battles): "First, we must understand that as long as Christ remains outside of us, and we are separated from him, all that he has suffered and done for salvation of the human race remains useless and of no value for us. Therefore, to share with us what he has received from the Father, he had to become ours and dwell within us. . . . All that he possesses is nothing to us until we grow into one body with him. . . . To sum up, the Holy Spirit is the bond by which Christ effectively unites us to himself." For a more comprehensive discussion, see Billings, *Calvin, Participation, and the Gift*.

3. Schweitzer, *Mysticism of Paul the Apostle*, 225.

4. The last five years have seen an explosion of studies, including Peterson, *Salvation Applied by the Spirit*; Macaskill, *Union with Christ in the New Testament*; M. Johnson, *One with Christ*; C. Campbell, *Paul and Union with Christ*; Billings, *Union with Christ*.

5. C. Campbell, *Paul and Union with Christ*, 29.

resurrection, baptism, ecclesiology, eschatology) in fact interrelate. If we are saved, it is because we have been united with Jesus and incorporated into his innocence by means of the atoning function of his sacrificial death and the gift of the Holy Spirit; we are now part of him, so we participate in his death and resurrection unto victorious new life. In the final analysis, then, an individual can be said to be righteous or justified—past, present, and future—when and only when he or she is "*in* the Messiah" or united to Jesus the king.

In this chapter, the heart of what I want to say about how union relates to an individual person's justification is this: properly speaking, at the present time Jesus the king is the only person who has already been *directly* judged by God (the Father), found to be in the right (justified), and vindicated. His resurrection from the dead is proof of his innocence—that he truly has been justified. Resurrection constitutes Jesus's deliverance and total vindication. Currently no other person has been directly justified and declared righteous *apart from him*. All other cases are reserved for the final judgment. And here *apart from him* does not mean in the absence of Jesus as merely an abstract atoning sacrifice that covers over sin; it means *apart from him* as the church's kingly representative, the one to whom we are united (as a head is united to the members of its body) by the Holy Spirit. Yet, in order to arrive at this conclusion, we must lay a foundation by exploring some key concepts within soteriology: *ordo salutis* and election.

Order of Salvation

In addition to speaking about the past historical process by which salvation has been and will be achieved (*historia salutis*), theologians have sought to describe the "order of salvation" (*ordo salutis*), the logical progression or activities by which God makes salvation applicable to an individual. That is, an *ordo salutis* seeks to describe the sequence by which God brings an individual to final salvation.

So what elements are found in an *ordo salutis*? And how does "justification" fit into it? To give a popular outline rooted in the Reformed tradition, one might speak of personal salvation as a process that begins with God's unfathomable eternal decree to save certain humans and continues with those humans sinning but then progressing onward to effectual calling, regeneration, faith and repentance, justification, adoption, sanctification, perseverance, union with Jesus, and finally glorification.[6] So even if justification has often

---

6. This is the *ordo salutis* defended by Murray, *Redemption—Accomplished and Applied*, 79–181. Cf. Hoekema, *Saved by Grace*.

been treated as the centerpiece of salvation, the moment of declaration of innocence before God, it has nevertheless traditionally been regarded as just one of many crucial steps on the road to personal salvation. But even so, there are difficulties with this approach.

Difficulties with Order of Salvation

Although undeniably systematizing the true order of salvation is a worthy goal, biblical scholars, myself included, generally remain wary of such systems. For even when such systems employ biblical terms as conceptual categories or organizational rubrics, they tend to foist alien concerns onto the biblical text rather than allowing the biblical narrative to supply the framework, and this leads to skewed emphases.[7] For instance, a common category in the order is "election." This is a biblical term (*eklektos* and cognates), and it is indeed sometimes used in the Greek Old Testament and the New Testament to emphasize God's sovereignty in choosing specific individuals and groups for various purposes. But as it is mobilized by systematicians, the tendency is to treat it as a special "salvation" category pertaining to God's eternal (or slightly later) decree to save or damn certain individuals, when in fact the word means merely "choosing" and frequently doesn't have eternal salvation or condemnation in view at all, especially not with regard to the individual. My intention is not to suggest that systematics is unnecessary or unhelpful in clarifying Scripture through philosophical inquiry; my point is rather that the biblical story has not always been correctly aimed for systematic inquiry.

To illustrate the problem, consider the definition of election given by noted systematician Louis Berkhof: "*that eternal act of God whereby He, in His sovereign good pleasure, and on account of no foreseen merit in them, chooses a certain number of men to be the recipients of special grace and of eternal salvation.*"[8] This definition is surely constructed in conversation with the biblical data, but it is certainly not a definition that any first-century follower of Jesus could or would have supplied. When election is reified as a distinct

---

7. For a serious recent attempt to define an order of salvation for Paul, see Gaffin, *By Faith, Not by Sight*. Although Gaffin helpfully seizes upon union as a key to Paul's soteriology (and upon our present participation in the Christ's resurrection), unfortunately his broader attempt to defend an order of salvation in Paul must be regarded as unsuccessful. For he disallows any renovative or transformative dimension to justification (e.g., p. 55) and in so doing falsely separates the righteousness associated with "justification" and "sanctification" in unstable ways. Moreover, biblical statements pertaining to groups are occasionally assumed to apply to an individual without sufficient warrant (e.g., pp. 120–22).

8. Berkhof, *Systematic Theology*, 114 (emphasis original).

theological category in such a manner, it is then made to fit into an overarching scheme of additional reified categories that are likewise slightly artificial (calling, regeneration, justification, sanctification, glorification). In this manner a whole system is created that is considerably distant from any system that a first-century follower of Jesus could have held. This is a problem because the thought structures native to our biblical texts should inform subsequent systematization in a more holistic way.

Moreover, since salvation has been discussed in the church throughout its lengthy history, certain systematic ways of analyzing "order of salvation" and accompanying schools of thought have come to dominate the conversational landscape. These systems are often put forward not only as competitors but as the only possible options—as if one must choose between the Catholic, Reformed (Calvinist), Arminian, Barthian, or existential system wholesale, and one cannot select parts of one and parts of another. This lock-stock-and-barrel approach is flawed, however, for it is doubtful that the scriptural evidence conforms to any of these systems entirely. (And I hope that the reader will likewise resist labeling the results obtained here as Reformed, Arminian, semi-Pelagian, or Catholic, as this present author would reject these descriptions.)

In contradistinction, biblical scholars when systematizing (that is, when doing "biblical theology") tend to describe how the various terms such as "election" function in ancient texts while resisting the tendency to treat these terms as overarching, reified categories or as discrete stages in an "order of salvation" except inasmuch as they seem to function consistently as such for specific ancient thinkers.[9] So it is crucial to allow the narrative flow of Scripture, considered historically, to control the categories and meanings if we are to understand the Bible's vision of salvation. When we do so, it becomes apparent that we must reckon with Scripture's emphasis on *corporate* election if we are to make sense of justification.

God Chooses the Son

Some statements in the Bible affirm that God the Father had saving purposes before time began. God chose Israel, and the Messiah within Israel, for the sake of bringing salvation to the world through him.[10] In fact, Scripture

---

9. For a convincing synthesis that pays attention to how ancient thought structures (such as "election") functioned at the worldview level for Second Temple Jews and early Christians, see N. T. Wright's treatment of monotheism, election, and eschatology throughout his multivolume series Christian Origins and the Question of God (for a primer, see Wright, *New Testament and the People of God*, esp. 215–338).

10. See Wright, *Paul and the Faithfulness of God*, 1:774–836.

is clear that God chose *the Son* (1 Pet. 1:20; Luke 9:35 echoing Isa. 42:1 and Ps. 2:7) and *the church in the Son* (Eph. 1:11; 1 Pet. 1:2) for salvation in eternity or ages past. But how this election of the Son and the church relates to the salvation of this or that *individual* must be teased out. The Bible does suggest that God knows the future and controls its unwinding in intimate detail (Prov. 19:21; Acts 2:23; 17:26; Isa. 46:10). Moreover, God directs saving outcomes by working with, not against, personal free will (Acts 13:46; 28:24; Phil. 2:12–13). So philosophical consistency together with general biblical evidence may lend probability in favor of the individual-election conclusion, as the time-transcending God works with our free will.

Nevertheless, within biblical theology, foreordained individual election may not be a safe starting point, for even if it is allowed (perhaps even encouraged) by the general biblical evidence and is philosophically consistent, at the same time it runs roughshod over *the election story* the Bible wants to tell: God's election of the Messiah through Israel's election in order to save Jew and gentile alike within his elect church. In fact, there is not a single statement in the Bible that unambiguously indicates that God preselects *specific individuals* before they are born (apart from the Son) for eternal salvation[11]—and the same can be said for eternal separation.[12] Nor does the Bible stress an individual-first sequence of salvation, but a community-first sequence. The Bible is not really interested in telling a story about God's predestining election of individuals, even if such a view is compatible with the biblical witness.[13] So if the Bible is reticent to articulate an election-based individual theology of salvation, then might it not be wise for us to follow suit?

11. The closest the Bible comes to affirming individual predestining election is Acts 13:48. This verse states that the gentiles rejoiced upon hearing Paul's message, "and as many as were appointed [*ēsan tetagmenoi*] to eternal life gave *pistis* [*episteusan*]." But God's *fore*ordained or *prior* choosing (e.g., before time) is in all likelihood *not* emphasized here (to suggest otherwise is weak exegesis as it overloads the perfect passive participle *tetagmenoi* with inappropriate temporal and theological weight); rather it merely emphasizes that God is sovereign over appointment to eternal life even at the individual level. The timing of this appointment is not specified other than that it is prior to or simultaneous with these individuals giving *pistis*. This passage appears to assume both free will and divine sovereignty (on which see "Irresistible Grace and Free Will?" in chap. 5), but does not comment on eternal predestination or the security of eternal life with regard to these individuals.

12. Regarding predetermined eternal separation, Judas is described as having departed to "his own place" (Acts 1:25), but this does not necessarily imply *fore*ordained reprobation, even when John 6:70–71 and Mark 14:21 are added.

13. Even the famous "election" passage, "Jacob I loved, but Esau I hated" (Rom. 9:11–13), does not directly pertain to individual election unto eternal life or reprobation. Rather it pertains to God's sovereign choice to use individuals and peoples (Jacob/Israel, Esau, Pharaoh) in diverse ways to bring salvation to Jew and gentile alike through the Son. As Bird (*Evangelical Theology*, 519) puts it, "The concept of election in Romans 9–11 is fundamentally corporate and ethnic."

In short, it is crucial that we recognize the primacy of God's choice of the Son as Messiah, and the church in the Son, as central to biblical theology. We must also recognize that God graciously takes the initiative in stimulating personal salvation for individuals (John 6:44; 15:16), so even the ability to render allegiance to Jesus the king is a gift (Eph. 2:8; Acts 18:27). But God's prior choosing of specific individuals for eternal life or reprobation remains at best on the outer fringes of the story our biblical authors want to tell about salvation.

Justification as Union, Not Order

All of this is pertinent to a discussion of justification (and related *dikaio-* terms) for three reasons. First, as with "election," we need to be wary lest we reify "justification" and "righteousness" in ways foreign to Paul or early Christianity. Much as with election, it is prima facie doubtful that the earliest Christians thought in terms of a theology of justification. That is, they used *dikaio-* language as a helpful metaphor but did not isolate it as a distinct step of salvation or an object of separate inquiry. In fact, as we will see momentarily, since the *dikaio-* word group involves past, present, and future dimensions, it encroaches on other "stages" in the traditional order of salvation, because these are best considered not as stages at all. So justification is best regarded not as a discrete additional step in the midst of calling, regeneration, sanctification, and glorification, but as a metaphor explaining union that is informed and bounded by these other terms.

Second, Paul, when he gives his famous "order of salvation," is not speaking about a *sequential progression* that an *individual* must be moved through, but rather about God's actions, holistically considered, as events that have been *accomplished* on behalf of the *collective* people of God:

> For those God *foreknew* he also *predestined* to be conformed to the image of his Son, in order that he might be the firstborn among many brothers. Now, those he predestined, he also *called*; those he called, he also *justified*; those he justified, he also *glorified*. (Rom. 8:29–30)

Since Paul is speaking of a *group*, we cannot apply his words about foreknowledge and predestination to assert that specific individuals have certainty of final salvation without considering how an individual enters and stays within the boundaries of this group.

To show why this is so, consider a comparison to the modern business world. Imagine that the president of a corporation has been awarded a secure contract from a stable government. The president's entire company will certainly and necessarily receive the benefits through the accomplished work. In fact, current employees have already received the first payment from the contract as a guarantee that the full amount will be delivered in the future. The company's present and future health is guaranteed by the first installment. But if some individuals choose to leave the company, severing ties with the president, then present and future benefits are revoked. New employees may join the company at any time. Loyal employees may die, but even in death they finish employment as full employees, guaranteed all associated benefits. The president's prior actions guarantee the future of the company in whole and also the future welfare of all individual employees that remain affiliated, but there is no such guarantee for any who choose to revoke allegiance to the president, leaving his company.

In weighing this analogy, consider Jesus the king as the president who has been chosen by God the Father to receive not just a secure contract but an unwaveringly certain one, because he has already fulfilled its terms. His company is the church, whose benefits are not just absolutely guaranteed but also presently enjoyed, as the first installment (the benefits accrued through the union-securing Spirit) has already been paid out. No member of the body of the Christ can be unwillingly fired or forced out by external pressures, but if a person were to entirely cease giving allegiance to the Lord (and the Lord's people), then she or he would be denied the benefits secured through Jesus's contract.

Whether or not such a cessation is possible is a matter of dispute among Christian theologians and is beyond the purview of this study. But the more important point here is that although Romans 8:29–30 gives rock-solid promises of eternal security for the *collective* people of God, these promises only lend assurance to the individual who remains "in the Messiah"—that is, within the body or group. Since Paul has the collective in view here, his words about foreknowledge, predestination, calling, justification, and glorification apply to the company as a whole, but he does not speak to the security of individual membership in the company. Contrary to the conclusion of many systematic theologians,[14] Paul says nothing here directly about the election of specific individuals to eternal life (or condemnation) or about the inevitability of final salvation for any such chosen individuals.

Notice further that Paul does *not* say, "Those whom he justified he also *will glorify*," but rather "those whom he justified he also *glorified*" (Rom. 8:30). That is, just like "justified," the verb "glorified" is in the aorist indicative, the verbal form in Greek that is most often used to represent past events in a holistic fashion. In other words, glorification is not spoken of as future

---

14. E.g., Grudem, *Systematic Theology*, 671, 692–93, 790; Demarest, *Cross and Salvation*, 127–29, 217–18, 228.

here, for *glorification* (just like justification) has a past, present, and future dimension. So, Paul is probably not delineating a progressive order of salvation designed to climax with *future* glory.

Since Paul understands union as a whole, under ordinary circumstances, to have begun decisively at baptism (that is, not specifically at the moment of immersion in the water but at the event holistically considered), it is best to see the *past* dimension of our glorification as individuals in the midst of the collective church as also having begun, for Paul, at baptism. At baptism, repentance was embodied by the washing away of sins in the water, allegiance (*pistis*) was publically confessed, and the Spirit was invoked with the laying on of hands—so baptism was not separate from declaration of allegiance and Spirit-infilling, but rather it was the larger context in the midst of which these activities transpired.[15] In regard to baptism, Paul speaks of our union with Jesus the Messiah in death: "We were buried therefore with him by baptism into death" (Rom. 6:4a). Yet then Paul goes on to speak of glory in association with resurrection life: "Just as the Christ was raised . . . through the *glory* of the Father, we too might walk in newness of life" (Rom. 6:4b). In so doing, Paul connects not only Jesus's resurrection life with the glory of the Father but also our own since we have come to participate in the resurrection power of the king through baptism and the gift of the Holy Spirit. Those who are in the Messiah have already come to share in his glory (2 Cor. 4:6; 8:23) as a past reality, but that glory is presently being actualized by the Spirit in the midst of the people of God (2 Cor. 3:7–11).

Paul's words about our past, present, and future glory, then, are conditioned on our ongoing participation with the Messiah. So it is not surprising that *present* glory is most clearly seen when we suffer in the Christ (2 Thess. 2:14), as suffering shows that we truly are participating in the Christ's death-unto-glorious-life (Rom. 8:17). Those who are in the Christ are currently in the process of transformation into a greater glory: "And all of us who with unveiled faces are beholding as in a mirror the glory of the Lord are being transformed into the same image from glory into glory, even as by the Lord, that is, by the Spirit" (2 Cor. 3:18). Finally, those who are in the Messiah will be fully glorified alongside the Messiah in the future—as numerous passages

15. On Christian baptism, see esp. Rom. 6:4; 1 Cor. 12:13; Gal. 3:27; Eph. 4:25; Col. 2:11–14; cf. Acts 2:38; 22:16; 1 Pet. 3:18–22. Tertullian (*On Baptism* 6–8; *On the Soldier's Crown* 3–4) describes and interprets the typical baptismal procedure as he knew it. The candidate had already shown and pledged repentance and "faith" (*fides*). Then, after entering the water, she or he publically confessed "faith," renounced the devil, was baptized in the threefold name, emerged from the water, and partook of a honey/milk mixture. This was immediately followed by an anointing with oil, the laying on of hands, and a benediction that invoked and invited the Holy Spirit to descend on the individual (cf. Justin Martyr, *1 Apol.* 61, 65; Ps.-Hippolytus, *Apostolic Tradition* 21–22). See Ferguson, *Baptism in the Early Church*, esp. 196–98, 340–45, 853–57.

indicate (e.g., Rom. 5:2; 2 Cor. 4:17; Col. 1:27; 3:4). So Paul's "he also glorified" (Rom. 8:30) speaks not of a sequence culminating in *future* glory, but of glory as the past, present, and future reality for all those who are in the Christ.

Third, the construal of Romans 8:29–30 as delineating an order of salvation is often connected to a faulty way of reading Romans as a whole, in which Romans 3–4 is felt to articulate the first step in individual salvation, "justification by faith," and Romans 5–8 is felt to describe "sanctification" while announcing our future "glorification."[16] But this is wrongheaded. As Michael Gorman puts it:

> This series is often taken as a reference to the *ordo salutis*, the order of God's saving acts toward the individual. But in context the last three verbs are more precisely an elaboration of what God has done to create a family of Christlike (which is to say Godlike) siblings. Paul's point is not to define an order so much as to stress the effectiveness and totality of God's saving action.[17]

In other words, Paul in Romans 8:29–30 is not giving an order by which an individual comes to be saved—predestination, calling, justification, glorification. Rather, he is bringing to a climax his description of how the collective people of God are united with the Messiah's death and resurrection. If Paul were giving an order, it would be odd for him to fail to mention purportedly crucial steps such as regeneration and sanctification. So this is a further indication that delineating an order is not Paul's intention at all. Paul's point is not that God's predestination of an individual leads to calling, justification, and finally glory, but that union with the Christ in his death and resurrection is constituted by a past, present, and future calling, justification, and glorification for the collective people of God. Our justification and glorification are not mere stages of salvation but its past, present, and future substance if we are "in the Christ."

Resurrection for Justification

Once we have come to appreciate the corporate nature of election—God has chosen his Son, Jesus the king, and the people of God only "in" the king—and

16. For a thoroughgoing deconstruction of this traditional way of reading Romans, see D. Campbell, *Deliverance of God*, esp. 62–95.

17. Gorman, *Becoming the Gospel*, 283. Gorman critiques this type of reading similarly elsewhere: "Chapters 5 through 8 of Romans do not present a narrative sequence of the believer's life in Christ, as is often thought. Rather, they present a set of various explanations of the meaning of participating in the narrative of Christ, that is, salvation as Christlike *dikaiosynē* ["righteousness"] and *doxa* ["glory"], or cruciform theosis. . . . The material content of Romans 5–8 . . . is not supplemental to the gospel or justification but constitutive of them" (281).

have better located justification as constitutive of salvific union rather than as a discrete stage in an individual's *ordo salutis*, then we are in a better position to understand what is otherwise an odd conundrum in Paul's Letters: we are accustomed, correctly, to regard our justification as effected through Jesus's atoning sacrifice on the cross (e.g., Rom. 3:25; 5:9), so why in Romans 4:23–25 would Paul speak not of the cross but of *resurrection* as purposed toward our justification?

> But the words "it was counted to him" were not written for his [Abraham's] sake alone, but for ours also. It will be counted to us who give *pistis* to him who raised from the dead Jesus our Lord, who was delivered up for our trespasses *and raised for our justification*. (Rom. 4:23–25)

For many of us, justification is exclusively about how Jesus's sacrifice on the cross resulted in our innocence. But with his "raised for our justification," Paul surprisingly also connects Jesus's *resurrection* to our justification. Why? We are ready to answer this question, at least in brief—and the answer helps pave the way for an analysis of how justification relates to the puzzling and vitally important phrase "the righteousness of God."

When Paul speaks of justification to his churches, he speaks of it as the past and present possession of his churches because through *union* those who confess Jesus as king truly share in Jesus's death *and his resurrection unto new life*. Justification is not only about what happened on the cross; it also depends on Jesus's *resurrection*. Through *pistis* we are *united* to Jesus in such a way that his *resurrection* (which liberated him from death and served as proof of the genuineness of his own justification) forms part of the basis of the church's past, present, and future *justification*. Because the head has been "raised for our justification," the body and its members are justified too. That is, the church is delivered through Jesus's resurrection so that union with his resurrection guarantees our own. Paul explains in more detail how both the cross and resurrection are bound up with God's justifying activity in his use of the compact phrase "the righteousness of God."

Reconsidering the Righteousness of God

At the epicenter of the debate about how justification works is the meaning of Paul's phrase "the righteousness of God."[18] Disagreement about the

---

18. The meaning of the "righteousness of God" and its relationship to justification is disputed. On the history of interpretation, see McGrath, *Iustitia Dei*. Regarding God's justifying activity

meaning of this phrase is at the heart of the Catholic-Protestant divide—and
there is still no firm consensus today regarding its meaning. But that should
not discourage us from attempting to offer ever-more satisfying definitions.
Nor, since disagreement prevails, should we come to the conclusion that
we have no idea whatsoever about Paul's meaning, for since Paul uses the
phrase (or references it) ten times, these occurrences give parameters that
bound possible meanings. Moreover a better understanding of "the righteousness of God" might help us move beyond Reformation-era disputes
toward a better, truer synthesis. My aim here is to present the biblical data
and to suggest an overarching framework for how the "righteousness of God"
connects to justification.[19] This, of course, does not by any means exhaust
all that systematic theologians can or should say about such matters, but
I hope that this is a helpful sketch of how Scripture should shape further
inquiries.

The Scriptural Evidence

The principle biblical evidence pertaining to "the righteousness of God"
for Paul can be consolidated as follows.[20]

We first meet the phrase "the righteousness of God" in Romans 1:17. In
a chain of "for" clauses, Paul explains why he is eager to preach the gospel
in Rome:

> *For* I am not ashamed of the gospel, *for* it is the power of God for salvation to
> everyone who gives allegiance, to the Jew first and also to the Greek. *For* in it
> the righteousness of God is revealed by allegiance for allegiance, as it is written,
> "The righteous one shall live by allegiance." *For* the wrath of God is revealed
> from heaven against all the ungodliness and unrighteousness of men, who by
> their unrighteousness suppress the truth. (Rom. 1:15–18)

(Greek: *dikaioō*), Augustine famously contributed to the medieval synthesis by interpreting the
Latin *iustificare* as "to make righteous" rather than "to declare righteous," taking justification
to be a comprehensive restoration of the individual as righteousness gradually increases (see
pp. 38–54). Meanwhile, reacting to medieval scholastic understandings of "the righteousness of
God" as the quality that compels God to judge sinners as guilty and the righteous as innocent,
Luther, working from the Greek, determined that it instead is the righteous status that humans
passively and instantly receive from God as a declared gift by "faith" (pp. 218–35).

19. Luther's understanding of the righteousness of God as a gift has been questioned by those
favoring a relational framework. For example, N. T. Wright (see esp. *What Saint Paul Really
Said*, 95–111; *Paul and the Faithfulness of God*, 2:925–66) understands it to be God's covenant
faithfulness and not the gift of right standing before God per se. For a thorough (and, at least
to my mind, convincing) critique of Wright's view, see Irons, *Righteousness of God*; cf. Piper,
Future of Justification, 179; Westerholm, *Justification Reconsidered*, 65–73.

20. Rom. 1:17; 3:5; 3:21; 3:22; 3:25; 3:26; 10:3–4 (×2); 2 Cor. 5:21; Phil. 3:9; cf. James 1:20.

We learn, then, that the reason Paul believes that the gospel is the power of God for salvation is that it reveals the righteousness of God in association with a new movement in salvation history (cf. Rom. 3:21). We also discover that the revelation of *the wrath of God* from heaven against unrighteousness is so closely associated with the revelation of *the righteousness of God* that the same judging activity of God appears to be in view. This conclusion is reinforced in Romans 3:5: "But if our unrighteousness demonstrates the righteousness of God, what shall we say? Surely God is not unrighteous when he inflicts wrath on us?" So Romans 1:17 and 3:5 show that the righteousness of God is freshly revealed in the gospel, clarify how the gospel is truly the power of God for salvation, and indicate that it is closely bound up with God's wrath against unrighteousness. The righteousness of God is also revealed *by allegiance for allegiance*—that is, probably, by the Messiah's allegiance to God and for the purpose of fostering our allegiance to the Messiah.[21]

Meanwhile, in Romans 10:3–4 and Philippians 3:9 the meaning of the righteousness of God is constrained in a different way. In Romans 10:3–4 we discover that Paul's compatriots who are outside the Christ have stumbled, not because they did not have zeal, but because they did not have appropriate knowledge concerning the righteousness of God: "For, being ignorant of the righteousness of God and seeking to confirm their own righteousness, they did not submit to the righteousness of God. For the Messiah is the end/goal of the law for righteousness to everyone who gives allegiance."[22] Thus, the righteousness of God is something that Paul believes his compatriots had been ignorant of, had sought to confirm on their own, and had failed to submit to, and he believes it has reached its end/goal in the Christ for everyone who gives allegiance. Meanwhile, Paul gives a closely related statement in Philippians 3:9. Paul in his pre-Jesus days had felt that he had a profit on his ledger, which he further describes as "a righteousness of my own." Yet he concludes that it was in fact rubbish, for he did not have the only thing that can count as profit, the allegiance-based righteousness of God. Furthermore, this righteousness of God is very closely associated with participation in the Christ—in his suffering unto death and his resurrection life (Phil. 3:10–11). So what Paul says about Israel apart from the Messiah in Romans 10:3–4, we find reinforced on the level of the individual in Philippians 3:9–11.

Additionally, we learn something absolutely vital about the righteousness of God from 2 Corinthians 5:21—we can "become" it in the Messiah: "The

21. For discussion, see "Reconsidering 'by Faith for Faith'" in chap. 2.
22. For the translation of *stēsai* as "to confirm" or "to validate," as a slight variation of the traditional "to establish," see Barclay, *Paul and the Gift*, 538.

one who did not know sin, he was made sin for our sake, that in him we might become the righteousness of God." Several observations should be made. First, we become the righteousness of God only "in the Christ." Second, the Messiah-king was made sin "for our sake" or, better, "on our behalf" (*hyper hēmōn*)—that is, for the purpose of our becoming the righteousness of God, or to achieve this result. So there is at least a one-way exchange (the Christ was made "sin," and since it was not his it must be ours). But if the righteousness of God is something that is the Messiah's possession or describes his status in an analogous way to how sin is our possession or describes us, then a two-way exchange is quite possibly implied (our becoming the Messiah's "the righteousness of God").[23]

Romans 3:21–26 contains the highest density of "righteousness of God" language. It has been saved until last because it is the most central. Two additional points about the righteousness of God are fairly straightforward here. Paul declares that "the righteousness of God has now been manifested apart from the law" (3:21), meaning that prior to the Christ event it was *not* present, but it is now present *apart from performing the commandments* enshrined in the Mosaic law. For as Paul has thoroughly demonstrated, "no one will be 'justified' [or declared righteous] through works of law" (Rom. 3:20; cf. 3:28). Nevertheless, the righteousness of God is "*attested* by the Law and the Prophets" (Rom. 3:21), meaning the Old Testament bears witness to it. The Old Testament attests God's judging activity (saving and condemning) and its results. So this freshly unveiled righteousness of God cannot be attained through performing the commandments, yet it is somehow witnessed to by the Law and the Prophets.

As Paul continues, he describes in Romans 3:22 the righteousness of God as "through the *pistis* of Jesus the Christ" and "for all who give *pistis*." Whether the first clause, "through the *pistis* of Jesus the Christ," intends "through the faithfulness of Jesus the Christ to God" or "through our faith in Jesus the Christ" remains a matter of scholarly debate.[24] Nevertheless the second clause, "for all who give *pistis*," suggests with its "for" language that the righteousness of God is a status or gift that is attainable. All have sinned and lack the glory of God, but this is counterbalanced by God's free gift, as all in the Messiah

23. Piper, *Future of Justification*, 174–80, helpfully points out dimensions of exchange in this text.

24. See discussion of the subjective genitive ("the faithfulness of Jesus Christ") and objective genitive ("faith in Jesus Christ") in "Allegiance in Paul's Letters" in chap. 4. Against the objective in Rom. 3:22, consider that it is extremely difficult to explain how human faith in Jesus the Christ could be instrumental in revealing "the righteousness of God" in 3:21, since this is a prior divine action that was already being attested by the Law and the Prophets. For discussion, see D. Campbell, "Romans 1.17," 275–77; Kugler, "ΠΙΣΤΙΣ ΧΡΙΣΤΟΥ," 249–50.

Jesus are "justified." The Messiah was put forward by God as a *hilastērion* ("mercy seat"), the place where atonement was made, which involved the satisfaction of God's wrath and the removal of sins. Paul says that this was a demonstration of God's righteousness, as God had "passed over" or left unpunished previous sins. It was a further demonstration of the righteousness of God in the present moment, so that "he might be just and the justifier of the person by the *pistis* of Jesus" (Rom. 3:26). In sum, the righteousness of God is "for" those who give allegiance and is bound up with God's making Jesus the place of atonement—where God's wrath was satisfied and sins were wiped away. The righteousness of God is also established, probably, through Jesus's allegiance to God as the Messiah.

Defining the Righteousness of God

If we synthesize our observations about the "righteousness of God," the following seven statements emerge as key.[25] The righteousness of God is

1. something that the people of God ("we") become in the Messiah;
2. nearly always associated with *pistis*—whether with the Messiah's allegiance to God or our allegiance to Jesus as the Messiah, or both;
3. tightly linked with atonement and exchange;
4. associated with God's judgment—both his wrathful judgment of sin and his saving judgment unto new resurrection life;
5. frequently connected with union or participation with the Messiah;
6. attested in the Old Testament but cannot be obtained through performing the commandments of Moses either on the individual or corporate level;
7. revealed in the gospel but was not available prior to the Christ event.

In seeking to bring these emphases together into a coherent whole, we must ask ourselves, What story might Paul have had in mind that could produce these multifaceted associations with regard to the righteousness of God? Perhaps the following best brings together Paul's description.

Israel was called to be the people through whom God's righteousness would be made manifest and would be mediated to the nations (e.g., Isa. 51:7; 62:2).

---

25. D. Campbell's analysis (*Deliverance of God*, 683–88) indicates that the righteousness of God in Rom. 1:17 and 3:21–26 must be described in the following terms: (1) as an event; (2) singular—that is, uniquely focused on the Christ event; (3) saving; (4) liberating—that is, involving deliverance from previous oppression; (5) life giving; (6) eschatological/resurrecting; and (7) with genitive flexibility—that is, a definition must maintain flexibility with regard to how "God" relates to "righteousness."

As such, the law of Moses was a righteous standard that held the promise of life, but it was unable to deliver on that promise because of the reign of sin and its death-dealing consequences (Rom. 4:25; Gal. 3:21). Instead of life, the law brought a heightened awareness of sin in the form of the covenant curses (Rom. 5:20; Gal. 3:10). God chose the Messiah, the king, as a righteous representative figure within Israel to bear the sins of Israel (and through Israel, the world): "From the distress of his soul he shall see and be satisfied; by his knowledge *the righteous one*, my servant, *will make many righteous*, and he will bear their iniquities" (Isa. 53:11). In bearing the sins and establishing the righteousness of the many, Jesus as the king was fulfilling a fundamental purpose of Israel: to create one worldwide family in the Messiah characterized by the "righteousness of God."

Jesus the Christ-king is the righteous one, the one who lives through allegiance—just as Scripture attests, "the righteous one will live by allegiance" (Hab. 2:4; Rom. 1:17; Gal. 3:11). But this allegiance to God the Father meant coming "in the likeness of sinful flesh and for sin, in order to condemn sin in the flesh" (Rom. 8:3). It meant "becoming a curse of the law for us" (Gal. 3:13). It meant allowing himself to be put forward as the *hilastērion*, the mercy seat (Rom. 3:25). There the wrath of God, an expression of his righteous judgment against all the ungodliness and wickedness of the world, was focused on Jesus as the *designated Messiah*, the representative king-in-waiting, the one chosen and anointed as king. In his body sin was condemned, but Jesus, because of his *pistis* (allegiance) to God even unto death, was not condemned. Jesus, because he was the sinless, righteous one, was raised up by God unto resurrection life and installed at God's own right hand. As the *enthroned Messiah* his kingly rule has begun. He has now poured out the Holy Spirit so that all who give allegiance to him might be united to him—to his death, his resurrection, and his enthroned glory.

For Paul, then, the righteousness of God is *God's resurrection-effecting verdict that Jesus the wrath-bearing, sin-atoning, allegiant king is alone righteous—a verdict that all who are united to Jesus the representative king share.* This death-unto-resurrection-life verdict is made effective for us as an unmerited gift when we are united by allegiance alone to the death and resurrection of Jesus the king via the Holy Spirit.[26] The result is that "in the

26. This definition is my own (esp. the stress on allegiance), but its formulation depends in part upon discussions by D. Campbell, *Deliverance of God*, 683–704, and esp. Jipp, *Christ Is King*, 244–71. Irons, *Righteousness of God*, esp. 272–336, convincingly shows that, contra N. T. Wright, the phrase does not mean "covenant faithfulness" but the righteous status that God confers (e.g., Rom. 3:21–22) and secondarily the righteous status attained by those who are found to be "in Christ" (e.g., 2 Cor. 5:21)—although I find unstable Irons's restricted understanding of

Messiah-king" we "become the righteousness of God"; that is, we become the family that has died with the Christ and that has been reconstituted "in him" by God's declarative (innocence-creating) yet transformative (resurrection-effecting) verdict. Cleared of guilt, final salvation means above all else joining the family that shares the Messiah's resurrection life. Scripture is clear that this righteousness is properly *the king's righteousness*, not our own righteousness, for we receive this resurrection-effecting verdict only "in the Christ"—that is, initially, presently, and finally only through *pistis*-securing union with Jesus the king, when God declares us righteous "in him."

Imputed Righteousness

So in the past, present, and future our right standing before God is an alien righteousness, for it properly belongs only to Jesus the Christ, and it is ours also only through union with him. Luther, Calvin, and their spiritual descendants in the Protestant Reformation rediscovered and rightly celebrated this. Luther was fond of saying that the Christian is simultaneously just and a sinner. By this Luther did not mean that the Christian remains helplessly trapped, forever wallowing in sin's filth. He meant that God reckons the one who has faith, however filthy he or she might be at that moment, to be righteous in the presence of God. For Luther, the justified Christian has victory over sin, will progress in holiness, and will produce the fruit of good works. Luther meant that as far as our justification proper is concerned, we are declared to be in the right in the presence of God by virtue of our "faith alone" in God's promises to us in Jesus, because Jesus's righteousness is *imputed* to us. For Luther and likeminded Reformers, Jesus's alien righteousness is like a clean garment that is once and for all laid over an individual's filthy rags at the moment of "faith," so that when God judges us he looks only upon Jesus's righteousness; the result is that we are freed from sin's bondage and liberated to progress in holiness.[27]

But here we run into an obstacle. Not only is *pistis* capable of a richer definition, but the transactional idea of the Christ's righteousness being imputed to us so that it *covers* our unclean sins is nowhere to be found in Scripture. There are passages that urge the Christian to "put on the Lord Jesus Christ" (Rom. 13:14) or that affirm that "as many of you as were baptized into the Messiah have put on the Messiah" (Gal. 3:27) and so forth. Meanwhile, there

---

justification that would seem to close it off from reconciliation (see pp. 341–42). On deliverance and transformation, see further my subsequent comments in note 33 below.

27. For the metaphor of Jesus's righteousness as a garment, passively received, that covers our filthy sin, see, e.g., Luther, *Preface to the Latin Writings*.

are texts that speak of God counting or reckoning righteousness on the basis of *pistis* (e.g., Rom. 4:5, 9–11). One passage speaks of the Messiah as having become "wisdom for us from God, and also our *righteousness*, holiness, and redemption" (1 Cor. 1:30), but the context does not pertain to legal declaration. Finally, several of the passages reviewed above speak of our genuine sharing in the righteousness of God as that righteousness has been manifested or made available through and in the Christ (e.g., 2 Cor. 5:21; Phil. 3:8–9). But these various images are not combined.

So, contrary to some expressions within the Lutheran and Reformed traditions, Scripture does *not* affirm in an unqualified fashion that the Messiah's righteousness becomes ours by virtue of *imputation* in the abstract "transactional exchange" or the instantaneous "covering over" sense of this word apart from a prior or simultaneous union. Imputation in this sense is not a preferable biblical concept, category, or term.[28] The language of imputation can be preserved if it retains a more modest valence as a subset of union with the Christ-king. Paul favors the language not of *covering* for imputation, but of *counting* or *reckoning* or *considering* (*logizomai*) for those who are found to be "in the Messiah" (e.g., Rom. 4:3–11, 22–24; 2 Cor. 5:19; Gal. 3:6). Imputation can be maintained from a biblical standpoint only if it is predicated on a prior or simultaneous union and if it is regarded as a counting or reckoning.[29]

When we recognize the limitations in traditional Protestant constructions of imputation, we are in a better position to recognize how the Catholic position on justification offers clues that lead ultimately to a more scripturally faithful understanding of the whole doctrine, even though the Catholic position also needs to be reworked in light of advances in biblical scholarship. The Catholic tradition prefers organic metaphors such as *impartation* or *infusion* in speaking about how justification transpires. Although penned nearly five hundred years ago, the Council of Trent's "Decree Concerning Justification" remains the Catholic Church's most authoritative statement on justification.[30]

---

28. For discussion of traditional Protestant understandings of imputation and their limitations, see Bird, *Saving Righteousness of God*, 60–87; Seifrid, *Christ, Our Righteousness*, 174–75; Wright, *Paul and the Faithfulness of God*, 2:951. These and other studies show that there is no direct NT equivalent to "imputation" as defined and understood by the Reformers and especially their descendants inasmuch as union was not consistently foregrounded.

29. Piper (*Future of Justification*, 123–25) and Schreiner (*Faith Alone*, 179–90), while preferring to maintain imputed righteousness, both correctly stress the necessity of a prior union.

30. The "Decree Concerning Justification" was crafted in Trent's sixth session and was issued on January 13, 1547. All citations are from Schroeder, *Canons and Decrees of the Council of Trent*. Justification is described by the Council as "not only a remission of sins but also the sanctification and renewal of the inward man through the voluntary reception of the grace and gifts whereby an unjust man becomes just" (§7).

Infused Righteousness

Trent teaches that justification, although secured by the merit of Jesus's sacrifice, is not a direct human participation in God's *own* (or Jesus's own) righteousness; that is, justification is "not that by which God himself is just" (§7; cf. canon 10). Although won by Jesus's merits, as a gift it becomes *our own righteousness* through the sacrament of baptism, and it is subsequently developed as God's grace comes alongside us. Moreover, although baptism is the instrumental means by which it comes about, justification has one and only one formal cause: a renewal of the spirit of our mind through the Holy Spirit.[31] The virtues of faith, hope, and charity are "infused" in the act of baptism/justification (§7). This infusion waters the seed of true righteousness that has been *imparted* by the Holy Spirit (received by our cooperation), and this righteousness then grows with God's assistance to the degree that we allow, so that our righteousness/justification might increase (§10). Good works performed with God's grace increase a person's justification, and this increase in justification is necessary to receive the final "crown of justice" at the end of life (§16). Anyone who thinks otherwise is declared cursed and cut off from Christ (canon 24).

So, according to Trent, although we as Christians can have firm hope, we cannot be absolutely confident that our righteousness will increase sufficiently to avoid condemnation, for it is our own (not the Christ's) and depends on our cooperating perseverance (§§11–13). In fact, those who commit a mortal sin (serious and intentional) after baptism lose their justification and must undertake the sacrament of confession and penance in order for justification to be restored (§§14–15).

In sum, for Catholics, as an undeserved gift won by Jesus's merits, God imparts a true seed of righteousness into the heart of the individual at baptism. That righteousness is not a direct participation in the Messiah's righteousness; it is the individual's own righteousness, albeit provided by Jesus's benefits and given by grace. This seed of righteousness can blossom into sufficient righteousness for final salvation through the sacraments and perseverance in good works.

31. Regarding the instrumental and formal cause of justification, the "Decree Concerning Justification," §7, states: "The instrumental cause [of justification] is the sacrament of baptism, which is the sacrament of faith, without which no man was ever justified; finally, the single formal cause is the justice of God, not that by which He Himself is just, but that by which He makes us just, that, namely, with which we being endowed by Him, are renewed in the spirit of our mind, and not only are we reputed but we are truly called and are just, receiving justice within us, each one according to his own measure, which the Holy Ghost distributes to everyone as He wills, according to each one's disposition and cooperation."

Reflecting on Righteousness

Can Trent's formulation help us better understand justification? Yes. But there are also some difficulties that must be discussed first. The Reformers correctly judged, contrary to Trent but according to Scripture, that the formal cause of justification (the "not guilty" verdict rendered over the individual in the past, present, and future) is not a graciously imparted righteousness *that becomes our own*. Rather the formal cause is God's declaration of Jesus as righteous and our union with him as such, so that we share in his resurrection-effecting verdict.

To emphasize an infused righteousness *that becomes our own* and is *gradually nurtured* (achieved in collaboration with God's grace as one participates in the sacraments), as does Trent, is to fail to recognize that the individual who gives *pistis* participates immediately, truly, and fully in the forensic, once-for-all-time declaration of complete "righteousness" that has already been rendered over Jesus the king. The formal cause of our justification is God's resurrection-effecting declaration of the representative king's righteousness, not a righteousness that has become our own (however graciously given) except inasmuch as we are joined to his righteousness so that we come to share in it (all of which Paul terms the "righteousness of God"). The one who gives allegiance has been reconstituted in the king and is a new creation, a new person, and he or she joins with others who collectively have become "the righteousness of God," but only *in the Messiah* (2 Cor. 5:17, 21; Gal. 6:16; Eph. 4:24; Col. 3:10). As such, the formal cause of justification cannot be enhanced or increased by our cooperation as we labor in the sacraments, trusting that God will meet us by increasing our justification through our actions.

Meanwhile, although the official Catholic dogma on justification advanced at Trent needs to be reworked in light of advances in scriptural understanding—especially the formal cause—it does get several important things right. According to the Catholic view, a person's initial justification does indeed stand at the fountainhead of a lifelong process of becoming increasingly righteous. Generally Protestants agree, tending to call the latter "sanctification." But Trent is helpfully clear about this matter, for it straightforwardly affirms that Scripture does not make a clean conceptual division between initial righteousness (traditionally "justification" proper for Protestants) and subsequently enjoyed righteousness (traditionally part of "sanctification" for Protestants). All too often Protestants have treated these as separate, self-contained categories, with the righteousness of "justification" alone deemed relevant for an individual's final salvation, and the

righteousness of "sanctification" regarded as merely the inevitable outworking of a prior justification.[32]

Protestants urgently need to reassess their grammar of salvation. For such
distinctions between initial righteousness (so-called justification) and subsequent righteousness (so-called sanctification) simply cannot be consistently
maintained by a careful exegesis of the specific terms, thought structures,
and categories actually used by even a single one of our biblical authors.
Such terminology promotes an individualistic one-time transaction model of
justification and in so doing does not deal seriously with justification's past,
present, future, communal, and creational dimensions. In the final analysis
Scripture does not make consistent qualitative distinctions between the declared righteousness of the Messiah attained at our initial moment of justification (when we are united with him) and our righteousness in the Messiah
as subsequently nurtured and maintained by the Holy Spirit, as if one or the
other were more primal or important for our final salvation.[33]

Any saving righteousness that we enjoy is predicated on God's justifying
actions. And this righteousness is ours (past, present, and future) by allegiance alone only "in the Christ" as that allegiance is upheld—and all of
this without speaking of sanctification as part of an *ordo salutis*. And since
allegiance (*pistis*) is not disembodied, this involves both a recognition of our
bankruptcy apart from Jesus the righteous king and our enacted loyalty to
him. Hence good works are necessary. These good works involve an enfleshment of *pistis*, an enacted loyalty, an "obedience of faith" (Rom. 1:5) and
are necessary, as the final judgment will be (at least in part) on the basis of
works.[34] So Trent, in stressing the necessity of perseverance in good works,

32. The distinction goes back to Calvin, *Institutes* 3.11.6 (Battles), who asserts that righteousness (or justification) and sanctification are inseparable but distinguishable. He compares
the situation to *light* and *heat* from the sun, saying that just as reason "forbids us to transfer the
peculiar qualities of one to the other" even though they are inseparable, so also with *justification*
and *sanctification*. Calvin's only evidence, however, is 1 Cor. 1:30, which lists "justification"
(*dikaiosynē*) and "sanctification" (*hagiosmos*) as separate items. But it cannot be demonstrated
from Scripture that Paul consistently treats these terms (or the like) as coterminous but separable
categories within regeneration as Calvin imagines, or as discrete stages within an *ordo salutis*.

33. The language of "justification" (*dikaio-*) is generally forensic and declarative, but it also
involves deliverance and transformation. See, among other probable texts, Rom. 1:17; 3:20 (in
light of Ps. 143:2); 3:21–22; 4:25; 5:16–19; 6:16; and esp. Rom. 6:7 ("For the one who has died
has been set free [*dedikaiōtai* or 'has been justified'] from sin"); 2 Cor. 5:21. On this and on the
related imagery in Rom. 8:1–4, 33–34, see Leithart, "Justification as Verdict and Deliverance";
Stegman, "Paul's Use of *Dikaio-* Terminology"; Gorman, *Becoming the Gospel*, 212–96. The
dikaio- word group occasionally entails concepts such as life, resurrection, and liberation from
sin that move beyond declaration to ontological change.

34. See "Obedience of Faith and Law of the Christ" in chap. 4 and "Works and Allegiance
Alone?" in chap. 5.

offers helpful directives that Protestants should consider, even if some of its specific formulations are problematic.

A recent Catholic-Protestant effort to come to agreement about justification makes strides in the right direction. The document resulting from this effort, titled "Joint Declaration on Justification" (1999), was issued by the Catholic Church's Pontifical Council for Promoting Christian Unity and the Lutheran World Federation. Thus, it is not yet affirmed officially by the highest levels of Catholic authority, nor has it been affirmed by all Lutheran fellowships. Nevertheless, in the document it is jointly affirmed that justification "means that Christ himself is our righteousness, in which we share through the Holy Spirit in accord with the will of the Father" (§15). Furthermore, it is also jointly agreed that "persons are by faith united with Christ, who in his person is our righteousness" (§22). Although some have given only a lukewarm reception to this document, I think it makes huge steps toward truth and unity.[35] This new agreement that *the Christ himself is our righteousness* and that salvation is through *pistis*-union with the Christ is both a major breakthrough in ecumenical relations and a very promising realignment (or clarification) for Catholics of Trent's teachings.

For maximal clarity, subsequent ecumenical work should add that Jesus as our atoning, representative Messiah-king is our *declared, realized, and effective righteousness*, and that we genuinely share in the king's liberating righteousness by *pistis alone* as we are declared righteous in him by God upon our own confession of allegiance and come to share in the Holy Spirit (ordinarily at baptism). The Messiah's righteousness (that is, the resurrection-effecting verdict that he possesses) is then maintained and infused by our collaboration with the Holy Spirit, so that in him we become the righteousness of God (that is, we share in the Christ's resurrection-effecting verdict). This *pistis* is not primarily "faith" or "trust" or "belief" in the validity of God's promise that we are justified (righteous) in Jesus—and this misplaced emphasis characteristic of the Reformation era still holds sway today. Rather, this *pistis* is especially submissive and embodied *allegiance* to Jesus as the ruling Messiah, an allegiance that forges and maintains union with Jesus the righteous king.

One can only hope the preliminary statements in the "Joint Declaration" will be subsequently reaffirmed and strengthened within Catholicism by more authoritative conciliar documents and within Protestantism by confessions and official denominational position papers (and the like). The righteousness of God, God's resurrection-effecting verdict rendered over Jesus the anointed

35. For diverse responses to the "Joint Declaration," see Aune, *Rereading Paul Together*.

king, alone suffices for us as we remain in union with Jesus the enthroned king through rendered *pistis*—intellectual agreement with the gospel, declared allegiance, and embodied loyalty.

Incorporated Righteousness

As we have seen, both the traditional Lutheran/Reformed view of *imputed* righteousness and the Catholic position favoring *imparted* and *infused* righteousness preserve valid insights into justification. Both also have shortcomings. Accordingly, rather than *imputed* or *infused* righteousness, new terminology should be considered.

Imputed righteousness correctly reminds us that Jesus the Messiah has been declared righteous and totally vindicated, and that our own justification, past, present, and future, is predicated on his righteousness. Yet unless classical notions of imputation are reduced from instantly "covering" to an in-the-Christ "reckoning" or "considering" (per *logizomai* in Gal. 3:6 and elsewhere)—which does not really clarify how the "reckoning" transpires, then imputation cannot be regarded as a biblical concept or term. That is, apart from a prior (or simultaneous) *union* with the Messiah, imputed righteousness collapses. The declared righteousness (received status of innocence unto resurrection life) that properly belongs to the Messiah alone is declared ours through union with Jesus as the crucified, vindicated, and enthroned king. Salvation is sharing in Jesus's life, death, resurrection, and kingly glory.

Meanwhile, imparted righteousness also fails to front union sufficiently. The Bible's description of justification does not suggest that we are given a righteousness (through Jesus's merit) that then becomes our own when it is imparted as a gift at baptism, nor does it suggest that we work with God's grace (through the sacraments) to increase our own deposit of righteousness in order to receive final justification.[36] This is precisely why the realigning affirmation that "Christ himself is our righteousness" by the Catholic com-

---

36. While it is true that God's grace is sacramentally present to us in multitudinous ways (far beyond the seven formalized for Catholics in the Middle Ages as the sacraments), at the same time Paul is emphatic that we can secure righteousness only through *pistis* to Jesus the king, not by participating in an enumerated list of prescribed activities (see "Works of Law as Rule Performance" in chap. 5). The sacraments can be (and undoubtedly usually are) undertaken as acts of allegiance. They can joyfully be performed and celebrated as such! But when Catholic dogma (e.g., Trent) insists that right standing with God is inescapably bound up with completing prescribed sacramental activities (e.g., reconciliation or penance) as a required condition for final justification, because they contribute to the growth of a righteousness that has become our own, then this conclusion must be resisted as both unscriptural and dangerous. The realignments offered by the "Joint Declaration" give hope that Catholic and Protestant understandings of justification are in the process of being clarified and updated.

mission responsible for the "Joint Declaration" is such an encouraging step forward in Catholic-Protestant dialogue.

On the other hand, infused righteousness does front union, and so it is a helpful metaphor; but it is inadequate as a standalone description of how we attain a right standing before God.[37] Infused righteousness remains helpful inasmuch as we are limbs of the body of Jesus the Christ (e.g., Rom. 12:5; 1 Cor. 12:12; Eph. 3:6), much as in John's metaphor of Jesus as the vine and ourselves as the branches (John 15:1–5). So we might think of declared allegiance and initial receipt of the Holy Spirit as the first moment of grafting into Jesus the king (creating the union), and enacted loyalty as ensuring the continual flow of benefits (that which maintains the union). An organic metaphor, such as infusion, that suggests the flowing over of the Messiah's righteousness and resurrection life into us upon declaration of allegiance is totally appropriate so long as it is clear that the righteousness communicated properly belongs to Jesus as the Christ and only derivatively to us (that is, it is never imparted so that it becomes our own independently). Nor is this simply a one-time infusion, but rather it is critical that the life-giving sap of righteousness (received status of innocence unto resurrection life) continues to link the individual to King Jesus via the Holy Spirit. In other words, perseverance is required. This lifelong infused righteousness (which is shared but originates and flows from the Christ to us) does pertain to our final justification as, scripturally speaking, it is not different in quality than the righteousness associated with initial justification.

In bringing this chapter to a conclusion, we may ask whether there is a phrase that can capture the valid insights in imputed and infused righteousness, minimize inadequacies, and stay near to the Bible's own idiom. In answer, rather than imputed or infused righteousness, it is better to speak of in-the-Messiah righteousness or incorporated righteousness.[38] *In-the-*

---

37. Since gradually infused righteousness does not result in that individual's own *perfect* righteousness—for we continue to fall short of God's glory by sinning in many ways (as Trent [esp. canon 23] readily acknowledges for everyone except the Virgin Mary)—it proves to be a theologically insufficient formal cause for past, present, or future justification. The perfect righteousness that God's justice demands (Gal. 3:10; 5:3–4; James 2:10) can only be met by imperfect sinners through an allegiance-forging union with the representative king, so that we immediately and fully share in the righteousness of God associated with the Messiah's perfect atoning sacrifice and resurrection.

38. See Bird, *Saving Righteousness of God*, 60–87. While suggesting "incorporated righteousness," Bird nevertheless feels imputation is still a sufficiently accurate shorthand for systematic purposes. I agree with Bird, Piper, Schreiner, and others that imputed righteousness can be retained if it is clear that imputation depends on *union* and is restricted to "counting" or "reckoning." Yet in the end I judge that it is better to shift to discourse that is less loaded with Reformation-era baggage and that more straightforwardly reflects NT teachings.

Messiah or *incorporated righteousness* can be defined as *the saving perfect righteousness of Jesus the Christ that is counted entirely ours when we join the Spirit-filled body that is already united to the righteous one, Christ the kingly head.* That is, this alien righteousness, this righteous standing that properly belongs to Jesus alone, becomes ours derivatively when we give allegiance to Jesus as the sovereign king, at which moment the life-giving Spirit that already envelops the allegiance-yielding community also enters into us. At the moment of allegiance-generated, Spirit-enabled union, the individual is born again, is declared and truly is *fully* righteous in God's sight, and can properly be described as having eternal life because and only because she or he is united to Jesus the king and so shares his totally righteous standing. Paul envisions all of this ordinarily happening as part of the baptismal process.

As nearly all Christians agree, perseverance in allegiance is required.[39] If the union were to be severed by an unrepentant cessation of *pistis* (allegiance to Jesus as Messiah-king), then the continuing presence of the union-securing and fruit-producing Spirit would be decisively ruptured; the born-again person would experience spiritual death. That individual would no longer be justified, righteous, or innocent before God; eternal life would no longer be a present possession. Christian traditions disagree about whether or not such a severance is possible. Reformed and some Lutheran Christians prefer to speak of the impossibility of rupture ("eternal security").[40] Meanwhile, Catholic, Orthodox, and some Protestant traditions believe that it is possible for an individual to enter decisively into saving union but then to depart through an unrepentant turning away.[41] This debate should not, however, obscure the larger point about which Christian theologians are nearly unanimous: it is

---

39. As an exception, consider those associated with the free-grace movement such as Hodges (*Absolutely Free*) and Stanley (*Eternal Security*) (see "Not Reducible to Intellectual Assent" in chap. 1). On salvation despite temporary disloyalty, see "Struggling with Sin?" in chap. 5.

40. For a vigorous defense of perseverance and eternal security, see Schreiner and Caneday, *Race Set Before Us*. Consider the summarizing remarks of Piper, *Future of Justification*, 181–88, here 184, as representative of the eternal security position: "Through faith alone, God establishes our union with Christ. This union will never fail, because in Christ God is for us as an omnipotent Father who sustains our faith, and works all things together for our everlasting good. The one and only instrument through which God preserves our union with Christ is faith in Christ—the purely *receiving* act of the soul." Unfortunately, in my judgment, Piper's summary here is faulty because it is built on assumptions about what "faith" (*pistis*) and "grace" (*charis*) mean that are implausible for the NT time period (e.g., faith is not a "purely receiving act of the soul"). See discussion of how these two terms are inclusive of an active, embodied obedience in chaps. 4 and 5, respectively.

41. For arguments against eternal security, see McKnight, "Warning Passages of Hebrews." Students may especially appreciate the diverse statements and responses in Pinson, *Four Views on Eternal Security*.

necessary for an individual to persevere in *pistis* throughout the course of her or his lifetime in order to attain final salvation.

Justification and Allegiance Alone

In sum, the language of justification is controversial and complex. The location of justification as a discrete stage in an individualized *ordo salutis* is problematic. Ultimately Scripture does not give much attention to justification as a discrete stage within the sequence of an individual's salvation, preferring to speak in collective terms about God's election of Jesus the king and derivatively of the election of the people of God only in and through him. Properly speaking, only Jesus the Christ alone has been justified and glorified, but a person's present justification and glorification is real through union with his death and resurrection. This righteousness is best described neither as imputed nor as infused, but rather as incorporated.

It is necessary for final salvation that we (individually and collectively) be declared innocent by God. Toward that end, we must participate in "the righteousness of God," the resurrection-effecting verdict rendered by God over Jesus the Messiah, which occurs by *pistis* alone when the Holy Spirit unites us with him. Paul understands this union to be secured through the baptismal process, at which time repentance is embodied by the washing away of sins in the water, allegiance (*pistis*) is publically confessed, and the Spirit is invoked. For Paul *the righteousness of God is God's resurrection-effecting verdict that Jesus the wrath-bearing, sin-atoning, allegiant king is alone righteous—a verdict that all who are united to Jesus the representative king share.* Salvation means sharing in the righteousness of God, the verdict that Jesus the anointed king received unto resurrection life. Scripture is clear that this righteousness is properly *the king's righteousness*, not our own righteousness, for we receive right standing "in the Christ" initially, presently, and finally only through *pistis*-securing union with Jesus the king when God declares us righteous in him. Accordingly, our ongoing and future justification depends on the maintenance of our righteousness-union with Jesus the saving king. We are saved past, present, and future through allegiance alone as that allegiance forges a union with the Messiah through the Holy Spirit.

Our past and present justification is not a legal fiction, for if we have given allegiance (*pistis*) to Jesus the king, we genuinely share in the unshakable, irreversible verdict of innocence that the resurrected Jesus enjoys. Jesus will never be judged again in the future. Jesus the king already stands justified, and so does every person who gives allegiance, because they are incorporated into his righteousness, found to be "in him." In this indirect sense the Christian does not come under judgment but has eternal life, because the one who gives allegiance is united to the head, King Jesus. That person has died, and his or her life is now "hidden with the Christ in God," so that when the Christ appears, that person as a member of the Christ's body will also appear with the Christ in glory (Col. 3:3–4).

Although indirectly already justified and glorified, those who remain loyal to the Messiah will still be *directly* justified and glorified in the future when each one passes through the final judgment. At that time the union-securing allegiance to the Messiah (as established by intellectual affirmation of the truthfulness of the gospel, sworn fealty, and embodied loyalty) must be present in order for the individual to be declared innocent ("justified"). Since genuine allegiance cannot be disembodied, allegiance will be manifested by good works performed in union with Jesus the Christ through the Holy Spirit and judged accordingly.

True allegiance is enacted. But inasmuch as we remain "in him," participating in his Spirit-filled corporate body, that final judgment has already truly been traversed, because his resurrection life is already at work in our bodies and hence in our embodiment. We have been declared "righteous" (and truly are righteous) as the life-giving, good-works-producing Spirit flows in us, for we are united to the righteous one, Jesus the king.

—————— FOR FURTHER THOUGHT ——————

1. What's the difference between the history of salvation and the order of salvation? Why are both worthy of attention?

2. What are some problems with classic articulations of an order of salvation?

3. What is the difference between individual and corporate election? Why might the difference be important for how we understand justification?

4. If justification, for Paul, is not best described as a step or a stage in an individualized order of salvation, then how is it best described?

5. For Paul, how does justification relate to glorification?

6. What does the resurrection of the Messiah have to do with our justification? What do we learn through this about the meaning of the interconnection between Jesus the king's righteousness and the meaning of "the righteousness of God"?

7. If "the righteousness of God" is considered merely God's fairness in judging, what biblical data would this fail to account for? Likewise, what is excluded if it is merely considered God's saving activity? Or God's gift of right standing?

8. Why might it be important to see that God's justifying activity goes beyond declaration to liberation?

9. What is imputed righteousness? What does it accurately express? What are some of its limitations?

10. What is imparted righteousness? Infused righteousness? What do these terms accurately express? What are some limitations?

11. Within the model of incorporated righteousness, how can a sinner come to be declared righteous in God's presence?

9

PRACTICING ALLEGIANCE

The gospel was given as an unchanging, permanent proclamation by Jesus and the apostles to the church for the sake of the world. But at the same time we have our own cultural ideas about the gospel and salvation—ideas that have been informed by our familiarity with the original but also, for both better and worse, by subsequent church history and our own contemporary culture. The gospel can never be modified, but it can be clarified, and it must uniquely inform each generation. Our ability to successfully retrieve the gospel today depends on our adroitness in negotiating these ancient and modern horizons.

Accordingly, the bulk of this book has been purposed toward exposing ancient meanings and contrasting them with contemporary understandings. How were the gospel, "faith," works, and salvation understood by the earliest Christians? And how did these categories interface with related topics such as justification, sanctification, baptism, the final judgment, and heaven? By pursuing a historically informed approach throughout this book, it is hoped that new light has been shed on that old but ever-fresh story.

The whole of this book intends to be practical for the church—not as a how-to manual but in casting vision—to help clarify central theological matters so that today's church can more effectively achieve its mission. This final chapter seeks to tease out the implications of the salvation-by-allegiance-alone thesis by making a couple directed comments about specific applications for the church today. But I want to begin with an analogy that seeks to combine several facets of our study into one comprehensive image.

Comparisons can help us understand and remember complex information, but we also must recognize their limitations. For example, when God
is compared to a lion (e.g., Job 10:16; Jer. 49:19; Hos. 5:14), we must bear in
mind that there are ways in which God is very much like a lion (e.g., able to
bring swift disaster) and other ways in which he is not at all like a lion. God
is not yellowish-brown in color, nor does he have four velvety paws—with
all due respect to C. S. Lewis! So please recognize that all metaphors limp,
and this one may be so poorly contrived that it merely crawls. Nevertheless,
with a little encouragement from the apostle Paul, who exhorts us to take
up "the shield of 'faith'" (Eph. 6:16), I invite you to consider the metaphor
of a shield.

The Shield of Allegiance

As a portion of the full armor of God, we are instructed to take up "the shield
of 'faith'" so that we can "extinguish all the flaming darts of the evil one"
(Eph. 6:16). I want you to imagine *pistis*—what has traditionally been called
"faith" but what I have argued is better comprehensively regarded as "allegiance" when discussing salvation—as a circular shield that can ably protect
you from the schemes of the evil one, preserving you for eternal life. For the
allegiance to be saving, each person must have their own unique allegiance
shield. And all three surfaces of the shield—the inside, the edge, and the
front—must be properly crafted in order for the shield to serve its purpose of
securing eternal life. But how does one first acquire a shield of allegiance? As
was discussed in chapter 5, ultimately it can only come from outside oneself,
as a gift from God, when this gift is freely received.

For your shield to be effective, it must have a sturdy interior. In fact, for
it to be a saving shield of allegiance, only one type of interior will suffice.
Looking at the inside of your shield, the portion you hold close to your body,
you find the eight stages of Jesus's life story (the gospel) indelibly etched into
the metal, signifying that you, as the owner of the shield, mentally agree with
their truthfulness.

The Gospel: An Outline
Jesus the king

1. preexisted with the Father,
2. took on human flesh, fulfilling God's promises to David,
3. died for sins in accordance with the Scriptures,

4. was buried,

5. was raised on the third day in accordance with the Scriptures,

6. appeared to many,

7. *is seated at the right hand of God as Lord*, and

8. will come again as judge.

If you can affirm the truthfulness of the eight stages that comprise the gospel, then you can heft the shield, and the first component of saving allegiance is in place.

Then your eyes are drawn to the edge of the shield (the flat but circular surface that binds the inside of the shield to its outer face). Again, one and only one thing can appear on the edge for it to function ably as a saving-allegiance shield. You see the words "I profess that Jesus is Lord" embossed there, encircling the entire shield—that is, you see your own personal confession of loyalty. These are the words you spoke (exactly or in essence) when you first committed yourself to the service of Jesus as the true king of heaven and earth. It is this edge that holds the entire shield together, and fittingly so, for the confession of loyalty is the formal gateway to salvation—but it is inseparable from the whole shield of allegiance.[1]

Now, flipping the shield over, on the front side you see something strange. The metallic front of your shield is decorated with a marvelous engraving. It is a picture of your own image—wait!—it is a picture of Jesus the Christ. Stunningly, somehow the front of the shield is liquid metal, a moving picture—a picture of *your own image in the process of being transformed into the superimposed image of Jesus the resurrected king*. It a picture of your own current life story in process. You, through embodied fidelity to Jesus, are increasingly taking on his character qualities and participating in his proper stewardship over creation. You are becoming conformed to his image. Again, this enacted fidelity is not an optional extra but is a crucial portion of the allegiance shield. And on the front of the shield above this fluid image you notice a fixed banner announcing the royal household to which you belong. The color of the banner is crimson and white, and it reads "Child of God."

After a lifetime of weary battles, your shield of allegiance (which is already your present possession) will have served its purpose. Many of your comrades will still be fighting the battle, but, having died while remaining in Jesus the Messiah, your time for waging war will have ended. Yet at some

---

1. On how initial allegiance relates to the baptismal process, see "Justification as Union, Not Order" in chap. 8.

distant point in time, after the final battle, you will hear the blast of a re-
sounding trumpet! Those who are dead in the Christ will be raised (1 Thess.
4:16–18). Suddenly your renewed, transformed body, identical to the transformed image on the shield, will leap from the dust of the earth and begin
to walk about, fully embodied. Now changed so that you fully conform to
the image of the king, you journey into the new creation, faintly recognizing
the dim impressions from the old heaven and earth that have been drawn
by God into the new. Already having begun to reign with the Christ and
to share in his glory in your previous life, in your resurrected body you are
now ready to reign over creation with him fully as a nondistorted image of
God.

Each surface of the shield is necessary for a saving allegiance—mental
affirmation of the truthfulness of the gospel, declaration of fealty to Jesus
as the sovereign ruler, and embodied loyalty to Jesus as the king. The goal
of salvation is resurrection life: to join with Jesus the king and the rest of
God's people in ruling the new creation; to become a true idol of God now
conformed to the image of the Christ Jesus.

Toward a Better Gospel Invitation

We have been commissioned to share the good news about Jesus the Christ far
and wide, to extend God's saving offer of kingdom citizenship. How can we
do it more effectively? There are countless ways to present the gospel—casual
conversations, formal sermons, classroom teaching, books, tracts, songs, street
performances, protests, dances, plays, revivals, prayer meetings, mission trips.
The list could go on. Not all methods are equally effective. Nor is there an
ideal, archetypical technique for sharing the gospel—as if finding the right
program or formula is the key to unlocking the mysterious human heart. The
New Testament itself implicitly warns against a one-size-fits-all solution, as it
evidences a diversity in style, genre, approach, and technique. So the best way
to present the gospel will largely depend on the Spirit's leading with respect
to the specific people, contexts, and situations.

But in every case, for it to be a gospel invitation, it must be *the actual gospel*
that is presented in proper relationship to larger ideas of "faith," works, and
salvation, not a pale approximation. So while we can't specify the best method
or program, we can discern appropriate content and safeguard against common missteps. Drawing together many of the leading themes of this book,
the remarks that follow are offered in the hope that they can contribute to a
more accurate and effective gospel proclamation.

The Gospel Foregrounds Jesus as King

This point should be regarded as absolutely nonnegotiable: a true gospel invitation must summon the hearer toward a confession of allegiance to Jesus as the king or cosmic Lord. Although none of the eight elements that make up the full gospel can be excluded as nonessential (see the next subsection), one carries extra weight: *Jesus is seated at the right hand of God as Lord.* Why? First, this element shows that saving *pistis* is not primarily faith in forgiveness of sins or trust in God's promise to make us righteous (although it involves those things too), but is above all allegiance to Jesus as the Christ, the one who shares in God's very throne. Jesus as the universal *Lord* is the primary object toward which our saving "faith"—that is, our saving allegiance—is directed. We must stop asking others to invite Jesus into their hearts and start asking them to swear allegiance to Jesus the king. Second, all the other elements that make up the gospel refer to past or future events in Jesus's career, whereas the kingdom of God has been launched and Jesus is *presently* ruling the entire cosmos. Accordingly, the presence of the king and his kingdom fundamentally determines all current and future reality. *The present-tense moment of choice in a gospel invitation should always be understood to be a response to the present-tense reality of Jesus's kingly rule.*

Most of the confusion about the gospel in our contemporary church culture stems from a failure to see that "Jesus is the king" is the high point of the good news. In a "salvation culture" it may be eagerly acknowledged that "Jesus is Lord," but Jesus's cross is what saves us, not his resurrection or lordship, so that lordship can be freely ignored without risking salvation. This is a dangerous error. A "gospel culture," on the other hand, recognizes that "Jesus is king" is integral to the good news itself, affirming that we indeed are saved by Jesus's sacrifice and resurrection, but these are only personally effective when allegiance to Jesus as king forges a union with him.

Jesus's Story, Not a Procedure

If we find ourselves in a salvation culture rather than a gospel culture in the church today, it is also because we have failed to give the gospel its due as a grand, sweeping cosmic drama that encompasses Jesus's *entire* career. Instead the gospel is treated as a step-by-step process focused on saving the individual hearer. In this process, the hearer is gradually made aware of her or his sinfulness and need for a savior, and God's provision through "faith" in Jesus's death for sins. While this process captures portions of the truth, it introduces serious distortions, so it is absolutely imperative that we recognize that this is not the gospel. Any authentic gospel invitation must recount (or

otherwise presuppose or imply) its eight constituent parts noted above. These
are the nonnegotiable elements that together make up the full gospel.

Can the Gospel Be Reduced?

These eight elements that constitute the whole gospel can remain condensed or be expanded in great detail, but any gospel invitation that leaves
out a portion of the gospel can put the hearer at risk of misunderstanding
or of an insufficient response—for the hearer has not received or responded
to the complete gospel. Above all, because the error is so common, it must
be emphasized that the gospel cannot be accurately reduced to a forgiveness
transaction, as in the slogans "I am trusting in Jesus's righteousness alone" or
"Believe that Jesus died for your sins and you will be saved." For forgiveness
of sins is just one element in the gospel, and these slogans do not aim saving
pistis at the climax of the gospel.

Similarly, the gospel cannot be reduced to behaving in a cross-shaped manner or to social programs. Saint Francis of Assisi is often remembered to have
said, "Preach the gospel at all times; use words if necessary." This is a clever
saying (although its origination with Saint Francis is historically dubious),
because we all recognize that sometimes actions do speak more forcefully than
words. But it is dreadfully wrongheaded to suggest that *the gospel* is best (or
even adequately) proclaimed by actions unencumbered by words. It is also
off-base to think that Christian social activities, such as providing assistance
to the poor, are the gospel—even though it is popular in some quarters to
call such activities the "social gospel." Such actions *might* serve to remind
those who benefit of part of the gospel story *once they hear it elsewhere* or
if they already know it. But the actions themselves only become a gospel
proclamation derivatively, when the recipient hears the full gospel elsewhere
and then is able to make the link between the actions and the full narrative.[2]
Because we are uncomfortable sharing the gospel, afraid that we will turn
someone off or be perceived in the wrong way, we can convince ourselves that
the gospel is best communicated with actions, not words. But the true gospel
is not reducible to Christian activities.

This does not mean that all eight elements of the gospel must be slavishly
rehearsed in any single gospel presentation. That is, the risk of ill effects
because of selective omission of some of the elements is minimal in some
contexts. For example, if a person is proclaiming the gospel in a church setting, Jesus's preexistence with God and arrival in the Davidic line are probably

---

2. For further reflections on this point, see Carson, "What Is the Gospel?—Revisited,"
147–70, esp. 158.

already known and accepted facts, so they need not always be spelled out. Or they might be evoked by mentioning a gospel-related fact, such as Jesus's virgin birth. Similarly, it is obviously not necessary to mention Jesus's burial every single time the gospel is presented, for it is implicit in Jesus's death and resurrection. So the eight elements need not be doggedly reproduced for every gospel invitation. Still, there are several reasons that a fuller narrative should be preferred.

Retaining the Entire Gospel Story

Although omission of certain elements will sometimes be sensible, nevertheless gospel invitations should err on the side of completeness so that the church can recover the storied dimension of the gospel. For when we proclaim the entirety, it implicitly positions the reader to see that the proper response to the story is not just "faith" in the sense of belief or trust, but is allegiance to the enthroned king. There are three further reasons that the complete narrative is preferable.

First, the full gospel keeps the focus squarely on Jesus rather than on the self, compelling the self to be swept up into the saving story of Jesus, rather than allowing the self to remain at the center. The gospel proper is not a salvation procedure focused on the individual. It is the universe-wide story of Jesus's entire revealed life—from preexistence to anticipated return—a story that unveils God's saving power for the whole created order. It is a salvation story into which the individual can be whisked up when he or she joins the allegiant community. Gospel culture facilitates total integration of the forgiven self into the cosmic Jesus story; salvation culture encourages the self to stanch the flowing sin-wounds by applying a forgiven-so-I-can-go-to-heaven tourniquet, but it does little to remove the self from the center.[3]

Second, hearing a good story is more compelling than analyzing a list of propositions. A salvation procedure says: "Let me walk you through a few facts, and let's see if I can get you to agree with them, and if so, then I challenge you to take action." When an audience is marched half-willingly through a salvation procedure, they can perhaps be excused for feeling that a slick salesman is trying to hoodwink them into buying a product. A good story immerses—and the gospel is the greatest of all stories. It allows the hearer to enter into another time, place, and space to recognize his or her own face among the hostile crowds wrongly putting Jesus to death. The hearer feels

---

3. For further remarks on leaving behind a salvation culture to create a gospel culture, see the whole of McKnight, *King Jesus Gospel*, but esp. 146–60.

the plot tension rise to a climax in the crucifixion, and then is flooded with glad relief when it resolves in the resurrection and enthronement.

When the full gospel is presented, the call to action is organically embedded in the story. Jesus the enthroned king has summoned everyone, including you and me, to turn away from all other allegiances and to give him exclusive loyalty. If we declare allegiance to him, he will send his Spirit so that we will be united with him—forgiven and liberated from sin—and can subsequently maintain allegiance (however imperfectly). When a gospel invitation retains its natural storied shape, the hearer does not feel like he or she has been manipulated into a halfhearted agreement with random factual propositions; the call to action emerges organically from the story into which the hearer has been drawn. Jesus has become the king by offering himself so that his enemies might receive forgiveness: will you repent from hostilities and pledge him your loyalty, receiving forgiveness and the gift of resurrection life?

Third, story is foundational to worldview construction and maintenance since (arguably) all comprehensive explanations of existence ultimately take a storied shape. True repentance that accompanies salvation entails a certain amount of worldview reconstruction, but for that reconstruction to transpire in harmony with reason, it must rely on a foundational master story or metanarrative. The gospel story of Jesus integrates and serves as the climax to the larger Christian metanarrative: the story of God's creation, the fall, the election of Israel, the gospel, the establishment of the missional church, and the future renewal of creation.[4] When we issue an invitation, preserving the gospel as the complete story of Jesus's career and as the capstone to the Christian metanarrative helps the repentant sinner to undertake a gospel-centered rather than salvation-centered worldview reconstruction. Remembering that *pistis* is not directly equivalent to the English word *faith* also helps us avoid the false idea that Christian salvation is beyond, or contrary to, evidence or reason. Since Jesus's kingship is the fitting capstone to the whole biblical story, is the fulfillment of scriptural prophecy, and accords with our experience, allegiance to Jesus as the cosmic king is based on evidence and is reasonable.

God's Holistic Transformative Power

A better gospel invitation will maintain an emphasis on personal forgiveness of sins and eternal life as an effect of receiving the good news but will not emphasize heaven. Heaven is best regarded as a temporary abode where we

---

4. For a primer, see Bartholomew and Goheen, *Drama of Scripture*.

await the real goal, God's new creation (which is really a radical restoration of the present creation). Rather than focusing on heaven as the place where the disembodied soul experiences bliss after death, we should speak of the aim of salvation in holistic terms.

In the gospel, God's power to make things right is revealed, and the effects are personal, social, and cosmic. Human salvation is directed toward God's intention to restore individuals, communities, and the world as the kingdom of God continues to break into history. When we give allegiance, we become new creatures set free from the enslaving power of sin. As we worship the Son of God, who is the authentic, original image of God, our own distorted Adamic image is transformed, so that we are personally renewed. As we are transformed into the image of Jesus the Christ, we bring God's wise service, stewardship, and rule to one another and to the remainder of creation. Paul in fact declares that the whole creation waits in eager expectation for the full revelation of the sons (and daughters) of God (Rom. 8:19). That is, the frustrated creation is groaning as it yearns for the sons and daughters of God (refreshed in their glorious visage so that they are fully authentic image-bearers) to take up their God-intended role as stewards.

When allegiance is given to Jesus the king, God's making all things right, his holistic salvation, moves forward, for we increasingly are able to mediate God's presence to others and to the rest of creation. It begins as individuals are united to Jesus and to one another in the church, and then it spills out to the world. Someday the whole creation will attain to its full measure of life-sustaining fruitfulness. The citizens of the new Jerusalem will gaze directly at the face of Jesus the king, the Lamb of God. And the final transformation into the image of Jesus the Messiah will be complete, so that "the earth will be filled with the knowledge of the glory of the LORD as the waters cover the sea" (Hab. 2:14).

False Assurance, Perseverance, and Works

A better gospel presentation will not give total assurance of the security of final salvation on the basis of the acceptance of the gospel invitation. It may be pastorally pleasant to say, "If you prayed this prayer with me, and you sincerely asked Jesus into your heart, then you can have complete confidence that you are now eternally saved and on the road to heaven." This sort of comfort is precisely what the audience loves to hear, making it tempting to give it, but unfortunately it is a *false assurance*. To suggest otherwise is dangerous. Those who remain "in the Christ" do have perfect assurance of final salvation in and through him, but we cannot have perfect assurance that any single person without doubt is "in the Christ."

That this is false assurance should be recognized even by those who hold to "once saved, always saved" or "eternally secure" theological convictions. For since a person can be self-deceived about the sincerity of "faith," and since even an unregenerate person produces some good works, a person can never have complete assurance that he or she is "in the Christ," only overwhelming confidence. And if an individual's inability to attain perfect assurance must be affirmed even by those who hold to the "once saved, always saved" conviction, how much more is it true for those who are unpersuaded by that position? Christian theologians may disagree about whether it is possible for an individual to start along the path of salvation but then depart permanently from the path, but there is virtually no disagreement regarding the need for all who start along the path to persevere in order to attain ultimate salvation (see "Incorporated Righteousness" in chap. 8). So a better gospel presentation will emphasize that allegiance (*pistis*), once rendered, *must persevere* through God's assistance for it to result in final salvation.

The role of works in final salvation is a closely related matter. Although it is a finer theological point that is probably more suitable for leaders to ponder than to be directly featured as part of a gospel invitation to non-Christians, those presenting the gospel should be equipped to handle questions about works in final salvation. Since at the final judgment we will be assessed for eternal life at least in part on the basis of our works, a better gospel invitation will not polemicize in an unqualified fashion about "faith, not works," but will leave room for good works (not good works produced on our own through rule-keeping, but good works embodied in allegiant union with Jesus) in our final justification. For such good works are indicative of enacted and maintained *pistis*. Our own past, present, and future verdict of "righteous" depends entirely on our past, present, and future union with the Christ, so that by *pistis* we share his righteousness through the good-works-producing Holy Spirit. For final salvation, declared allegiance must be embodied and maintained as the Holy Spirit enables us to perform good works pleasing to God.

In sum, we have perfect assurance in the Christ, so we do not want to discourage the truly allegiant so that they lack firm assurance. But since at the same time, because we cannot be absolutely certain that any person is in fact "in the Christ," we should not offer total instantaneous assurance of final salvation when presenting the gospel. Instantaneous assurance compromises the allegiance-demanding gospel and spiritually endangers anyone who blithely accepts it.

Public Allegiance

Finally, a better gospel invitation will not allow the definitive decision to give allegiance to Jesus as king to remain a private matter. All such decisions must originate with a personal conviction in the mind/heart/will, and it is perfectly acceptable to give ample space for private reflection as part of a gospel proclamation. But it should not be suggested as part of a gospel invitation that privately agreeing or praying a certain prayer or "trusting in your heart" has a saving effect on its own. Perhaps a private declaration of allegiance in the heart is saving, perhaps not. But in any case when Scripture describes what is necessary for salvation, it does not speak of a private conviction as saving unless it is acknowledged to others.[5] For us to ratify our saving union with Jesus, God instructs us to declare our allegiance in the presence of others through baptism. So any gospel invitation should provide an obvious mechanism so that anyone who has responded can immediately bear witness to another. Meanwhile, the invitation should also encourage anyone who has responded to certify the change of allegiance publicly through baptism or rededication as soon as is feasible.

So what does a better gospel invitation look like? When sharing God's saving message, we must stop asking others to invite Jesus into their hearts and start asking them to swear public allegiance to Jesus the king. We must also urge that there is only one path to final salvation, the path of discipleship.

Discipleship Is Salvation

Dallas Willard describes a typical view of "faith" and salvation that he encountered many times among professing Christians, including pastors. He calls it "bar-code faith."

> Think of the bar codes now used on goods in most stores. The scanner responds only to the bar code. It makes no difference what is in the bottle or package that bears it, or whether the sticker is on the "right" one or not. The calculator responds through its electronic eye to the bar code and totally disregards

5. See "Dimensions of Allegiance" in chap. 4. Regarding private (nonpublic) yielding of *pistis*, although *pistis* does have dimensions of interiority (emotion, cognition, and virtue) in the NT, it does not denote an interior movement of the will in the NT era in the fashion stressed by Augustine and the Reformers. Rather it is primarily an outward manifestation of trust or loyalty. See Morgan, *Roman Faith and Christian Faith*, 11–12, 28–30, 224–30, 444–72. Of course, this is not to say that an interior movement of the will is absent from the *pistis* word family in the NT, but it does prove that it is unlikely that our NT authors seized upon that as the truly essential thing apart from its outward, bodily expression.

everything else. If the ice cream sticker is on the dog food, the dog food is ice cream, so far as the scanner knows or cares.[6]

Willard explains that much popular Christian theology regards "belief" (or the like) as the bar code and God as the scanner. As soon as a Christian has "faith" in Jesus, then they receive the bar code. When they are scanned, then, they are considered "righteous" and are deemed "saved" by God because, and only because, the bar code has been successfully attached to them. It doesn't matter whether they are good or bad, truly righteous on the inside or utterly depraved through and through. All that matters is that they have the "righteous" or "forgiven-in-Jesus" bar code.

Willard is rightly very critical of this bar-code faith and its accompanying vision of salvation. God is not a robotic scanner. We intuitively know that it is absurd to treat him as such, especially with regard to something as important as salvation. But why, precisely, is this bar-code faith deficient? Willard is not able to say directly; he is only able to point out that the scheme of salvation to which it refers is too narrow. The saving purview of the gospel is wider than mere "sin management." Salvation involves total transformation into Christlikeness through an obedient *discipleship*. Yet we still know that "faith" in Jesus is required for forgiveness. So are we saved by "faith," obedient discipleship, or both? Clearly for Willard it's both, but he hasn't really explained how these two categories touch.

By this point the solution for how they touch should be evident. Although contemporary Christian culture tends to separate personal salvation and discipleship, *allegiance* is where they finally meet—and they don't just meet, they embrace. For when we discover that saving "faith" means above all allegiance to Jesus the king, the intimacy between discipleship and salvation is easy to recognize. A person is not first "saved" by "faith" in Jesus's death for sins and then, once that is secured, plugged into a discipleship program as an optional extra in hope that he or she might "grow." On the contrary, a person is first saved when she or he becomes a disciple by declaring allegiance to Jesus the king—that is, when a person agrees to submit obediently to Jesus's wise and sovereign rule so as to take up his way of life. If subsequently a person entirely ceases to maintain allegiance, that individual has left the road of discipleship, the one and only road to final salvation. We are only and ever (past, present, and future) saved by discipleship to Jesus, for to be a disciple is to have declared and enacted *pistis* unto Jesus the king. Yet if discipleship and salvation coalesce in allegiance, then what does this mean practically for

6. Willard, *Divine Conspiracy*, 36.

how a disciple should live as she or he walks the path toward final salvation? Should discipleship primarily involve imitating the Messiah? Is it about a personal relationship with Jesus?

A Subject-to-King Relationship with Jesus

When I was an undergraduate, the Christian world was swept by a tidal wave of feverous what-would-Jesus-do enthusiasm. One day hardly anyone was talking about what Jesus might or might not do, and then suddenly, seemingly almost overnight, WWJD T-shirts, bracelets, necklaces, and bumper stickers could be spotted everywhere. In fact, if a person was not sporting some visible WWJD bling, then commitment to the cause could be questioned. The basic sentiment was noble, I suppose, even if it could (and did) devolve into all manner of silliness—if Jesus were in my place right now, would he go to the big dance after the game? Of course he would; only John the Baptist would stay at home and miss something this cool! But would he wear khakis or blue jeans? Would he invite Jessica or Samantha? . . . hmm. In those stirring times, a good Christian, so it seemed, could not make any decision without running through the what-would-Jesus-do gauntlet.

When "be like Jesus" enthusiasm begins to bubble over in unhelpful directions, how can salvation by allegiance alone help us practically? The centrality of the allegiance metaphor reminds us that Jesus is first and foremost *the king* to whom we have sworn loyalty; we are his *subjects*. His role is to rule; our part is to obey so that we become fitting servant-rulers too by willingly submitting to and then enacting his kingdom principles: openhanded love, radical forgiveness, spreading the good news, generosity to the poor, trust for daily provisions, and purity of heart. Similarly, when we begin to feel that Jesus is above all a best friend (or worse, a boyfriend), or at least that we would like him to be, it is probably time to remind ourselves that although Jesus is truly a friend and brother, he is the king, the enthroned Son of God, and what secures us to him is above all our allegiance to him as such. In other words, it is important to have a *personal relationship* with Jesus (Jesus knows his sheep, calling each by name, and his sheep know his voice; see John 10), but we dare not forget when personally relating to Jesus that he is *the mighty Christ*.

When Imitation Is Allegiance

All this being said, nevertheless the *imitatio Christi* tradition is strong—rooted in both Scripture and classic spirituality—and as such it certainly should be warmly embraced if aimed in the right direction.[7] Unfortunately the biblical statements that best inform us what Jesus would do are probably not going to help us decide whether to go to the big dance. Instead they announce that we should seek to follow Jesus's entire life pattern of death to self. For example, Paul states:

> Have this mind among yourselves, which is yours in the Messiah Jesus, who, though he was in the form of God, did not consider equality with God a thing to be grasped, but made himself nothing, taking the form of a servant, entering human existence in the likeness of humankind. And being found in human form, he humbled himself, becoming obedient to the point of death, even death on a cross. Therefore God highly exalted him and granted him the name that is above every name. (Phil. 2:5–9)

What would Jesus do? For the sake of others he would leave his lofty station in heavenly glory alongside the Father, take on the humble posture of a human, and do so even to the point of an embarrassing and excruciating death on a cross. In so doing he would trust that God would see the action and exalt him at the proper time. Those who have embraced the gospel of Jesus the king are following this pattern of self-emptying today.

For over ten years, a pastor-friend with a young family has resisted the lure of a higher salary and prestige in the pastorate (even though he is extraordinarily capable), choosing to serve at poor churches in low-income, inner-city, racially tense environments rather than "moving up" to a comfortable suburban megachurch. In so doing he and his family have accepted considerable hardship, but are quietly yet powerfully living out the story of the crucified Messiah.

Another friend has temporarily left a stable career in education, foregoing a salary for several years in order to teach children of medical missionaries. Her fidelity to the Lord Jesus means using the gifts of her college degree and prior teaching experience to move downward in service to others.

A different friend works a full-time job in finance and is a lay pastor (including preaching at least once a month). He and his wife have four young children. Yet in the midst of this busyness, he and his wife delight in God's Word. I am sure they deserve an extra hour of sleep or relaxation. Yet, because the Word of God truly is their daily bread—life-giving for themselves and for others through them—they spend an hour reading the Bible together each morning before work.

7. The high point of the imitation-of-Christ tradition was arguably reached in 1441 by Thomas à Kempis, *Imitation of Christ*.

Meanwhile, a family in our church has recently taken in foster children in obedience to Jesus's instructions to provide special care to the poor and those in social distress. *Pistis* includes embodying the gospel, following the Christ pattern.

In Philippians 2:5–9, Paul encourages the church to live out the gospel pattern of self-emptying in imitation of Jesus the king. In a related gospel statement, Paul exhorts the Corinthians to give willingly and self-sacrificially:

> I say this not as a command, but to prove by the earnestness of others that your love also is genuine. For you know the grace of our Lord Jesus, the Christ, that though he was rich, yet for your sake he became poor, so that you by his poverty might become rich. (2 Cor. 8:8–9)

What would Jesus do? Although he was rich, he would become poor for us; that is, he would live out the narrative that is the gospel. He invites us to follow this same pattern. As Michael Gorman so eloquently puts it, to be allegiant to Jesus means "becoming the gospel" for the sake of others, to live out the pattern established by the Christ's career and so to be joined fully to his life.[8]

The gospel is holistic. That is, we must be careful not to overspiritualize the gospel, as *pistis* involves active allegiance to Jesus the king. Remembering Jesus's words that "No one is able to serve two masters. . . . You are not able to serve God and money" (Matt. 6:24), a Christian I know carries out his loyalty to Jesus the king each year by giving all of his checking and savings accounts to charity. He and his family start over from zero each year.

Jesus took up his cross as a settled disposition of God-will rather than self-will. His disciples must learn, by God's grace and habitual practice, to do the same. Our final salvation depends on it, for this is what it means to be allegiant to Jesus as Lord. Jesus urges the crowds and his disciples, saying,

> If anyone would come after me, let him deny himself and take up his cross and follow me. For whoever would save his life will lose it, but whoever loses his life for my sake and the gospel's will save it. For what does it profit a man to gain the whole world and forfeit his life? (Mark 8:34–36)

Continuing, Jesus announces that he as the Son of Man will be ashamed of anyone who is ashamed of him, the crucified one, when he comes in the glory of his Father. Jesus's disciples must take up the cross not as an optional extra but because allegiance to Jesus and his gospel means that acquiring his death-to-self disposition is the only way in the end to find that you have a self that

8. Gorman, *Becoming the Gospel*.

belongs in his eternal kingdom. Putting allegiance into practice in the church today will involve following Jesus's pattern of dying to the old self and its self-serving allegiances and reorganizing a new life in accordance with Jesus's principles. Those interested in learning more about this spiritual transformation, this "renovation of the heart" (as Dallas Willard terms it), will find that many Christian writers, ancient and modern, can lend sound advice.[9]

Discipleship and salvation are not separable categories. Why is this of practical import for the church? The church must not think of evangelism or mission (traditionally, "getting people saved") and discipleship (traditionally, "growing people in Christ") as separate or even separable tasks—and church programming needs to be reconfigured accordingly.[10] Evangelism programs are only accurate and compelling when they are not merely an invitation to forgiveness but an invitation to full-orbed discipleship. Programs for discipleship are only accurate and compelling when discipleship is understood to be absolutely required for the allegiant outworking of salvation.

The invitation to begin the journey of salvation can never be anything less than a call to discipleship, for nothing less will result in final salvation. And final salvation is not possible apart from the path of genuine discipleship, the path of increasingly becoming conformed to the image of Jesus the king, who died in our place on the cross so that we might be forgiven and released from the stranglehold of sin. A gospel-centered *allegiance* is where discipleship and salvation meet in the church—and when they meet, they kiss.

From Apostles' Creed to Pledge

The introduction to this book suggested that the sensibilities of allegiance might prove helpful in rethinking matters pertaining to salvation. I have a final suggestion for how the church might become more allegiant. The suggestion is simple and, at least to my mind, highly practical. Each week children in the United States place their right hands over their hearts, face the flag, and pledge allegiance. Other countries have similar allegiance ceremonies—and all of us who participated in such ceremonies as children (or who still do as adults) can attest to their power for creating and maintaining loyalty. The Apostles' Creed needs to be mobilized so that it functions like a flag pledge—to become the Christian pledge of allegiance for the universal church.

9. In addition to repeated meditation on the Bible itself, beginners on the journey of Christian discipleship should especially consider Willard, *Renovation of the Heart*; Lewis, *Mere Christianity*; and Foster and Smith, *Devotional Classics*.

10. See Carson, "What Is the Gospel?—Revisited," esp. 164–66.

The Apostles' Creed is not merely a convenient summary of Christian beliefs. It is a concise presentation of the allegiance-demanding gospel.[11] In this study we discovered that the gospel in earliest Christianity was an eight-part story that encompasses Jesus's entire life, from his preexistence with the Father until his return in glory. Although it may be necessary to review chapter 2 to see why fully, notice that *all* of these elements (except #6, which is assumed) are in fact present in the Apostles' Creed:

The Apostles' Creed	The Eight-Part Gospel
I believe in God,	Jesus the king:
the Father almighty,	
Creator of heaven and earth,	
and in Jesus Christ, his only Son, our Lord,	
who was conceived by the Holy Spirit,	(1) preexisted with the Father,
born of the Virgin Mary,	(2) took on human flesh, fulfilling God's promises to David,
suffered under Pontius Pilate,	
was crucified, died and was buried;	(3) died for sins in accordance with the Scriptures,
he descended into hell;	(4) was buried,
on the third day he rose again from the dead;	(5) was raised on the third day in accordance with the Scriptures,
he ascended into heaven,	(6) appeared to many,
and is seated at the right hand of God the Father almighty;	(7) *is seated at the right hand of God as Lord*, and
from there he will come to judge the living and the dead.	(8) will come again as judge.
I believe in the Holy Spirit,	
the holy catholic Church,	
the communion of saints,	
the forgiveness of sins,	
the resurrection of the body,	
and life everlasting. Amen.*	

* This is the version used by the Roman Catholic Church (revised 2011).

When a person says the Apostles' Creed, he or she is restating the gospel of the earliest church in outline form—the story of how Jesus came to be the cosmic Lord. As such, the Apostles' Creed could easily be used by churches as a trinitarian pledge of allegiance to Jesus the king. Instructions could be given, for instance, to focus the eyes above the cross (or to focus the eyes of the heart if no cross is visible) when saying the Apostles' Creed, intended as a pledge.

The cross is the place of Jesus's death and victory over sin, the instrument by which he was "lifted up" in glory to the right hand of God. Jesus is now enthroned at the right hand of the Father, so looking above the cross would

11. For an introduction to the Apostles' Creed, see Bird, *What Christians Ought to Believe*.

serve as a reminder of how Jesus's actions on the cross resulted in his present status as exalted high priest and as king of heaven and earth. And as king, Jesus, together with God the Father, has sent the union-securing Spirit to indwell the church. This pledge could be done in liturgical and nonliturgical churches with minimum effort. The results, however, could be marvelously transformative for the worldwide church.

In liturgical traditions where the Apostles' Creed (or the closely related Nicene Creed) are already said as part of the standard worship service, leaders or celebrants could simply assist the congregation in recognizing that the creed is not a mere statement of common belief but is the allegiance-demanding good news. Invite the congregation weekly to view the creed as a pledge of loyalty. Before the creed is affirmed together, each week the celebrant could say something like "The Apostles' Creed tells us that Jesus rules at the right hand of God as king. Now we will affirm the gospel together as we declare our allegiance to Jesus as the king" or "Now let us pledge allegiance to Jesus the king, who is currently ruling at the right hand of God. This is the good news of our Lord Jesus, the Christ." Or if the liturgy is extremely fixed so that interpretative words cannot be added immediately before or after the creed is affirmed, a homilist could begin each sermon by reminding the congregation that the creed is the gospel; when the congregation affirms it, a declaration of loyal obedience to Jesus the king is intended. Over time the congregation would come to see the primary significance of the creed accordingly.

In nonliturgical traditions there might be more resistance among congregants to using the Apostles' Creed as a pledge in the worship service. Pastors, worship leaders, and others who belong to such traditions should nevertheless do it anyway. The Apostles' Creed is one of the earliest articulations of the gospel, expressed in a minimally expanded form. As such, it contains an implicit demand for all those who would affirm it to express loyalty to Jesus the king. If the congregation can come to see the value of the Apostles' Creed as the Apostles' Pledge of Allegiance, it may in fact prove to be a gateway to further liturgical riches.[12]

It is a well-known Christian truism that a person must have faith or believe in Jesus to be saved. I have been arguing that this truism is in fact a dangerous half-truth. With its anti-evidential, anti-rational, and "leap" connotations, the English word *faith* is of limited value when discussing eternal salvation in

12. Many churches with a nonliturgical heritage are in the process of rediscovery; see Ross, *Evangelical versus Liturgical.*

our present cultural climate. Meanwhile *belief* is also inadequate, because in contemporary idiom it suggests that we are saved merely by having the right facts squeezed into our brains. It primarily means "acknowledging as real or true" but does not sufficiently capture the connotation of enacted loyalty. But at the same time we must acknowledge that this half-truth does indeed contain genuine truth that must not be cast aside. We must find a vocabulary and grammar that extends beyond faith and belief, augmenting or replacing these terms when necessary, so that we emphasize active loyalty to Jesus the king.

The gospel is the transformative story about the career of Jesus—namely, how he became Jesus *the Christ*, that is, Jesus the king, Lord of heaven and earth. Jesus became the king through his willing participation in the saving events of the gospel, especially his trusting allegiance to God the Father in undertaking crucifixion unto death. That allegiance was vindicated when Jesus was raised to new life *and enthroned* at God the Father's right hand. In this sequence of action, God demonstrated fidelity to his Son, his people, the world, and indeed all creation. Jesus's enthronement is not something extra beyond the gospel, but its climax. To respond to the gospel above all means to publicly acknowledge allegiance to Jesus the universal king. On both the divine and the human side, the salvation story overflows with allegiance.

So, in the final analysis, salvation is by allegiance alone. That is, God requires nothing more or nothing less than allegiance to Jesus as king for initial, current, and final salvation. As such, while continuing to affirm the absolute centrality of the cross, the atonement, and the resurrection, the church must move away from a salvation culture that spins around the axis of "faith alone" in the sufficiency of Jesus's sacrifice. It must move toward a gospel culture that centers upon "allegiance alone" to Jesus the enthroned king. With the Apostles' Creed as a pledge of allegiance, the rallying cry of the victorious church can become "We give allegiance to Jesus the king." For as the creed reminds us, Jesus the Christ is "our Lord" and he "is seated at the right hand of God," and as such he both merits and demands our unreserved loyalty.

—— FOR FURTHER THOUGHT ——

1. Consider what three things are essential to allegiance. How are these various aspects interrelated? In light of this, can you think of your own analogy that helps explain what is necessary for saving allegiance?

2. In comparing allegiance to a shield, a military analogy has been invoked. There are possible risks and rewards for the church in combining such images. Do you think it is prudent for national flags (e.g., the American

flag) to be hung in a church? Do you think patriotic hymns have a place in the church? Where should the boundaries be, and why?

3. If you were writing a tract that extended a gospel invitation to the reader, how would you begin? What would you emphasize the most? Why?

4. Why is allegiance where discipleship and salvation kiss?

5. How does allegiance inform what a personal relationship with Jesus should look like? How does it inform what it means to imitate Jesus?

6. What's the difference between a creed and a pledge? Why might the Apostles' Creed also be suitable as a pledge?

7. Give at least three specific, practical suggestions that might help you personally become more allegiant to Jesus the king during this forthcoming week, month, or year.

8. Give at least two specific, practical suggestions that might help your local church (or another congregation that you know about) shift from a salvation culture to an allegiance culture during this forthcoming week, month, or year.

Bibliography

Allen, R. Michael. *Justification and the Gospel: Understanding the Contexts and Controversies*. Grand Rapids: Baker Academic, 2013.

Allison, Dale C., Jr. *Constructing Jesus: Memory, Imagination, and History*. Grand Rapids: Baker Academic, 2010.

Anderson, Gary A. *Charity: The Place of the Poor in the Biblical Tradition*. New Haven: Yale University Press, 2013.

Augustine. *The Trinity*. In *The Works of Saint Augustine: A Translation for the 21st Century*. Part 1, vol. 5. Translated by Edmund Hill. Hyde Park, NY: New City Press, 1991.

Aune, David E., ed. *Rereading Paul Together: Protestant and Catholic Perspectives on Justification*. Grand Rapids: Baker Academic, 2006.

Barclay, John M. G. *Paul and the Gift*. Grand Rapids: Eerdmans, 2015.

Bartholomew, Craig G., and Michael W. Goheen. *The Drama of Scripture: Finding Our Place in the Biblical Story*. 2nd ed. Grand Rapids: Baker Academic, 2014.

Bates, Matthew W. *The Birth of the Trinity: Jesus, God, and Spirit in New Testament and Early Christian Interpretations of the Old Testament*. Oxford: Oxford University Press, 2015.

———. "A Christology of Incarnation and Enthronement: Romans 1:3–4 as Unified, Nonadoptionist, and Nonconciliatory." *Catholic Biblical Quarterly* 77 (2015): 107–27.

———. *The Hermeneutics of the Apostolic Proclamation: The Center of Paul's Method of Scriptural Interpretation*. Waco: Baylor University Press, 2012.

Bauckham, Richard. *Jesus and the God of Israel: God Crucified and Other Studies on the New Testament's Christology of Divine Identity*. Milton Keynes: Paternoster, 2008.

———. *The Theology of the Book of Revelation.* Cambridge: Cambridge University Press, 1993.

Beale, Greg K. *The Book of Revelation: A Commentary on the Greek Text.* New International Greek Testament Commentary. Grand Rapids: Eerdmans, 1999.

———. *Handbook on the New Testament Use of the Old Testament: Exegesis and Interpretation.* Grand Rapids: Baker Academic, 2012.

———. *The Temple and the Church's Mission.* Downers Grove, IL: IVP Academic, 2004.

———. *We Become What We Worship: A Biblical Theology of Idolatry.* Downers Grove, IL: IVP Academic, 2008.

Beale, Greg K., and David H. Campbell. *Revelation: A Shorter Commentary.* Grand Rapids: Eerdmans, 2015.

Beale, Greg K., and Mitchell Kim. *God Dwells among Us: Expanding Eden to the Ends of the Earth.* Downers Grove, IL: InterVarsity, 2014.

Beilby, James K., and Paul R. Eddy, eds. *Justification: Five Views.* Downers Grove, IL: InterVarsity, 2011.

Berkhof, Louis. *Systematic Theology.* Grand Rapids: Eerdmans, 1941.

Billings, J. Todd. *Calvin, Participation, and the Gift: The Activity of Believers in Union with Christ.* Oxford: Oxford University Press, 2007.

———. *Union with Christ: Reframing Theology and Ministry for the Church.* Grand Rapids: Baker Academic, 2011.

Bird, Michael F. *Evangelical Theology: A Biblical and Systematic Introduction.* Grand Rapids: Zondervan, 2013.

———. *The Saving Righteousness of God: Studies on Paul, Justification and the New Perspective.* Milton Keynes: Paternoster, 2007.

———. *What Christians Ought to Believe: An Introduction to Christian Doctrine through the Apostles' Creed.* Grand Rapids: Zondervan, 2016.

Bird, Michael F., and Preston Sprinkle, eds. *The Faith of Jesus Christ: Exegetical, Biblical and Theological Studies.* Peabody, MA: Hendrickson, 2009.

Bovon, François. *A Commentary on the Gospel of Luke.* 3 vols. Hermeneia. Minneapolis: Fortress, 2002–13.

Calvin, John. *Calvin's Commentaries.* 22 vols. Reprint, Grand Rapids: Baker, 2005.

———. *Institutes of the Christian Religion.* Translated by Ford Lewis Battles. 2 vols. Philadelphia: Westminster, 1960.

Campbell, Constantine R. *Paul and Union with Christ: An Exegetical and Theological Study.* Grand Rapids: Zondervan, 2012.

Campbell, Douglas A. *The Deliverance of God: An Apocalyptic Rereading of Justification in Paul.* Grand Rapids: Eerdmans, 2009.

———. *The Quest for Paul's Gospel: A Suggested Strategy.* London: T&T Clark, 2005.

———. "Romans 1.17—A Crux Interpretum for the ΠΙΣΤΙΣ ΧΡΙΣΤΟΥ Debate." *Journal of Biblical Literature* 113 (1994): 265–85.

Capes, David B. *Old Testament Yahweh Texts in Paul's Christology.* Wissenschaftliche Untersuchungen zum Neuen Testament 42. Tübingen: Mohr Siebeck, 1992.

Carson, D. A. "What Is the Gospel?—Revisited." In *For the Fame of God's Name: Essays in Honor of John Piper,* edited by Sam Storms and Justin Taylor, 147–70. Wheaton, IL: Crossway, 2010.

Collins, Adela Yarbro, and John J. Collins. *King and Messiah as Son of God: Divine, Human, and Angelic Messianic Figures in Biblical and Related Literature.* Grand Rapids: Eerdmans, 2008.

Crossan, John D. *The Historical Jesus: The Life of a Mediterranean Peasant.* San Francisco: HarperSanFrancisco, 1991.

Crump, David. *Encountering Jesus, Encountering Scripture: Reading the Bible Critically in Faith.* Grand Rapids: Eerdmans, 2013.

Danker, Fredrick W., ed. *A Greek-English Lexicon of the New Testament and Other Early Christian Literature.* 3rd ed. Chicago: University of Chicago Press, 2000.

Das, A. Andrew. *Paul, the Law, and the Covenant.* Peabody, MA: Hendrickson, 2001.

Demarest, Bruce. *The Cross and Salvation: The Doctrine of Salvation.* Wheaton, IL: Crossway, 1997.

Dodd, C. H. *The Apostolic Preaching and Its Developments.* New York: Harper & Row, 1964.

Downs, David J. *Alms: Charity, Reward, and Atonement in Early Christianity.* Waco: Baylor University Press, 2016.

Ferguson, Everett. *Baptism in the Early Church: History, Theology, and Liturgy in the First Five Centuries.* Grand Rapids: Eerdmans, 2009.

Foster, Richard J., and James Bryan Smith, eds. *Devotional Classics: Selected Readings for Individuals and Groups.* Rev. ed. New York: HarperCollins, 2005.

Fredriksen, Paula. "Paul's Letter to the Romans, the Ten Commandments, and Pagan 'Justification by Faith.'" *Journal of Biblical Literature* 133 (2014): 801–8.

Gaffin, Richard B., Jr. *By Faith, Not by Sight: Paul and the Order of Salvation.* 2nd ed. Phillipsburg, NJ: P&R, 2013.

Garlington, Don B. *"The Obedience of Faith": A Pauline Phrase in Historical Context.* Wissenschaftliche Untersuchungen zum Neuen Testament 38. Tübingen: Mohr Siebeck, 1991.

Gathercole, Simon J. *Defending Substitution: An Essay on Atonement in Paul.* Grand Rapids: Baker Academic, 2015.

———. *The Preexistent Son: Recovering the Christologies of Matthew, Mark, and Luke.* Grand Rapids: Eerdmans, 2006.

Gorman, Michael J. *The Apostle of the Crucified Lord: A Theological Introduction to Paul and His Letters.* Grand Rapids: Eerdmans, 2004.

————. *Becoming the Gospel: Paul, Participation, and Mission.* Grand Rapids: Eerdmans, 2015.

————. *Inhabiting the Cruciform God: Kenosis, Justification, and Theosis in Paul's Narrative Soteriology.* Grand Rapids: Eerdmans, 2009.

————. *Reading Revelation Responsibly: Uncivil Worship and Witness; Following the Lamb into the New Creation.* Eugene, OR: Wipf & Stock, 2011.

Green, Joel B. *Conversion in Luke-Acts: Divine Action, Human Cognition, and the People of God.* Grand Rapids: Baker Academic, 2015.

Grudem, Wayne. *Systematic Theology: An Introduction to Biblical Doctrine.* Grand Rapids: Zondervan, 2000.

Gupta, Nijay K. "'They Are Not Gods!': Jewish and Christian Idol Polemic and Greco-Roman Use of Cult Statues." *Catholic Biblical Quarterly* 76 (2014): 704–19.

Hays, Richard B. "Apocalyptic Hermeneutic: Habakkuk Proclaims 'The Righteous One.'" In *Conversion of the Imagination: Paul as Interpreter of Israel's Scripture,* edited by Richard B. Hays, 119–42. Grand Rapids: Eerdmans, 2015.

————. *Echoes of Scripture in the Letters of Paul.* New Haven: Yale University Press, 1989.

————. *The Faith of Jesus Christ: The Narrative Substructure of Galatians 3:1–4:11.* 2nd ed. Grand Rapids: Eerdmans, 2002.

Hodges, Zane C. *Absolutely Free: A Biblical Reply to Lordship Salvation.* Dallas: Redención Viva, 1989.

Hoekema, Anthony A. *Saved by Grace.* Grand Rapids: Eerdmans, 1989.

Hurtado, Larry W. *Lord Jesus Christ: Devotion to Jesus in Earliest Christianity.* Grand Rapids: Eerdmans, 2003.

Irons, Charles L. *The Righteousness of God: A Lexical Examination of the Covenant-Faithfulness Interpretation.* Wissenschaftliche Untersuchungen zum Neuen Testament 386. Tübingen: Mohr Siebeck, 2015.

Jewett, Robert. "The Redaction and Use of an Early Christian Confession in Romans 1:3–4." In *The Living Text: Essays in Honor of Ernest W. Saunders,* edited by D. E. Groh and R. Jewett, 99–122. Lanham, MD: University Press of America, 1985.

Jipp, Joshua W. "Ancient, Modern, and Future Interpretations of Romans 1:3–4: Reception History and Biblical Interpretation." *Journal of Theological Interpretation* (2009): 241–59.

————. *Christ Is King: Paul's Royal Ideology.* Minneapolis: Fortress, 2015.

————. "Reading the Story of Abraham, Isaac, and 'Us' in Romans 4." *Journal for the Study of the New Testament* 32 (2009): 217–42.

Johnson, Luke Timothy. *The First and Second Letters to Timothy.* Anchor Bible 35A. New York: Doubleday, 2001.

Johnson, Marcus P. *One with Christ: An Evangelical Theology of Salvation.* Wheaton: Crossway, 2013.

Keener, Craig S. *Acts: An Exegetical Commentary*. 4 vols. Grand Rapids: Baker Academic, 2012–15.

Kierkegaard, Søren. *Fear and Trembling*. Reprint, London: Penguin, 1986.

Kilner, John F. *Dignity and Destiny: Humanity in the Image of God*. Grand Rapids: Eerdmans, 2015.

Koester, Craig R. *Revelation and the End of All Things*. Grand Rapids: Eerdmans, 2001.

Kugel, James L. *In Potiphar's House: The Interpretative Life of Biblical Texts*. San Francisco: Harper, 1990.

Kugler, Chris. "ΠΙΣΤΙΣ ΧΡΙΣΤΟΥ: The Current State of Play and the Key Arguments." *Currents in Biblical Research* 14 (2016): 244–55.

Lane, William. *The Gospel according to Mark*. New International Commentary on the New Testament. Grand Rapids: Eerdmans, 1974.

Lee, Aquila H. I. *From Messiah to Preexistent Son: Jesus' Self-Consciousness and Early Christian Exegesis of Messianic Psalms*. Wissenschaftliche Untersuchungen zum Neuen Testament 192. Tübingen: Mohr Siebeck, 2005.

Leithart, Peter J. "Justification as Verdict and Deliverance: A Biblical Perspective." *Pro Ecclesia* 16 (2007): 56–72.

Lewis, C. S. *Mere Christianity*. Reprint, San Francisco: HarperOne, 2001.

Lindsay, Dennis R. *Josephus and Faith: Pistis and Pisteuein as Faith Terminology in the Writings of Flavius Josephus and in the New Testament*. Arbeiten zur Geschichte des Antiken Judentums und des Urchristentums 19. Leiden: Brill, 1993.

Lints, Richard. *Identity and Idolatry: The Image of God and Its Inversion*. Downers Grove, IL: InterVarsity, 2015.

Longenecker, Richard N. *Biblical Exegesis in the Apostolic Period*. 2nd ed. Grand Rapids: Eerdmans, 1999.

Luther, Martin. *Preface to the Latin Writings*. Reprinted in *Martin Luther: Selections from His Writings*, edited by John Dillenberger, 19–34. Garden City, NY: Anchor, 1961.

Macaskill, Grant. *Union with Christ in the New Testament*. Oxford: Oxford University Press, 2013.

Martyn, J. Louis. *Galatians: A New Translation with Introduction and Commentary*. Anchor Bible 33A. New York: Doubleday, 1997.

McCready, Douglas. *He Came Down from Heaven: The Preexistence of Christ and the Christian Faith*. Downers Grove, IL: InterVarsity, 2005.

McGrath, Alister E. *Iustitia Dei: A History of the Christian Doctrine of Justification*. 3rd ed. Cambridge: Cambridge University Press, 2005.

McKnight, Scot. *The Heaven Promise: Engaging the Bible's Truth about Life to Come*. Colorado Springs: WaterBrook, 2015.

———. *The King Jesus Gospel: The Original Good News Revisited*. Grand Rapids: Zondervan, 2011.

———. "The Warning Passages of Hebrews: A Formal Analysis and Theological Conclusions." *Trinity Journal* NS 13 (1992): 21–59.

Melanchthon, Philip. *Commonplaces: "Loci Communes" 1521*. Translated by Christian Preus. Saint Louis: Concordia, 2014.

Middleton, J. Richard. *A New Heaven and a New Earth: Reclaiming Biblical Eschatology*. Grand Rapids: Baker Academic, 2014.

Morgan, Teresa. *Roman Faith and Christian Faith: Pistis and Fides in the Early Roman Empire and Early Churches*. Oxford: Oxford University Press, 2015.

Murray, John. *Redemption—Accomplished and Applied*. Grand Rapids: Eerdmans, 1955.

Noll, Mark A. *The Scandal of the Evangelical Mind*. Grand Rapids: Eerdmans, 1994.

Novenson, Matthew V. *Christ among the Messiahs: Christ Language in Paul and Messiah Language in Ancient Judaism*. Oxford: Oxford University Press, 2012.

Origen. *Contra Celsum*. Translated by Henry Chadwick. Reprint, Cambridge: Cambridge University Press, 1965.

Peterson, Robert A. *Salvation Applied by the Spirit: Union with Christ*. Wheaton: Crossway, 2015.

Pinson, J. Matthew, ed. *Four Views on Eternal Security*. Grand Rapids: Zondervan, 2002.

Piper, John. *The Future of Justification: A Response to N. T. Wright*. Wheaton: Crossway, 2007.

Pitre, Brant. *Jesus and the Last Supper*. Grand Rapids: Eerdmans, 2015.

Ritner, Robert K. "'The Breathing Permit of Hor' among the Joseph Smith Papyri." *Journal of Near Eastern Studies* 62 (2003): 161–80.

Ross, Melanie C. *Evangelical versus Liturgical: Defying a Dichotomy*. Grand Rapids: Eerdmans, 2014.

Sanders, E. P. *Paul and Palestinian Judaism: A Comparison of Patterns of Religion*. Minneapolis: Fortress, 1977.

Schneemelcher, Wilhelm, trans. *The Acts of Paul*. In *The New Testament Apocrypha*, edited by Wilhelm Schneemelcher, 2:213–70. Translated in English by R. McL. Wilson. 2 vols. Louisville: Westminster John Knox, 1991–92.

Schreiner, Thomas R. *Faith Alone: The Doctrine of Justification*. Grand Rapids: Zondervan, 2015.

———. "Justification apart from and by Works: At the Final Judgment Works Will Confirm Justification." In *Four Views on the Role of Works at the Final Judgment*, edited by Alan P. Stanley, 71–98. Grand Rapids: Zondervan, 2013.

Schreiner, Thomas R., and Ardel B. Caneday. *The Race Set Before Us: A Biblical Theology of Perseverance and Assurance*. Downers Grove, IL: InterVarsity, 2001.

Schroeder, H. J., trans. *Canons and Decrees of the Council of Trent: Original Text with English Translation*. St. Louis: Herder, 1941.

Schweitzer, Albert. *The Mysticism of Paul the Apostle*. Translated by William Montgomery. 2nd ed. London: A&C Black, 1953. Reprint, Baltimore: Johns Hopkins University Press, 1988.

Seifrid, Mark. *Christ, Our Righteousness: Paul's Theology of Justification*. Downers Grove, IL: IVP Academic, 2001.

Seneca, Lucius Annaeus. *On Benefits*. Translated by Miriam T. Griffin and Brad Inwood. Chicago: University of Chicago Press, 2011.

Smith, Joseph. *The Pearl of Great Price*. Salt Lake City: Latter-Day Saints, 1878.

Sproul, R. C. *Faith Alone: The Evangelical Doctrine of Justification*. Grand Rapids: Eerdmans, 1995.

———. *Getting the Gospel Right*. Grand Rapids: Eerdmans, 1999.

Stanley, Alan P. *Did Jesus Teach Salvation by Works? The Role of Salvation in the Synoptic Gospels*. Eugene, OR: Wipf & Stock, 2006.

Stanley, Charles F. *Eternal Security*. Nashville: Thomas Nelson, 1990.

Stegman, Thomas D. "Paul's Use of *Dikaio-* Terminology: Moving Beyond N. T. Wright's Forensic Interpretation." *Theological Studies* 72 (2011): 496–524.

Stein, R. H. "Last Supper." In *Dictionary of Jesus and the Gospels*, edited by Joel B. Green and Scot McKnight, 444–50. Downers Grove, IL: InterVarsity, 1992.

Stevenson, James. *A New Eusebius: Documents Illustrating the History of the Christian Church to AD 337*. Revised by W. H. C. Frend. New ed. London: SPCK, 1987.

Thomas à Kempis. *The Imitation of Christ*. Translated by William Creasy. Notre Dame, IN: Ave Maria, 1989.

Thrall, Margaret E. *The Second Epistle to the Corinthians*. Reprinted in 2 vols. International Critical Commentary. London: T&T Clark, 2008.

Trobisch, David. *The First Edition of the New Testament*. Oxford: Oxford University Press, 2000.

Walls, Jerry L. *Heaven, Hell, and Purgatory: A Protestant View of the Cosmic Drama*. Grand Rapids: Brazos, 2015.

Walton, John H. *Ancient Near Eastern Thought and the Old Testament: Introducing the Conceptual World of the Hebrew Bible*. Grand Rapids: Baker Academic, 2006.

Watson, Francis. *Paul and the Hermeneutics of Faith*. London: T&T Clark, 2004.

Westerholm, Stephen. *Justification Reconsidered: Rethinking a Pauline Theme*. Grand Rapids: Eerdmans, 2013.

———. *Perspectives Old and New on Paul: The "Lutheran" Paul and His Critics*. Grand Rapids: Eerdmans, 2004.

Westphal, Merold. *Kierkegaard's Concept of Faith*. Grand Rapids: Eerdmans, 2014.

Wilkin, Robert N. "Christians Will Be Judged according to Their Works at the *Rewards* Judgment, but Not at the *Final* Judgment." In *Four Views on the Role of Works at the Final Judgment*, edited by Alan P. Stanley, 25–50. Grand Rapids: Zondervan, 2013.

Willard, Dallas. *The Divine Conspiracy*. San Francisco: HarperSanFrancisco, 1998.

———. *Renovation of the Heart*. Colorado Springs: NavPress, 2002.

Winter, Bruce W. *Honours for the Caesars: The First Christians' Responses*. Grand Rapids: Eerdmans, 2015.

Witherington, Ben, III. *Paul's Narrative Thought World: The Tapestry of Tragedy and Triumph*. Louisville: Westminster John Knox, 1994.

Wright, N. T. *The Challenge of Jesus: Rediscovering Who Jesus Was and Is*. Downers Grove, IL: InterVarsity, 1999.

———. *How God Became King: The Forgotten Story of the Gospels*. New York: HarperOne, 2012.

———. *Jesus and the Victory of God*. Christian Origins and the Question of God 2. Minneapolis: Fortress, 1996.

———. *The New Testament and the People of God*. Christian Origins and the Question of God 1. Minneapolis: Fortress, 1992.

———. *Paul and the Faithfulness of God*. 2 vols. Christian Origins and the Question of God 4. Minneapolis: Fortress, 2013.

———. *The Paul Debate: Critical Questions for Understanding the Apostle*. Waco: Baylor University Press, 2015.

———. *Paul: In Fresh Perspective*. Minneapolis: Fortress, 2005.

———. *What Saint Paul Really Said: Was Paul of Tarsus the Real Founder of Christianity?* Grand Rapids: Eerdmans, 1997.

Young, Stephen L. "Romans 1.1–5 and Paul's Christological Use of Hab. 2.4 in Rom. 1.17: An Underutilized Consideration in the Debate." *Journal for the Study of the New Testament* 34 (2012): 277–85.

Zetterholm, Magnus. *Approaches to Paul: A Student's Guide to Recent Scholarship*. Minneapolis: Fortress, 2009.

Author Index

Scripture and Ancient Writings Index